THE CARTHAGINIANS

The Carthaginians reveals the complex culture, society and achievements of a famous, yet misunderstood ancient people. Beginning as Phoenician settlers in North Africa, the Carthaginians then broadened their civilisation with influences from neighbouring North African peoples, Egypt, and the Greek world. Their own cultural influence in turn spread across the Western Mediterranean as they imposed dominance over Sardinia, western Sicily, and finally southern Spain.

As a stable republic Carthage earned respectful praise from Greek observers, notably Aristotle, and from many Romans – even Cato, otherwise notorious for insisting that 'Carthage must be destroyed'. Carthage matched the great city-state of Syracuse in power and ambition, then clashed with Rome for mastery of the Mediterranean West. For a time, led by her greatest general Hannibal, she did become the leading power between the Atlantic and the Adriatic.

It was chiefly after her destruction in 146 BC that Carthage came to be depicted by Greeks and Romans as an alien civilisation, harsh, gloomy and bloodstained. Demonising the victim eased the embarrassment of Rome's aggression; Virgil in his Aeneid was one of the few to offer a more sensitive vision. Exploring both written and archaeological evidence, *The Carthaginians* reveals a complex, multicultural and innovative people whose achievements left an indelible impact on their Roman conquerors and on history.

Dexter Hoyos writes on Latin teaching and ancient history. His books include *Unplanned Wars* (1998), *Hannibal's Dynasty* (Routledge, 2003), *Truceless War* (2007), and *Hannibal: Rome's Greatest Enemy* (2008). He has retired after 36 years at Sydney University to continue research work on Romans and Carthaginians.

PEOPLES OF THE ANCIENT WORLD

This series stands as the first port of call for anyone who wants to know more about the historically important peoples of the ancient world and the early Middle Ages.

Reliable, up-to-date and with special attention paid to the peoples' enduring legacy and influence, *Peoples of the Ancient World* will ensure the continuing prominence of these crucial figures in modern-day study and research.

THE ROMANS
An Introduction *Second Edition*
Antony Kamm

THE GREEKS
An Introduction to their Culture *Second Edition*
Robin Sowerby

THE PERSIANS
Maria Brosius

THE TROJANS AND THEIR NEIGHBOURS
Trevor Bryce

MYCENAEANS
Rodney Castleden

THE EGYPTIANS
An Introduction
Robert Morkot

THE BABYLONIANS
An Introduction
Gwendolyn Leick

THE ISRAELITES
An Introduction
Antony Kamm

THE
CARTHAGINIANS

Dexter Hoyos

LONDON AND NEW YORK

First published 2010
by Routledge
2 Park Square, Milton Park, Abingdon, Oxon OX14 4RN

Simultaneously published in the USA and Canada
by Routledge
711 Third Avenue, New York, NY 10017

*Routledge is an imprint of the Taylor & Francis Group, an
informa business*

Typeset in Sabon by Saxon Graphics Ltd, Derby

British Library Cataloguing in Publication Data
A catalogue record for this book is available from the British
Library

Library of Congress Cataloging in Publication Data
Hoyos, B. D. (B. Dexter), 1944-
The Carthaginians / Dexter Hoyos.
p. cm.
Includes bibliographical references.
1. Carthaginians. 2. Carthage (Extinct city)--Civilization.
3. Carthage (Extinct city)--History. I. Title.
DT269.C34H69 2010
939'.73--dc22
2009048666

ISBN 10: 0-415-43644-3 (hbk)
ISBN 10: 0-415-43645-1 (pbk)
ISBN 10: 0-203-85132-3 (ebk)

ISBN 13: 978-0-415-43644-1 (hbk)
ISBN 13: 978-0-415-43645-8 (pbk)
ISBN 13: 978-0-203-85132-6 (ebk)

TO THE MEMORY
OF MY FATHER, BEN
(1913–2009)

CONTENTS

Acknowledgements   *xi*
Keys to the Maps   *xiii*
Illustrations   *xxi*
Sources of Images   *xxiii*
Chronological Table   *xxvi*
Sources of knowledge   *xxxiii*

I   The Phoenicians in the West   1

      The Phoenicians 1
      Sidon and Tyre 2
      Settlements in the West 3

II   Carthage: Foundation and Growth   6

      Tales of the foundation 6
      Legends and truths 7
      Carthage: site and potential 12

III   State and Government   20
      Citizens and aristocrats 20
      Carthaginian names 23
      Praise from Greeks 24
      Chief magistrates: the sufetes 25
      Adirim: *the senate of Carthage 28*
      The mysterious 'pentarchies' 31
      The generals 33
      Nemesis of generals: the court of One Hundred
          and Four 35
      The assembly of citizens 36

CONTENTS

IV   The Carthaginian 'sea empire'   39

      Carthage and North Africa 39
      Carthage and the Etruscans 43
      First treaty with Rome 44
      Projection of power: Sardinia 45
      Projection of power: Sicily 47
      Carthage, Spain and the Atlantic 49
      Hanno's Periplus 51
      Himilco's voyage 54
      An expansionist policy? 55

V   Traders and landowners: Carthaginian society   59

      Trade and traders 59
      Land and landowning 62
      Workers and labourers 67
      Slaves 69

VI   The Cityscape of Carthage   73

      The growth of the city 73
      Temples and other sacred buildings 76
      Houses and shops 82
      Public buildings 86
      The land fortifications and the ports 88

VII   Religion and cultural life   94

      The gods and goddesses 94
      The 'tophet' and child sacrifice 100
      Literature at Carthage: did it exist? 105
      Visual art, including coinage 108

VIII Carthage in Africa   124

      Politics and rivalries: Mazeus-'Malchus' 124
      The Magonid ascendancy 128
      The end of the Magonids 132
      The ascendancy of Hanno 'the Great' 134
      Politics and war in the late 4th Century:
         Bomilcar's putsch 138
      The Libyans and Numidians 142

CONTENTS

IX   Carthage at War: Sicily   149

The Carthaginian war machine: the navy 149
Carthage's armies 153
Carthaginians and Greeks in the 5th Century 163
Carthage vs Dionysius I 166
Carthage and Timoleon 170
The age of Agathocles: Carthage at bay 172
Carthage and Pyrrhus 176

X   The First War with Rome, and After   178

The second and third treaties with Rome 178
The outbreak of the war 181
Phases of war: 264 to 257 183
Africa invaded and saved: 256 to 255 185
Victories, defeats, stalemate: 254 to 242 186
Peace and revolt 189

XI   The New Empire and Hannibal   193

The Sardinia crisis 193
The new empire in Spain 194
The coming of the Second Punic War 197
Hannibal invades Italy 199
Hannibal, master of southern Italy 201
Limitations and setbacks 202
Metaurus, Zama and peace 203
Hannibal's war: an assessment 205

XII   Revival and Destruction   207

Politics and reforms 207
Peace and plenty 208
Carthage and Numidia 211
Politics at home and war with Masinissa 213
The outbreak of the Third Punic War 214
The Third Punic War 216

XIII   Carthage in History   220

CONTENTS

Notes   224
Select Bibliography   234
Index   241

NOTE: Punic writing, like Phoenician and Hebrew, did not use vowels. Modern transliterations of Punic words and names therefore do not add vowels, but in places I add a written-out version of a word for greater clarity.

ACKNOWLEDGEMENTS

It is a special pleasure to acknowledge the encouragement, collaboration and help which many people and institutions have generously given as I prepared *The Carthaginians*. In first place I must thank Richard Stoneman for suggesting the topic and readily accepting my optimistic outline when he directed classical publications at Routledge. Routledge's support for the work has continued steadily since then, in spite of my slow work and distractions, and I owe much in the latest stages of composition to the firm and friendly guidance of my series editor Lalle Pursglove. Sydney University, my professional centre for thirty-six years, has provided invaluable facilities for my research even after I left full-time academic life for what I thoughtlessly supposed would be serene retirement. Sydney University Library in turn is one of the most supportive institutions that I know for scholarly work, in both its facilities and its staff.

The illustrations for the book I owe to a generous range of scholars and institutions. Professor M'hamed Hassine Fantar, Titulaire de la Chaire Ben Ali pour le Dialogue des Civilisations et des Religions at the University of Tunisia, gave me immediate permission to use images from his vividly illustrated book *Carthage: La cité punique,* and so did its publisher, CNRS Editions of Paris. The Institut National du Patrimoine in the Ministère de la Culture et de la Sauvegarde du Patrimoine, Republic of Tunisia, and its Directeur Général Professor Fathi Bejaoui have with equal generosity authorised me to reproduce images of Carthaginian materials held in the great museums of Tunisia. The Badisches Landesmuseum of Karlsruhe, Germany, in turn authorised me to use two evocative photographs in its possession.

Most images themselves are taken, in turn, from the splendid volume edited by Sabine Peters, *Hannibal ad Portas: Macht und Reichtum Karthagos,* published by Theiss Verlag of Stuttgart,

Germany, to accompany the wide-ranging exhibition of Carthaginian, Phoenician and related artefacts presented at the Badisches Landesmuseum in 2004. Theiss Verlag, through its executive in Programmleitung Mr Rüdiger Müller, has both encouraged my efforts and granted me the permission to make the necessary scans of images from that work.

The selection of coins I owe to the renewed kindness of my university colleague and friend Dr Stephen Mulligan of Sydney, who combines a distinguished professional career in haematology with an expert knowledge of Carthaginian numismatics. The high-quality coin images were made by Colin Pitchfork and Bob Climpson of Noble Numismatics Pty. Ltd., Sydney, who found the time for this task in spite of their own busy commitments.

Finally I must acknowledge the debt I owe to my wife Jann and daughter Camilla, whose support and love are the bedrock of my life, both in and outside scholarship.

MAPS

The maps have been drawn by the author to show the principal places mentioned in this book. The largest and most detailed maps of the Mediterranean world will be found in R. J. A. Talbert (ed.), *The Barrington Atlas of the Greek and Roman World* (Princeton Univ. Press, 2000).

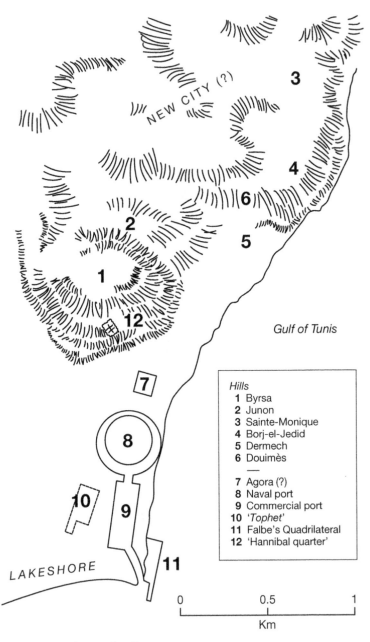

Gulf of Tunis

LAKESHORE

Hills
1 Byrsa
2 Junon
3 Sainte-Monique
4 Borj-el-Jedid
5 Dermech
6 Douimès
—
7 Agora (?)
8 Naval port
9 Commercial port
10 'Tophet'
11 Falbe's Quadrilateral
12 'Hannibal quarter'

0   0.5   1
             Km

Map 1A Carthage: the City

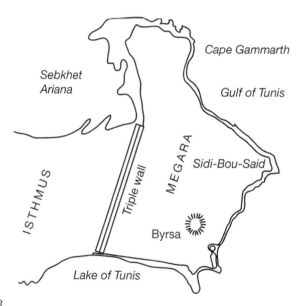

Cape Gammarth

Sebkhet
Ariana

Gulf of Tunis

MEGARA

ISTHMUS

Triple wall

Sidi-Bou-Said

Byrsa

Lake of Tunis

Map 1B

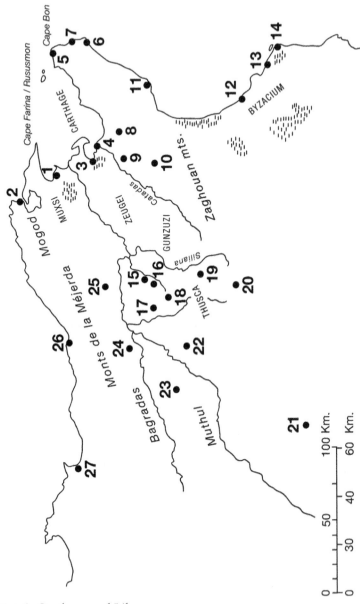

Map 2 Carthage and Libya

Key to Map 2

	Numerical	Alphabetical	
1	Utica	Aspis/Clupea	6
2	Hippacra	Bulla	24
3	Tunes	El Houaria	5
4	Maxula	Hadrumetum	12
5	El Houaria	Hippacra	2
6	Aspis/Clupea	Hippo Regius	27
7	Kerkouane	Kerkouane	7
8	Nepheris	Leptis	13
9	Uthina	Mactar	20
10	Ziqua	Maxula	4
11	Neapolis	Musti	18
12	Hadrumetum	Naraggara	23
13	Leptis	Neapolis	11
14	Thapsus	Nepheris	8
15	Thubursicu	Sicca	22
16	Thugga	Thabraca	26
17	Uchi	Thapsus	14
18	Musti	Theveste	21
19	Zama	Thubursicu	15
20	Mactar	Thugga	16
21	Theveste	Tunes	3
22	Sicca	Uchi	17
23	Naraggara	Uthina	9
24	Bulla	Utica	1
25	Vaga	Vaga	25
26	Thabraca	Zama	19
27	Hippo Regius	Ziqua	10

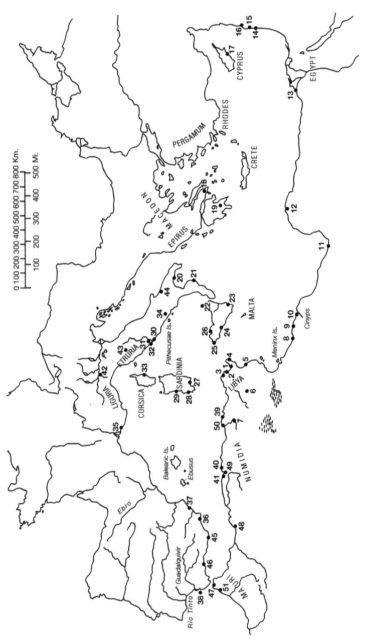

Map 3A The Mediterranean World

Key to Map 3A

	Numerical	Alphabetical	
1	Carthage	Abdera	45
2	Utica	Acragas	24
3	Hippacra	Akra Leuke	37
4	Kerkouane	Alalia	33
5	Hadrumetum	Alexandria	13
6	Theveste	Arae Philaenorum	11
7	Cirta	Athens	18
8	Sabratha	Caere	31
9	Oea	Cannae	44
10	Lepcis Magna	Capua	34
11	Arae Philaenorum	Carales	27
12	Cyrene	Carthage	1
13	Alexandria	Carthage in Spain	36
14	Tyre	Chullu	50
15	Sidon	Cirta	7
16	Ugarit	Citium	17
17	Citium	Croton	21
18	Athens	Cyrene	12
19	Sparta	Gades	38
20	Tarentum	Hadrumetum	5
21	Croton	Hippacra	3
22	Messana	Icosium	40
23	Syracuse	Iol	41
24	Acragas	Kerkouane	4
25	Motya	L. Trasimene	43
26	Panormus	Lepcis Magna	10
27	Carales	Lixus	51
28	Sulcis	Malaca	46
29	Tharros	Massilia	35
30	Rome	Messana	22
31	Caere	Motya	25
32	Pyrgi	Oea	9
33	Alalia	Panormus	26
34	Capua	Pyrgi	32
35	Massilia	Rome	30
36	Carthage in Spain	Rusicade	39
37	Akra Leuke	Sabratha	8
38	Gades	Sidon	15
39	Rusicade	Siga	48
40	Icosium	Sparta	19
41	Iol	Sulcis	28
42	Trebia River	Syracuse	23
43	L. Trasimene	Tarentum	20
44	Cannae	Tharros	29
45	Abdera	Theveste	6
46	Malaca	Tingi	47
47	Tingi	Tipasa	49
48	Siga	Trebia River	42
49	Tipasa	Tyre	14
50	Chullu	Ugarit	16
51	Lixus	Utica	2

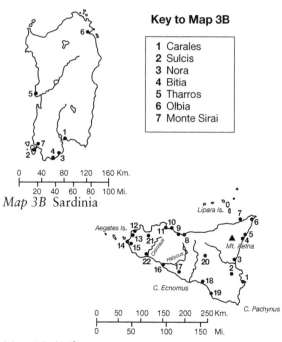

Key to Map 3B

1 Carales
2 Sulcis
3 Nora
4 Bitia
5 Tharros
6 Olbia
7 Monte Sirai

Map 3B Sardinia

Map 3C Sicily

Key to Map 3C

	Numerical	Alphabetical	
1	Syracuse	Acragas	17
2	Leontini	Camarina	19
3	Catana	Catana	3
4	Naxos	Drepana	13
5	Tauromenium	Enna	20
6	Messana	Gela	18
7	Mylae	Heraclea Minoa	16
8	Himera	Himera	8
9	Thermae Himeraeae	Leontini	2
10	Solous	Lilybaeum	15
11	Panormus	Messana	6
12	Mt Eryx	Motya	14
13	Drepana	Mt Eryx	12
14	Motya	Mylae	7
15	Lilybaeum	Naxos	4
16	Heraclea Minoa	Panormus	11
17	Acragas	Segesta	21
18	Gela	Selinus	22
19	Camarina	Solous	10
20	Enna	Syracuse	1
21	Segesta	Tauromenium	5
22	Selinus	Thermae Himeraeae	9

ILLUSTRATIONS

COVER   Statuette of a Carthaginian goddess with lioness-
head: Isis or, less likely, Tanit
   The lioness-head is an Egyptian motif, while the
goddess' robe is Greek in style; her legs are clasped by
huge wings, an Isis-cult motif (compare Illustration 21).
From Thinissut on the Cape Bon peninsula, after
146 BC: an example of surviving Carthaginian
cultural influence.

1   Sea walls, *c*. 400 BC: artist's reconstruction   74
2   Mausoleum at Thugga (2nd Century BC)   79
3   Stone *cippus* from Carthage: rectangular tower design
    and 'bottle' symbol on side   80
4   View of the '*tophet*' at Carthage   81
5   Painting of city in Jebel Mlezza tomb VIII   82
6   View of the 'Hannibal quarter' on Byrsa's southern
    slope   84
7   Another view of the 'Hannibal quarter'   84
8   Carthage 1958   86
    *Circular naval port in foreground, 'tophet' to the right
    of the rectangular commercial port, heights of
    Borj-el-Jedid and village of Sidi Bou Said in background.*
9   Carthage *c*. 200 BC: artist's reconstruction   89
    *The view is from the hill of Byrsa looking south, with
    the agora, the artificial ports and Falbe's
    Quadrilateral beyond.*
10 The artificial ports area *c*. 1922   90
    *The peninsula stretching beyond the rectangular port
    has developed far beyond its ancient extent.*
11 Entrance to house at Kerkouane, with 'sign of Tanit'   96
12 The 'Isis priestess' from Ste Monique tomb: marble
    lid of sarcophagus   97
13 Ivory mirror-handle depicting a goddess(?),
    c. 7th Century   109

14 Terracotta statuette of a goddess, 7th–6th Century   109
15 Mother and child at baking oven   110
16 Terracotta tondo: cavalryman and his hound   111
17 Fluteplayer from Carthage: terracotta statuette,
    4th Century   114
18 Bronze mirror (back), profile of a goddess   115
19 Terracotta head of Medusa   115
20 *Cippus* from Hadrumetum   116
21 *Stele* of a youth, from Hadrumetum   117
22 Ossuary of a priest from Ste Monique tomb,
    4th–3rd Centuries   118
23 Another Isis effigy: terracotta statuette   119
24 A selection of Carthaginian coins from Sicily and
    North Africa   122
25. Heavy-armed infantry on the march: jasper scarab from
    Kerkouane, 4th Century BC   159
26. Front and back parade armour (4th–3rd Centuries BC)
    found at Ksour Essaf, near Sousse   160

SOURCES OF IMAGES

1. From M. H. Fantar, *Carthage: La cité punique*, p. 39, by permission of the author and publisher.
2. From S. Peters (ed.), *Hannibal ad Portas,* p. 63: by permission of the Badisches Landesmuseum, Karslruhe, and Theiss Verlag, Stuttgart.
3. From *Hannibal ad Portas,* 221 no. 3: by permission of the Institut National du Patrimoine, Ministère de la Culture de la Sauvegarde du Patrimoine, Republic of Tunisia [hereafter the Institut National du Patrimoine, Tunisia], and of Theiss Verlag.
4. Freely licensed image (Creative Commons Attribution ShareAlike 2.5) from Wikipedia Commons at: http://images.google.com.au/imgres?imgurl=http://upload.wikimedia.org/wikipedia/commons/5/51/Tunisise_Carthage_Tophet_Salambo_04.JPG&imgrefurl=http://commons.wikimedia.org/wiki/File:Tunisise_Carthage_Tophet_Salambo_04.JPG&usg=_w1I_TucezbuF7-AgxLy8CWKZrds=&h=2000&w=3008&sz=3201&hl=en&start=3&um=1&tbnid=YnoFeRmUnbjiPM:&tbnh=100&tbnw=150&prev=/images%3Fq%3Dcarthage%2Btophet%26hl%3Den%26client%3Dfirefox-a%26rls%3Dorg.mozilla:en-US:official%26sa%3DN%26um%3D1, retrieved 19/10/2009.
5. From M. H. Fantar, *Carthage: La cité punique*, p. 31, by permission of the author and publisher.
6. From *Hannibal ad Portas,* p. 217, by permission of the Badisches Landesmuseum, Karlsruhe, and Theiss Verlag.
7. Public domain image from Wikipedia Commons, at: http://en.wikipedia.org/wiki/File:Quartier_Punique.JPG, retrieved 14/10/2009.

8. Public domain image from Wikipedia Commons at http://
commons.wikimedia.org/wiki/File:Carthage-1958-
PortsPuniques.jpg, retrieved 3/10/2009.
9. From M. H. Fantar, *Carthage: La cité punique*, p. 43, by
permission of the author and publisher.
10. Public domain image from Wikipedia Commons, at: http://
images.google.com.au/imgres?imgurl=http://upload.wikimedia.
org/wikipedia/commons/2/26/Carthage-1922-PortsPuniques.
jpg&imgrefurl=http://commons.wikimedia.org/wiki/
File:Carthage-1922-PortsPuniques.jpg&usg=__iVS0nYYJWV
O60XpepUgF4dmt5sI=&h=1797&w=2400&sz=357&hl=en&
start=1&um=1&tbnid=z_JOiB5MkF0OeM:&tbnh=112&tbn
w=150&prev=/images%3Fq%3DCarthage%2B1922%26hl%
3Den%26client%3Dfirefox-a%26rls%3Dorg.mozilla:en-
US:official%26sa%3DG%26um%3D1, retrieved 3/10/2009.
11. From M. H. Fantar, *Carthage: La cité punique*, p. 46, by
permission of the author and publisher.
12. From *Hannibal ad Portas*, pp. 284–5 no. 61: by permission of the
Institut National du Patrimoine, Tunisia, and Theiss Verlag.
13. From *Hannibal ad Portas*, p. 337 no. 5: by permission of the
Institut National du Patrimoine, Tunisia, and Theiss Verlag.
14. From *Hannibal ad Portas*, p. 233 no. 4: by permission of the
Institut National du Patrimoine, Tunisia, and Theiss Verlag.
15. From M. H. Fantar, *Carthage: La cité punique*, p. 62, by
permission of the author and publisher.
16. From *Hannibal ad Portas*, p. 271 no. 10: by permission of the
Institut National du Patrimoine, Tunisia, and Theiss Verlag.
17. From M. H. Fantar, *Carthage: La cité punique*, p. 102, by
permission of the author and publisher.
18. From *Hannibal ad Portas*, p. 291 no. 86: by permission of the
Institut National du Patrimoine, Tunisia, and Theiss Verlag.
19. From *Hannibal ad Portas*, p. 237 no. 20: by permission of the
Institut National du Patrimoine, Tunisia, and Theiss Verlag.
20. Reproduced by permission of the Institut National du Patrimoine,
Tunisia.
21. From *Hannibal ad Portas*, p. 259 no. 7: by permission of the
Institut National du Patrimoine, Tunisia, and Theiss Verlag.
22. From *Hannibal ad Portas*, p. 286 no. 64: by permission of the
Institut National du Patrimoine, Tunisia, and Theiss Verlag.
23. From *Hannibal ad Portas*, pp. 285 no. 63: by permission of the
Institut National du Patrimoine, Tunisia, and Theiss Verlag.

24. Coin-images reproduced by permission of Dr Stephen Mulligan, Sydney, and prepared by Noble Numismatics Ltd., Sydney.
25. From M. H. Fantar, *Carthage: La cité punique*, p. 111, by permission of the author and publisher.
26. Reproduced by permission of the Institut National du Patrimoine, Tunisia.

CHRONOLOGICAL TABLE

All dates are BC unless marked otherwise

Foundations

1103	traditional date for foundation of Gades
1101	traditional date for foundation of Utica
813	Timaeus' foundation-date for Carthage (and Rome) and story of Elissa-Dido
753	foundation of Rome (most widely accepted date)

Expansion of Carthage

c. 640	Colaeus of Samos trades with Tartessus
c. 600	Phocaean Greeks found Massalia
c. 580	Pentathlus unsuccessfully tries to found a Greek city in western Sicily
550–500	Carthage imposes dominance over much of Sardinia and over western Sicily
c. 540	Phocaean refugees settle at Alalia in Cyprus
c. 540–530	career of Mazeus or 'Malchus'
c. 535	Carthaginian and Etruscan fleet defeated by Phocaeans off Alalia; Phocaeans abandon Alalia

The Magonid family in power

c. 530	Mago achieves dominance in Carthage's affairs
c. 530–396	ascendancy of Mago's sons and descendants, the Magonids
c. 525	Carthaginians control island of Ebusus
c. 515	Dorieus of Sparta's colony near Lepcis Magna expelled

c. 510	Dorieus killed in western Sicily
c. 510–500	Hasdrubal the Magonid killed in Sardinia
c. 509	Carthage's first treaty with Rome
c. 500–450	Atlantic voyage of Hanno, recorded in his *Periplus*, and Himilco's voyage to north-western Europe
c. 500	Thefarie Velianas' shrine to Astarte-Uni at Pyrgi, Etruria
c. 485	Carthaginians at war with Acragas and Syracuse in Sicily
480	Battle of Himera and death of Hamilcar the Magonid
480–410	Carthage at peace with Sicilian Greeks
after 480	progressive subjugation of Libyans
474	Syracuse defeats Etruscans at sea off Cumae, Campania
415–413	Athenian expedition against Syracuse

War and peace with the Sicilian Greeks

409–405	Carthaginian campaigns against Sicilian Greeks
406	Sack of Acragas by Hannibal son of Gisco and his colleague Himilco
405	rise to power of Dionysius I at Syracuse; peace with Carthage
398–396	Dionysius' new war with Carthage
398	Syracusans sack Motya
396	plague epidemic at Carthage; suicide of Himilco; end of Magonid dominance
	Carthage institutes cult of Demeter and Kore (Persephone) to atone for impieties in Sicily
	Great Libyan Revolt, put down by Mago
393–392	Sicilian campaigns of Mago, ended by new peace with Syracuse
390s/380s	creation of the court of One Hundred and Four
383–(?)381	Mago's second war with Syracuse
379/378	Carthage re-establishes town of Hipponium in southern Italy
370s–360s	plague again rages at Carthage; revolts by Libyans and Sardinians, eventually crushed
368	Dionysius I launches new war with Carthage, but dies; war flickers out
c. 368	Carthaginian senate bans study of Greek (temporarily)
367–357	rule of Dionysius II at Syracuse

360s–350s	ascendancy of Hanno the Great at Carthage
c. 350	conspiracy and fall of Hanno the Great
357–344	wars, coups and anarchy in Greek Sicily
348	Carthage's second treaty with Rome

Carthage against Timoleon and Agathocles

345	new Carthaginian intervention in Greek Sicily
343	Timoleon arrives in Sicily. Suicide of Mago after setback outside Syracuse
341	May/June: battle of the river Crimisus and end of Carthage's war in Sicily Gisco son of Hanno the Great recalled from exile
341–320s	ascendancy of Gisco
334	Alexander the Great captures Tyre, threatens Carthage with future attack
325	Carthage mediates in Sicilian Greek quarrels
319	Carthage mediates in Syracusan civil strife, first opposing but then supporting Agathocles
317	Agathocles takes power at Syracuse
315–314	Carthaginian general Hamilcar mediates in fresh inter-Greek conflicts
312	Agathocles attacks Carthaginian territory in western Sicily
311	new general, Hamilcar son of Gisco, occupies much of eastern Sicily; besieges Syracuse
310	(14 August) Agathocles' invasion fleet sails to Cape Bon; he wins victories in Libya; many or most Libyans revolt from Carthage
309	Hamilcar's second attack on Syracuse defeated; he is captured and killed; Carthage's Sicilian Greek allies break away. Agathocles dominates Libya but cannot take Carthage
308	Bomilcar's failed coup in Carthage Agathocles, reinforced by Ophellas' army from Cyrene, captures Hippacra and Utica; returns on his own to Sicily. Plundering campaigns by his son and lieutenants across Libya and into Numidia; Carthaginians defeat the invaders
307	Agathocles returns to Africa, but is defeated; abandons his sons and soldiers to return to Syracuse; collapse of the Greek invasion. Libyans subdued

306	peace between Carthage and Agathocles restores old status quo supposed date of supposed 'Philinus-treaty' with Rome

War with Pyrrhus and the First Punic War

289	death of Agathocles; fresh upheavals among Sicilian Greeks
288	Mamertine mercenaries seize Messana
c. 280	Hicetas, tyrant of Syracuse, invades Carthaginian Sicily
280/279	Carthaginian land and sea forces besiege Syracuse; Syracusans appeal for help to Pyrrhus in Italy
278–276	Pyrrhus' campaigns against the Carthaginians
276	Pyrrhus returns to Italy
275/274	Hiero becomes effective leader of Syracuse
273/272	Hiero makes peace with Carthage
272	Tarentum surrenders to Rome; Rome now effective ruler of Italian peninsula
264	escalating crisis over Mamertines of Messana; outbreak of war between Carthage and Rome
264–241	First Punic War
260	Rome's first grand fleet defeats Carthaginians off Mylae, Sicily
256–255	failed Roman invasion of North Africa under Regulus
249	Roman naval defeats off Drepana and Camarina (last Carthaginian victories in the war)
247	Hamilcar Barca appointed general in Sicily Hanno the Great captures Theveste in Numidia
241	(10 March) Roman naval victory off Aegates Islands; peace treaty ends First Punic War

The dominance of the Barcids

late 241–early 237	Great revolt (Truceless War) of mercenaries and Libyans in North Africa
238/237	Hamilcar Barca becomes dominant at Carthage
237–228	Hamilcar's campaigns in southern Spain create new Carthaginian province
228–221	his son-in-law and successor Hasdrubal dominates Carthaginian affairs from Spain

227/226	Hasdrubal founds Spanish Carthage ('New Carthage' to Romans)
221	Hannibal, son of Hamilcar, becomes chief general and leader of Carthage
219	Hannibal besieges and after 7 months sacks Saguntum in eastern Spain

The Second Punic War

218	Hannibal marches over the Alps into Italy; victory at river Trebia, northern Italy (December)
218–211	elder Scipio brothers' campaigns in Spain against Carthaginians
c. 218–210	construction of Carthage's artificial ports south of the *agora* (suggested dating)
217	(22 June) Hannibal's victory at Lake Trasimene, Etruria
217–216	Hannibal's operations against Fabius the Delayer and his military successors
216	(2 August) victory of Cannae, Apulia; Capua defects to Carthage
216–212	much though not all of southern Italy defects from Rome
215	Hannibal's alliance with Philip V of Macedon
214	Carthage's alliance with Syracuse
213	Marcellus opens siege of Syracuse
212	Tarentum defects to Hannibal
	Romans open siege of Capua
	Syracuse captured and plundered by Marcellus
211	destruction of the elder Scipios in southern Spain
	Hannibal's march on Rome; surrender of Capua to Romans
209	younger Scipio (later Africanus) captures Spanish Carthage; Fabius the Delayer recaptures Tarentum
208–206	Scipio defeats Carthaginians in Spain and conquers Carthaginian province
207	Hasdrubal, brother of Hannibal, marches into northern Italy; (21 June) defeated and killed at river Metaurus
207–203	Hannibal confined to far south of Italy
204–203	Scipio invades North Africa, defeats Carthaginians and their Numidian ally Syphax; Carthage makes

	peace with Rome. Hannibal recalled from Italy with his army
202	peace denounced or ignored by Carthage and Hannibal; (19 October?) battle of Zama; Carthage, urged by Hannibal, seeks fresh terms
201	second peace treaty with Rome: end of Carthage as a great power. Masinissa king of all Numidia

Carthage's last half-century

200–196	Rome's second war with Philip V, crippling Macedon as a great power
197(?)–193	Carthage in dispute (over territory?) with Masinissa of Numidia
196	Hannibal as sufete enacts financial and political reforms
195	Hannibal forced into exile by his political enemies, with Roman connivance
192–188	Antiochus III, the Great King of the east, defeated in war with Rome. Rome becomes dominant power from the Atlantic to the Euphrates
182	supposed dispute between Carthage and Numidia over territory
174–172	third(?) dispute with Numidia over territory
mid-160s	Masinissa seizes Emporia; Rome adjudicates in his favour
150s	factional politics at Carthage embittered by Masinissa's encroachments
153 or 152	Masinissa seizes all Carthage's western Libyan lands
150	Masinissa attacks more Carthaginian territory; Carthaginian offensive against him ends in disaster Carthage threatened with Roman armed intervention; fails to appease Rome

The Third Punic War and the destruction of Carthage

150–149	(winter) Rome declares war on Carthage. Carthage offers total submission to Roman wishes
149	(spring) consuls land at Utica and demand that Carthaginians abandon their city Carthage declares war on Rome; siege of the city begins

	Masinissa dies, aged over 90; Scipio Aemilianus settles Numidia's affairs
149–148	Carthaginians in the city hold out, supported by field army at Nepheris and by much of Libya
147	Scipio Aemilianus, now consul, reinvigorates the siege; improvised Carthaginian fleet defeated outside the ports
147–146	(winter) Scipio destroys field army at Nepheris; Libya capitulates
146, spring	Scipio's troops break into Carthage; Byrsa capitulates; Carthage burned. Remaining Carthaginian lands become Roman province of 'Africa'

Carthage under the Romans

122	abortive effort to found a Roman colony on site of Carthage
112–105	Rome at war with Numidia under Masinissa's grandson Jugurtha
46	Julius Caesar annexes Numidia as province of 'Africa Nova'
	Caesar refounds Carthage with Roman colonists
AD 160–240	Tertullian: Carthaginian, Roman and Christian writer
AD 193–211	Septimius Severus of Lepcis Magna reigns as first Roman emperor from Africa; honours memory of Hannibal

SOURCES OF KNOWLEDGE

Archaeological evidence and ancient written works carry the story of the Carthaginians. Both are incomplete in many ways. Archaeological finds are limited because of costs, because the site of Carthage is again inhabited, and because what is found is not always easy to interpret. Inscriptions written in Punic, the Carthaginians' language, may be only partly legible, and the meaning of the words is often debated. Nonetheless, archaeology has not just added to our knowledge of Carthaginian civilisation but has revolutionised it.

The surviving written works are by Greeks and Romans, most of them living after the fall of Carthage and all of them interested mainly in her dealings and her cultural contrasts with their societies. Most ancient works do not survive complete either, so that a good deal which the ancient readers had available is now lost to us.

IMPORTANT ANCIENT WRITERS

Appian: an Alexandrian Greek and imperial bureaucrat of the later 2nd Century AD; wrote a history of Rome's wars down to Julius Caesar's time, treating each region in a separate book (that is, book-roll). His book *Libyca* narrates Rome's campaigns in Africa against Carthage; *Iberica*, all their wars in Spain; *Hannibalica*, the campaigns of Hannibal in Italy. Some books are only partly preserved. Appian is very dependent on earlier histories; his chosen sources for the Punic Wars were often imaginative. His own composition methods, too, left him open to mistakes (sometimes silly ones). Even so, his histories of these conflicts offer useful information, above all on the Third Punic War where he mainly though not exclusively relies on Polybius.

Cassius Dio: a Roman senator and consul who lived from about AD 163 to after 220, Bithynian by birth; of his *Roman History* in eighty books from Rome's foundation to his own times only some books survive in full, as do Byzantine excerpts from his earlier books and a virtual précis by the Byzantine John Zonaras down to 146 BC, as well as for some later periods. Dio is an intelligent writer, focused on Rome but prepared to be fair to other sides, and important too because he seems to have consulted older Roman sources (of the 2nd–1st Centuries BC) along with Greek authors.

Diodorus: a Sicilian of the later 1st Century BC; author of a *Library of History* in forty books, which he describes as a compressed world history taken from respected Greek predecessors. He seems to have compressed one at a time for lengthy stretches, though in places adding items from another source. This method can produce an uneven narrative, but Diodorus is still the main source for Greek Sicily's history and its dealings with Carthage, as well as an important one for Greece and the eastern Mediterranean. His sources for Carthage's wars in Sicily included Ephorus (4th Century) and Timaeus (early 3rd Century); on the Punic Wars he used Polybius. Of the original forty books, only 1–5 and 11–20 are now complete; excerpts, some long, others short, survive in Byzantine compilations.

Justin: a Roman writer of late but unknown date (between the 2nd and 4th Centuries) who made a précis of the forty-four-book world history by Pompeius Trogus, a Roman from Gaul of Augustus' time. The *Philippic Histories* avoid a detailed account of Rome and focus on the rest of the world from the Assyrians onwards, with short but notable treatments of Carthage's foundation-story and history from the 6th to the early 3rd Centuries. Trogus' sources are unnamed but no doubt included earlier extensive histories, especially Greek ones. Besides Justin's précis, a set of contents lists (*prologi*) of Trogus' books survives; at times these throw light on what Justin chose to include and exclude.

Livy: Titus Livius of Patavium (59 BC–AD 17) devoted most of his life to a monumental history of Rome in 142 books, bringing it down to the middle of Augustus' reign and consulting a broad range of older histories and other sources, Greek as well as Roman. Conscientious, relatively humane, and strongly patriotic, Livy found his history expanding almost unstoppably as he proceeded (he comments on this at the start of Book 31), while his own critical abilities stayed limited and his bias for Rome's side of events often over-coloured his narrative. Books 1–10 survive (down to 293 BC), then 21–45 (from 218 to 167): his history of the Second Punic War (Books 21–30) is the longest, and most famous, full-length account, while in later books he gives much information about Hannibal's later life. For this half-century he draws greatly on both Polybius and Roman authors – sometimes more or less paraphrasing Polybius while constantly adding details from elsewhere, which can have strange results. Unfortunately he is not that interested in Carthaginian affairs, though what he does narrate is valuable. Useful epitomes (*Periochae*) of nearly all the 142 books, of 4th-Century AD date, survive; most are brief, while those of Books 48–50 (the period of the Third Punic War) are much lengthier and offer important details.

Nepos: Cornelius Nepos, a contemporary of Cicero, included short biographies of Hamilcar Barca and his son Hannibal among a set of *Lives of Eminent Foreign Generals*. They provide useful items along with some foolish errors; his sources probably included Hannibal's literary Greek friends Silenus and Sosylus.

Plutarch: Greek philosopher and biographer of Greek and Roman leaders, including several who had dealings with Carthage (Dion, Timoleon, Pyrrhus, Fabius Maximus, Marcellus). Plutarch used a range of sources, mostly sound ones, and is important whenever he touches on Carthaginian matters.

Polyaenus: Greek writer of the 160s AD, author of eight books on military and naval *Stratagems,* largely on Greek commanders but with some examples from Carthaginian history. Unfortunately his methods are often careless and some of his anecdotes implausible.

Polybius: historian (about 200–118 BC) of the Mediterranean world for the period 264 to 146 BC, a leading Greek of Megalopolis in the Peloponnese. During years spent as an increasingly respected political hostage at Rome (167–150), and becoming a close friend of the eminent Scipio Aemilianus and a temperate admirer of Rome's political system, he composed his *Histories* in forty sizeable books, analytical and argumentative as well as narrative, to explain how the Romans could make themselves masters of the Mediterranean world in less than fifty-three years (219–167). He opens with a shorter narrative of events from 264, and later extended the work to end in

146 with the destruction of Carthage; he was an eyewitness of this tragedy. His sources, whom he often analyses and criticises, all wrote in Greek but included pro-Carthaginian and early Roman historians. Like others, Polybius is interested in Carthage largely where she interacted with the outside world, especially Rome. His ponderous style and complex treatment of issues caused only Books 1–5 to survive in full, but Byzantine compilers in the 10th Century made lengthy extracts from the rest, while shorter excerpts are quoted by ancient and Byzantine authors.

Strabo: Greek scholar of Augustan times, whose seventeen-book *Geography* of the known world deals with places, peoples, cultures and even economics. Book 17 covers Africa, including a rather short section on Carthage.

I

THE PHOENICIANS
IN THE WEST

THE PHOENICIANS

The Canaans (*Kn'nm*), as the ancient Phoenicians called themselves, had long been settled on the eastern shore of the Mediterranean before they made an impact on the west. The ancient Israelites called them *Ponim*, a name which in varying forms spread to the Greeks (as 'Phoenices') and the Romans ('Poeni'), and so to modern times.[1]

Trade became their forte, under the leadership of wealthy cities like Byblos – the earliest to achieve commercial riches – Arwad, Sidon and Tyre. Phoenicia lay conveniently at the crossroads of Near Eastern trade routes, both east–west and north–south, with tin and copper among their staples: tin originally from central Asia, copper from local mines and also from Cyprus, the 'copper' island par excellence. The cedar forests of Lebanon were another much-exploited resource, valued especially by timber-poor Egypt and important too to the peoples to Phoenicia's north and east, notably the Hittites, Assyrians and Babylonians. Textiles and even glass manufactures formed other elements in the Phoenicians' trading versatility.

With prosperity came outside pressures. New Kingdom Egypt sought to impose and hold control over Phoenicia's coasts and cities, with varying success; the 14th-Century BC collection of documents from Amarna in Egypt show how the kings of Byblos could communicate with the pharaohs on near-equal terms. But Egypt's weakness after 1200 BC, in the confusion of attacks by the mysterious 'Sea Peoples' and by Libyans overland from the west, along with her internal dissensions, allowed the Phoenicians a little time for complacency – as the long-suffering Egyptian envoy Wenamon, on another quest for timber around 1100, found in his dealings with Zakarbaal, king of Byblos.

Disruption and change happened elsewhere too. Assyria suffered setbacks in Mesopotamia and beyond, the Hittite kingdom collapsed, and the great Syrian port and entrepôt Ugarit was destroyed. When Assyrian power revived in the 11th Century, the Phoenicians did not escape its attention: they became vassals of the eastern empire. Their dependence was limited and did not hamper their business fortunes, nor did migrations of (it seems) Sea Peoples from the central and western Mediterranean to the coast to Phoenicia's south. This region, from then on called Philistia, with prosperous cities like Ascalon and Gaza, developed close ties with Phoenicia, while trade with Cyprus, Syria and other eastern lands recovered after a dip and increased in vigour during the 11th Century. Among Phoenician cities Byblos suffered eclipse, while Sidon and then Tyre became pre-eminent.

SIDON AND TYRE

Both were very old places already. The Tyrians remembered being first founded around 2750 BC (so they told Herodotus in the mid-5th Century, and archaeological finds support it). Nor had they invariably been friends: around 1340 we find the Sidonians blockading Tyre and her king writing to seek help – not very successfully – from Egypt. Sidonian tradition, represented on coins of the Hellenistic era, gave that city a more benign role as 'foundress' of Tyre: a garbled memory at best, but perhaps Sidon helped to repopulate her sister city soon after 1200 after other troubles. Sidon's power had been based both on prosperous trade from her two harbours, and on broad mainland acres. With a city area of 145 acres (58 hectares) and substantial territory along the coast and stretching inland, she was Phoenicia personified for the writers of Old Testament books like *Joshua* and *1 Kings*; and, as just noted, made life miserable at times for her sister city twenty-two miles to the south. From about 1000 BC on, however, Tyre outdid Sidon in energy and success, thanks at least in part to vigorous and extended commerce.

Tyre, whose Phoenician name was Sor, stood on an island just off the coast (until Alexander the Great's siege-mole joined it to the mainland). In its times of prosperity, its 130 acres housed an estimated thirty thousand inhabitants: Strabo, the geographer of Augustus' era, notes that its multi-storeyed buildings were higher than the skyscrapers in Rome. It too acquired fairly sizeable mainland territory, important for foodstuffs and the city's water supply, while the coastal waters yielded the shellfish that produced Tyre's famous 'purple', in fact scarlet, dye. The first of its enterprising leaders known to history was the famous Hiram (king *c.* 971–939), recorded in the Bible as a comradely contemporary of Solomon of Jerusalem, whose great temple he supposedly contributed to building. In the same period, Tyre's trading links with western lands blossomed.

Phoenician trading ships had been visiting Greece and lands further west from very early, with the versatile, and sometimes devious, Phoenician merchant finding mention in both the *Iliad* and the *Odyssey*. Of course they were not unique in these activities: Greek traders too ventured abroad, and are found for instance in Syria at the 9th-Century emporium now called Al Mina, and from the 8th Century on the island of Pithecusae (Ischia) near Naples. At these and other places, trading intercourse with both locals and Phoenicians was busy and mutually beneficial.

The Phoenicians' overseas commerce was celebrated and sometimes envied – as Old Testament diatribes against Tyrian wealth and pride vividly show. Merchants offered household goods and luxury items from their homeland and other eastern countries, and in return sought mainly raw materials: iron from the island of Elba, for instance; silver and lead from mainland Etruria and then from southern Spain. Ivory and tin were traded from beyond the Pillars of Hercules (the straits of Gibraltar) – tin coming from the 'Cassiterides islands', often but insecurely thought to be Cornwall or the Scillies, and ivory from the west coast of Africa. Trade exchanges necessarily were by barter: even after the Lydian kingdom in western Asia Minor devised coins around 600 as a way to pay for goods, it took some centuries for western states (Carthage included) to make use of them even in limited ways. Traders' ships would arrive at a harbour or anchorage, interested locals – including local grandees or their agents – would gather, and business would be done. Landing sites, at the mouths of rivers or on small, easily defended peninsulas, became regular trading places and, later on, the sites of colonial settlements from Phoenicia.[2]

SETTLEMENTS IN THE WEST

It was only after some centuries that Phoenicians began to settle overseas. Various ancient traditions accorded very early dates – around 1100 – to Gades (today's Cádiz), Lixus on the Atlantic coast of Mauretania (Morocco), and Utica on the Tunisian coast just north of Carthage, so that Carthage with her traditional date of 813 was seen as much the youngest of Tyre's daughters. On the other hand, a century and a half of archaeological effort on the western Mediterranean's many shores lends no support to tradition. The earliest levels of occupation, identified by finds of relatively datable Greek pottery imports, point to the 8th Century or, at most, late in the 9th. The driving force behind these foundations was Tyre.

By the middle of the 8th Century Tyre, though under pressure from Assyria, had won hegemony over its old rival Sidon: thus King Ithobaal I (887–856, father of the notorious Jezebel) also styled himself 'king of the Sidonians'. Tyrian commerce with lands overseas developed as well. The Cyprus copper trade was important enough for the city to establish a settlement-colony there during the 9th Century, apparently though not certainly at the already old town of Citium (Phoenician *Kty*; modern Larnaca) on the coast facing Phoenicia. An inscription of about 750 commemorates a governor or vice-regent (*soken*) of the 'New City': a name, or a term, used perhaps to denote the colony in contrast to an older community. It was a name with a future – in Phoenician, *Qart-hadasht*. Also worth noting is that the Phoenician name for Cyprus was Alashiya.

With the evidence from archaeology indicating foundation-dates for all the western colonies no earlier than Citium's, and many of them later, we have to infer that the Phoenicians led by Tyre chose to launch ambitious and consistent waves of colonisation during the later 9th and the 8th to 7th Centuries. They planted not trading-posts but urban settlements all across the southern, central and western Mediterranean coasts. Lixus, Gades and Utica were only three of many; in Spain the colonies also included Malaca, Sexi and Abdera on the Costa del Sol; the Sardinian creations included Bitia, Carales, Nora, Olbia, Sulcis and Tharros; in Sicily they founded the island town of Motya, and probably Panormus and Solous; and in North Africa, which they and the Greeks after them called Libya, the cities of Utica and Carthage at least, probably also Hippacra, Hadrumetum and, to the east, Lepcis Magna near today's Tripoli (others too are possible). The migrations were so prolific that before very long some settlers in southern Spain moved on to establish themselves on the island of Ebusus, as archaeological finds indicate – although the Carthaginians claimed otherwise, as we shall see.

The Tyrians had their own chronicles, which may have told a different story about the migrations. The later Jewish historian Josephus, citing Menander of Ephesus, a Greek researcher into Phoenician history, reports the chronicles dating Carthage to a hundred and fifty-five years after the accession of Hiram, thus around

816. These 'annals of Tyre' may also be the ultimate source for the Roman author Velleius' date of about 1103 for Gades and Pliny the Elder's of 1101 for Utica; and according to Pliny again, Lixus' temple of 'Hercules', in other words the Phoenician god Melqart, was older than the famous one at Gades. If such dates do have a basis, they may record when such shrines were first established at trading-sites; Pliny's date for Utica is actually that of its hallowed temple of 'Apollo', usually identified on Cypriot evidence as the god Reshef.

Phoenicians were as punctiliously pious as Romans, and merchants arriving to trade in a new region would commonly set up a sacred place for their protecting deity to watch over them. This may then have been recorded. The oldest Phoenician *stele*, or inscribed stone, in Sardinia apparently commemorates such an honour to the Cypriot god Pumay, at Nora in the south-west; it dates to around 800 or soon after, and Nora indeed had the reputation of being Sardinia's first Phoenician foundation.[3]

The extent of this colonial expansion in about a century and a half indicates that, while the Tyrians led, other Phoenicians took part too. Over-population may have been a factor, as some ancient writers like Sallust and Justin thought. Another may have been a need for new, copious and less contested raw materials, in an era of conflict-driven great powers in Phoenicia's neighbourhood – notably the resurgent Assyrians, whose kings exacted varied and always expensive tribute from the coastal cities. These stresses may in turn have created a third reason for some migrations overseas: domestic dissensions, blamed or credited by ancient writers as prompting the foundation both of Lepcis and, more famously, of Carthage.

II

CARTHAGE: FOUNDATION
AND GROWTH

TALES OF THE FOUNDATION

When the first colonists from Tyre established themselves on the great headland overlooking the Gulf of Tunis, they named their 'new city' appropriately, *Qart-hadasht*. To the Greeks this was 'Carchedon' and to the Romans 'Carthago'.

One Greek literary tradition about the foundation began as early as Euripides in the 5th Century BC and the historians Philistus and Eudoxus in the 4th; it is mentioned too by the 2nd-Century AD historian Appian as one of Carthage's own foundation-legends. It dated the city's beginnings thirty to fifty years before the sack of Troy – thus between 1234 and 1214 BC, far earlier even than the dates claimed for Gades and Utica – with two co-founders, Zorus and Carchedon. But as the Phoenician name of Tyre was Sor and Carthage's Greek name was Carchedon, while a 13th-Century date is out of the question, this version has little to recommend it, save as a warning of how inventive (not to mention perilous) some Greek and Roman tales can be.

A group of late 9th-Century datings is a different issue. Menander of Ephesus dated the event to 816 or thereabouts. Additionally he set it 'in the seventh year' of Pygmalion king of Tyre, whose forty-seven-year reign is variously dated from 831 or 820. A short work about natural wonders, from the time of the philosopher Aristotle or not long after, sets the foundation two hundred and eighty-seven years after Utica's, which would match Pliny's date of 1101 for the latter and 813 for Carthage herself, the year stated by Timaeus, a distinguished Sicilian historian who died around 260 aged over ninety. Timaeus placed it in 'the thirty-eighth year before the first Olympiad': thus thirty-seven before 776. The Augustan-era historian Pompeius Trogus, whose history of the Mediterranean world survives in Justin's abridgement, reported its first year as seventy-two before Rome's, in other words between 825 and 819 (the Romans oscillated over dates between 753 and 747 for their city). This literary near-euphony looks impressive. But how Timaeus got his date is unknown (he lived before Menander, but there were other, obscurer Greek writers on Phoenician affairs) and, rather unsettlingly, he dated the foundation of Rome to the same year. Trogus' source is equally unknown, although it looks as though it was a different one from Timaeus'.

Such dates, far distant from the authors' own times and based on earlier sources of untestable reliability, can hardly be accepted merely on trust. But the archaeological evidence from Carthage goes back at least to the decades before 750. Remains of stone houses built in the second quarter of the 8th Century have been unearthed at the foot of the hill which the Greeks and Romans called Byrsa (now the Colline de St Louis), 360 metres from the water's edge and the most southerly of a range of low coastal hills behind the ancient city-site. Again, very recently published carbon-14 analysis dates cattle and sheep bones found at the same site to the second half of the 9th Century, most likely between 835 and 800 – a result that is striking but also controversial, because associated with the bones are fragments of Greek Late Geometric pottery normally classified as 8th-Century. The debate on the likeliest date for Carthage's founding goes on, but that the late 9th Century may be right after all is now a real possibility.[4]

LEGENDS AND TRUTHS

Carthage's standard foundation-legend in Greek and Latin literature is famous. Elissa, afterwards named Dido, flees from her evil brother Pygmalion king of Tyre and settles with her followers in North Africa at a site they call Carthage. The most detailed version is found in Justin's epitome of Pompeius Trogus. The young king, having first cheated his sister out of an equal share of rule, afterwards murdered her husband, their uncle Acherbas (Sicharbas in another writer) – in Phoenician, Zakarbaal, Latinised as Hasdrubal – who was high priest of Tyre's chief god Melqart ('Hercules' in Justin). His hope of finding Acherbas' hoarded wealth was frustrated, for Elissa and a number of her supporters then left the city for exile overseas, taking with them the hoard and also the ritual objects sacred to Melqart. Their flight took them via Cyprus, there to be joined by the high priest of 'Jupiter' – probably the Phoenician chief god Baal, who was also worshipped on Cyprus – and eighty virgins, originally meant to be sacred prostitutes until marriage but now chosen by Elissa to be the first wives in the new community.

On arriving in Libya, the emigrants received a welcome from both the colonists already at Utica and, initially, from the local Libyans who (according to Justin) welcomed the prospect of 'mutually beneficial dealings'. They offered the newcomers, however, only such ground as an ox's hide could cover – but the resourceful Elissa cut this into thin strips to enclose the hill of Byrsa as her citadel (*byrsa* being Greek for oxhide), and the natives agreed to this on condition of a yearly rent. Later, with Carthage starting to prosper, the queen – loyal to Zakarbaal's memory – avoided being forced to marry a neighbouring king by committing suicide on a funeral pyre.

Whether any of this colourful story can be believed is debated. A constant problem with ancient accounts of Carthaginian history is that they are all supplied by authors writing in Greek or Latin; and only Josephus, or rather his source Menander of Ephesus, claims a Phoenician basis for his. The grounds for doubt and suspicion are potentially great, for (as noted above) Greek and Roman writers could bring imagination and inventiveness to their task; nor have we many ways of assessing their truthfulness. The Roman poet Virgil contributes memorably, but unhelpfully, by dating Dido to the time of the fall of Troy again, and telling of a passionate affair between her and the wandering Trojan hero Aeneas; her suicide was due to his sailing away to Italy. Many modern scholars grant nearly as little trust to the non-poetic ancient accounts.

Pygmalion, though, looks like a historical figure (the Phoenician name is Pumayyaton, derived from Pumay the god) even if, in Josephus' version, he became king aged nine and so was only a teenager when Elissa with her followers fled from Tyre, in his seventh year of misrule. There is more of a problem with his sister. She is famous under her alternative name Dido, which various Greek authors explained as Libyan for 'wanderer', though its real meaning and origin – and why she should bear two alternative names at all – are quite unclear. Nor, as far as we know, did the Carthaginians in historical times have (or do) anything to commemorate her as foundress, though Justin claims that they paid her divine honours. Certainly they had no other queens in their history or legends. The tale of the 'oxhide', *byrsa,* must in turn be a later Greek confection, for neither Phoenician migrants nor Libyan landlords in the 9th or 8th Centuries would have been using Greek.

Elissa's stratagem with the hide might well be an inventive Greek dig at her people's proverbial habit of slippery bargaining. These items and some others (Elissa's conscription of Cypriot girls, for instance – argued to be too akin to the first Romans' rape of the Sabine women) lead most modern scholars to dismiss Trogus' foundation story more or less entire.

Several features of it deserve thought, all the same. As even a summary shows, a strong Cypriot connection colours it. The name Elissa, in Phoenician Elishat, means 'woman of Cyprus' (the island's Phoenician name was Alashiya) while Pumayyaton is a name attested at Citium, including its last king in the later 4th Century. Citium was probably Cyprus' *Qart-hadasht*, as mentioned above, though its older name eventually won out. The girls saved by Elissa from sacred prostitution could be seen as intended servitors of Astarte the widely-venerated Near Eastern goddess (called elsewhere by other versions of the name, such as Astoreth, Attart, Atargitis). Her priestesses did indeed perform that function, and she was worshipped in Cyprus. So was Baal, whom Greeks and Romans generally identified with their Zeus and Jupiter, and it was his high priest who brought heavenly favour on the exiles by agreeing to accompany them along with his family – interestingly on the proviso that his priesthood be heredi-tary to his descendants, a practice common in Phoenicia.

With Elissa reportedly also taking Melqart's sacred objects with her from Tyre, Justin's story shows itself therefore alive to key aspects of Carthaginian religion, in which all three deities were important. Worth noting again is that it presents the Libyans as not just rejoicing in the prospect of 'mutually beneficial dealings' with the newcomers but indeed as starting a prompt trade with the new city – a natural and plausible detail, for Phoenician trade was already well established and colonists already dwelled not far away at Utica and perhaps Hippacra. A further stage in Justin's account is inter-esting too. Though the initial settlement, he implies, was on Byrsa itself, a warning omen then impelled the Carthaginians to move to another site, where they prospered. It has been suggested that the animal bones found near the shore below Byrsa and carbon-dated to the late 9th Century, yet with pottery fragments normally dated a century later, may have been dislocated from an initial settlement higher up the hill, perhaps in the course of urban development. This is hypothetical, for what stood on Byrsa before 146 BC is largely untraceable: its summit was cleared away in Roman times. Even so, it is intriguing that the report of a first and then a second site for the early city may not be pure imagination.

The name Byrsa itself is open to various explanations relevant to Phoenician colonists: a possible Phoenician word for measuring out, *parša* or *perša* (thus 'the measured space' – if so, a further sign that the Elissa story had a real Phoenician basis, while it would contribute too to the more fanciful Greek etymology), or one akin to Aramaic *birta*, a fortress; or as a third possibility, the Phoenician for 'sheep-well', *birša* (assuming that such a well, on the hill or the nearby shore, was important for the first settlers).

There are other points of interest. So far as we can tell, only the Carthaginians remembered a woman founder for their city. A woman leading men in any enterprise was rare in legend: apart from Elissa-Dido, perhaps only the legendary Assyrian queen Semiramis figures thus – and Elissa is favourably portrayed as a leader devoted, resolute and resourceful. If she was simply an invention, we might wonder what the point was, for the Carthaginians did not use it in propaganda form (for instance, to differentiate themselves from their Greek or Roman rivals), nor was Elissa given divine parentage or ancestry like Rome's founder. Timaeus claimed that the name Elissa meant *Theiosso* in Greek: 'divine woman' or the like, as *theos* was Greek for 'god'. The Phoenician word *'lt*, vocalised approximately as *elit*, did mean 'goddess'; some of Timaeus' information, then, may have come indirectly from Phoenicia or Carthage (even if partly wrong or distorted). His remark also recalls Justin's idea that Elissa became revered as divine.[5]

Another item merits mention: a gold pendant discovered in 1894 in an early burial at Douimès, one of the hilltops north-east of Byrsa. Inscribed in Phoenician letters of – it seems – the 9th Century, it offers a ritual greeting, 'for Astarte and for Pygmalion [*Pgmlyn*]' by a soldier named Yadomilk son of Paday or Pidiya (*Yd'mlk bn Pdy*) 'whom Pygmalion equipped'. If correctly dated – though some scholars are doubtful – it could attest a Tyrian military officer at Carthage's site around the foundation-date claimed by Timaeus. Livy, the Roman historian who was Pompeius Trogus' and Virgil's contemporary, in a lost part of his work named the commander of Elissa's fleet as one Bitias – so at least the ancient Virgil-commentator Servius attests – and it has been pointed out that Bitias could be a Greek form of *Pdy*. Livy's remark probably came in his survey of Carthage's history and culture prefacing his narrative of the First Punic War. The source that told him of Bitias and Elissa could, in turn, have been the one that Trogus was also to use.

It has even been argued that here we have evidence for Pygmalion and the kingdom of Tyre, not his sister with a breakaway group, being the real founders of the New City. The suggestion is not compelling, for if many important Tyrians migrated with Elissa, as Justin says, we should expect some military officers too – and a gold pendant was a valuable possession (all the more so in an era before coinage), not to be discarded even if Yadomilk had renounced his allegiance to the king. It was found amid items of rather later date, 7th or 6th Century, suggesting that it was kept by Yadomilk's descendants until placed in a grave on Douimès.[6]

The pendant itself does lend at least modest added support to the basic foundation story. That story, while clearly given dramatic colouring in Justin – notably the repeated theme of Elissa outwitting those who seek to exploit her, and her suicide-for-love – in essence tells how internal dynastic strife at Tyre caused the defeated party to emigrate and found a new city which quickly prospered. As a Phoenician colony instigated by civic dissension, Carthage was not unique, given the tradition that Lepcis Magna was another. Items in the story can relate to features known from elsewhere: thus Elissa's Cyprus stopover recalls the existence of Phoenician communities in the island and their religious cults. The possible archaeological evidence for a first settlement on Byrsa followed by a later move to lower ground could fit Justin's similar claim, though the broad hilltop continued to serve as Carthage's citadel until the end. Such features of the story suggest that even its dramatic colouring may go back to his and therefore Trogus' original sources.

The dynastic stresses at Tyre sketched by Justin, if they did occur, must have occurred alongside the social, economic and international factors actuating Phoenician colonising migrations over a century and more. As noted earlier, over-population may have been one factor. Another would be the pressure put on the Phoenicians by the resurgent empire of Assyria, which as early as 870 was receiving lavish gifts from them (seen by the Assyrian kings as tribute). By the mid-8th Century the Assyrians were exacting still more massive regular payments, notably of gold, silver, bronze, copper, iron and tin – raw materials which the Tyrians and their kinsmen could best acquire from the western lands but were now required to provide in quantities and regularity greater than the long-existing, often seasonal trading outposts could supply.

How to develop Mediterranean trade further and more profitably, how far to appease or to resist Assyria (both attitudes were tried during the 8th and 7th Centuries) and how to cope with population strains, were all interlinked issues for the ruling élites to handle and sometimes, no doubt, to disagree over. Again, with Greek traders travelling around the Mediterranean and doing good business at trading-posts like that on the island of Pithecusae (Ischia) near the bay of Naples, added need may have been felt for a more permanent Phoenician presence in or near resource-rich lands. When Greek colonies in their turn came to be founded in the western Mediterranean – the earliest at Cumae near Naples around 740, soon followed by Syracuse and others in Sicily and southern Italy – trade between them and the colonies from Phoenicia also developed, to mutual benefit.

On current evidence, then, which dates Phoenician colonies in the Mediterranean mostly to the century after 800, Carthage was not a late foundation as Greeks, Romans and perhaps Carthaginians themselves believed, but one of the earliest. She dates to no later than the earlier half of the 8th Century and may yet prove to have been founded in the late 9th. The romantic and dramatic story of Elissa quite possibly rests on a basic historical reality, even if efforts to treat all its details as sober fact should be avoided (especially those in poets, Virgil included). After a time, the Carthaginians re-established proper relations with their mother city, sending a yearly delegation with gifts (reportedly a tenth of the revenues) to Melqart's temple there. They also paid their annual rent to the Libyans, according to Justin; although in later times both sets of payments ceased.

CARTHAGE: SITE AND POTENTIAL

The early site of Carthage was Byrsa, its eastern slope and the narrow plain between the shore and this hill and its companions to the north-east – the hills now called Douimès, Junon, Borj-el-Jedid, and above it Sainte-Monique, these latter two beside the sea (Maps 1A and 1B). The area was the south-eastern side of a great arrowhead-shaped peninsula pointing into the gulf of Tunis, a deep arm of the Mediterranean. The site consists of the hills and the shore below them, while high ground to their north forms the capes now called Sidi bou Said and Gammarth. Rain was erratic, but fresh water could be had from a spring called 'the fountain of a thousand *amphorae*' (because of a huge find of these pottery vessels nearby) below the hill of Borj-el-Jedid, and from wells dug in the ground into the then high water-table. The northern edge of the arrowhead, ending in a tongue of land beyond Cape Gammarth, in ancient times edged a wide bay which is now cut off from the sea to form the salt lake called the Sebkhet Ariana. On the southern side of the penin-sula, its shore is bounded by the oval-shaped lake of Tunis, an inlet of the outer gulf. Between bay and lake a broad isthmus linked the peninsula to the mainland, where other hills and higher ridges inter-sected by narrow valleys stretched into the Libyan, now Tunisian, countryside.

This geographical position was unusually favourable, in a well-populated and productive region with river-valleys nearby – the Bagradas to the north of the site and the Catadas (Mellane) to the south – giving easy access inland, and local peoples willing to trade their mineral and agricultural products for goods both imported and Carthaginian-made. Carthage's defensible headland was standard for a Phoenician colony but, unlike most others, her site was spacious. Two centuries after the foundation, if not sooner, the city covered some 136 to 148 acres (55 to 60 hectares). This was as large as Tyre on its island, and over four times the size around 600 BC of the important Phoenician colony, name unknown, on Spain's Costa del Sol near modern Toscanos – and not much smaller than Pompeii's 66 hectares in AD 79. Meanwhile the fertile upland on the northern half of Carthage's arrowhead was later to become the garden suburb of Megara.

Between Cape Bon and Sicily the Mediterranean is narrowest, only 140 kilometres wide: an important feature for ancient ships, which could not travel for more than a few days without putting in to land for provisions. Two hundred and fifty kilometres north of Hippacra lies Sardinia, also beginning to receive a steady flow of Phoenician settlers from around 800 who readily developed two-way trade with Carthage. Utica and Hippacra, though much the same distance from both islands, lacked their sister colony's size and had more limited harbour facilities. If the Phoenician traditions about her founding have a factual core, Carthage also had close links to the ruling aristocracy of Tyre, with whom good relations were restored at least after Pygmalion's time – another advantage.

Carthage in her early centuries is hard to reconstruct in detail, because of developments in later times followed by her re-founda-tion under the Romans and by modern construction. The first settle-ment seems to have stretched eastward almost as far as the shore, as the sandy ground there has evidence of sites for the (pungent) prepa-ration of dried *murex* shellfish to make the famous, expensive and coveted scarlet dye for clothing. On the southern side of the colony, south-east of Byrsa, are traces of archaic potteries, iron foundries and other metallurgical workshops. From the start, Carthage was more than merely a middleman-centre for acquiring goods from other sources and selling them on to buyers elsewhere. At some date, incidentally, her ironmasters developed the technique of adding a quantity of calcium to their furnaces to neutralise the sulphur in iron ore, a process which much improved the quality of their iron products (and was not recovered until the Bessemer process in the mid-19th Century).[7]

Some recent discoveries, and excavations at a number of Phoenician settlements in southern Spain, indicate that the earliest city had a typical range of structures: temples and warehouses, shops and private dwellings – with the wealthiest and largest of these, each with its central courtyard, on Byrsa's slopes – all linked by streets of pounded earth, most of them only a couple of metres wide although the wealthier Byrsa quarter enjoyed at least one about three times wider. Such streets can be seen at the site of Kerkouane, a small city near Cape Bon destroyed in the mid-3rd Century. The layout of the streets varied: on the flat ground, they formed a grid pattern even in early Carthage; on Byrsa's slopes they radiated outwards down from the top while those crossing them followed the hill's contours. Stone or brick walls protected Byrsa at least, for traces of them have been found too; stone walls for the entire city-circuit would come later. A town square or space no doubt existed then, just as one did later on a site further south, where people gathered for markets, political functions, ceremonies and announcements. Not until the 5th and 4th Centuries did further expansion change the urban landscape.

On parts of the slopes and crests of Byrsa and the other hills they buried their dead in increasingly extensive cemeteries or necropoleis. These and other resting-places supply much of the material evidence for Carthaginian culture and commerce, for it was customary to entomb the deceased with offerings and mementoes to help them in the next world – jars or bowls with food and drink, figurines, lamps, rings, amulets and jewellery, some home-made and others imported. South of the settlement, close to some salty shore-lagoons, the colonists by 700 had established a special cemetery for infants' cremated remains deposited in pottery jars: a place for which excavators have borrowed the Biblical name '*tophet*' (Map 1A).

Past the seaside lagoons and a little to the south of the '*tophet*', the ancient shoreline passed around a sandy tongue of land partly closing the entrance to the lake of Tunis, then made a gentle curve northwards to form a natural roadstead where ships could anchor. It may not have been a wholly convenient anchorage for delivering goods in early times, due to the distance overland to the city and with the lagoons in between, but it was sheltered from the open sea, while barges and other boats could ferry at least some cargoes along the shore to and from the city. There was thus plenty of space for loading and unloading cargoes. It is possible that the low-lying area by this shoreline developed in the 7th and 6th Centuries into a 'lower city' – outside Carthage's own walls – for the artisans and labourers who worked at the harbour, built Carthage's merchant vessels and warships, and manned the potteries and foundries which have been found below Byrsa on the south.

This lakeshore was not the only landing point in the city's early centuries. The indented eastern shoreline, up to the steep slopes of Douimès and Borj-el-Jedid, allowed ships to anchor close to land or even to be beached in places. In the waters just offshore from the northern sector of the city are the broken remnants of a breakwater or mole, called 'Roquefeuil's Quadrilateral' after its French discoverer, which at some stage in Carthage's history was built to protect such an anchorage. These exposed waters all the same would be less appealing or safe as ships grew in size and so too did Carthage's mercantile traffic. The bay of Ariana, as it then was, on the northern side of the isthmus could also receive some ships. But it was no nearer to the city, and wagons or pack-animals would have to climb over Byrsa, Junon and the other hills to get down to Carthage. As a result it seems always to have been less important for shipping and cargo.

At the head of the lake of Tunis, fifteen kilometres from the open sea, stood the town of Tunes (the small ancestor of the modern metropolis), and on the lake's southern shore the Libyan town of Maxula, supposedly the home of the king whose marriage demand forced Elissa to die. From there the coast trends east and then north-eastwards, past more coastal heights, to become the mountainous and fertile peninsula of Cape Bon, imposingly visible from Carthage. The coast beyond this lake stretched north-westwards to Utica, then a seaport like all Phoenician colonies, while Libya's principal river, the Bagradas – in Greek Macaras, today the Mejerda – met the gulf of Tunis between the two cities. The coastline has receded some distance since then to leave Utica's site inland, thanks to silting, and the river has also changed its lower course more than once over the centuries. Not far north of Utica, the narrow eastward-pointing promontory of Rususmon (the cape of Eshmun, Apollo's Promontory or sometimes the *Promonturium Pulchri*, 'Fair One's Cape', to Greeks and Romans; today Ras Sidi Ali El Mekhi, or Cape Farina) formed the northern limit of the gulf of Tunis, the home waters of Carthage.

Probably the Carthaginians from the start controlled the rest of the land on their own peninsula, for they needed a security zone and some ground where produce could be grown; and as just mentioned, the land outside the colony later developed into the semi-rural suburb called Megara. As noted earlier too, Justin reports them paying their Libyan neighbours a yearly fee for the site (not always willingly) until after 480. Disappointingly he does not say which Libyans or how large a fee, or whether this paid for territory outside the colony too. The last is likely enough: it would be virtually unknown in the ancient world for any town to possess nothing but the land inside its own walls.

The Libyans who were their neighbours were part of the ethnic group today called Berbers, who dwelt along the coasts and uplands of North Africa from the region of modern Libya to the Atlantic. The high plateaux and long mountain valleys of this vast area, a virtual subcontinent north of the Sahara desert, supported semi-nomadic communities and small permanent settlements, often and perhaps regularly focused around dominant family groups or clans. The peoples in the far west came to be called Mauri; to those east of the Mauri – that is, occupying roughly the broad uplands of modern Algeria – the Greeks gave the name Nomades, or nomads, while the Romans called them Numidians. The communities in Carthage's and the other Phoenician colonies' hinterland were the easternmost of the Numidians, though Greek and Roman writers prefer to call them Libyans.

The rulers of the countless North African communities are usually termed kings by the same writers (like Iarbas king of Maxula in the Elissa story), though many or most were kinglets at best. Not until much later did some larger kingdoms arise. From the Carthaginian, not to mention Greek and Roman, point of view these peoples were unsophisticated barbarians, but this did not prevent the Phoenician colonists in North Africa from treating them with careful respect. Much of the country inland from Carthage was very productive, as were parts of Numidia; the inhabitants – while themselves wary of the eastern immigrants – were receptive to many aspects of the settlers' culture and ready, as Justin insists, to do business. One Numidian product came to be particularly valued: their small but tough and agile horses, and the warriors who rode them with superlative skill. Numidians would provide the prized cavalry of Carthaginian armies and make history under the leadership of generals like Hamilcar Barca and his son Hannibal.

Some relations between the Phoenicians in North Africa, Carthaginians included, and the local peoples grew still closer. Intermarriage was frequent enough for Justin to depict Elissa's own followers as keen for her to marry her Libyan suitor. He implies, too, that the city soon grew powerful partly because locals came to live there. In turn Aristotle in the 4th Century noted (approvingly) the Carthaginians' habit of easing population pressures in the city by sending out citizens to settle at inland centres: this no doubt furthered intermarriage. In later times too, the people of the other Phoenician colonies were sometimes called 'Libyphoenicians', a name which the Roman historian Livy, and the source he consulted, ascribed to their mixed descent. Diodorus in turn records that the Libyphoenicians had the right of intermarriage with Carthaginians.[8]

Naturally there was intermarriage too with people from more distant countries and cities with which Carthage had contacts. The dedicator of a votive *stele*, of uncertain date, in the '*tophet*' (the infants' cemetery) gave his name as Bodmilqart son of Istanis, son of Ekys, son of Paco – Greek ancestors, or possibly Egyptian.[9] Hamilcar the general at Himera in Sicily in 480 had a Sicilian mother, although this had no effect on his implacability towards the Sicilian Greeks. A sister of Hannibal's and then a niece both married Numidian princes; then Sophoniba, daughter of a leading aristocrat, was married some years later to two kings of united Numidia in succession, Syphax and Masinissa. Meanwhile both Hannibal and his brother-in-law in the 220s took Spanish wives. And Hasdrubal, one of the last generals defending the city against Roman attack in 149, was a grandson on his mother's side of Masinissa (and so a cousin of the famous Jugurtha, the Numidian king who fought the Romans a generation later). The Carthaginians, then, from quite early times were almost if not just as much North African and, more generally, western as they were Phoenician.

By 750, the New City was doing business with her Phoenician homeland, Egypt and Greece, as well as with her North African neighbours. The steady growth of Phoenician settlements, as further colonies were set up elsewhere in North Africa, in Sicily, Malta, Sardinia, the southern coasts of Spain, and the Atlantic coast of Morocco, further promoted trade. Greek settlements in the central Mediterranean were spreading too, chiefly in Sicily – notably Syracuse, Acragas and Messana – and southern Italy, for instance Cumae just west of Naples, Naples itself, Rhegium and Tarentum. In the 8th and 7th Centuries both migrant movements, Phoenician and Greek, coexisted peaceably. Though the historian Thucydides later wrote that Phoenician traders in eastern Sicily withdrew to its western parts when Greek colonists arrived, no clashes are mentioned in these early centuries. In fact, apart from Sicily the two migrations kept largely to separate lands: there were no Phoenician colonies in south Italy, for instance, and no Greek ones in North Africa west of Cyrene, or in southern Spain west of Cape de la Nao near Cartagena.

Carthage's North African territories also expanded, though the early stages can be seen only dimly. The Cape Bon peninsula was an obvious area to reach for, given its closeness to the city and its fertile valleys. Just south of the cape, in the sea-cliffs near today's village of El-Haouaria, sandstone quarries (now called the 'Grottes Romaines') were exploited from the mid-7th Century for building works at Carthage. Then sometime before 500, perhaps as early as the 7th Century again, a small town was founded on the coast nearby, about fifteen kilometres north of Kelibia. As its Punic name is unknown, it is called by its modern one, Kerkouane – the one purely Punic town to be excavated in modern times, since it was abandoned in the Roman invasion of 256–255 and never reoccupied. Carthage may have contributed to establishing the little town, which prospered on farming and fishing, and others nearby: notably Neapolis on the northern edge of the gulf of Hammamet, a place known by its Greek name which in fact means New City – in Punic, therefore, another *Qart-hadasht*.

Effective Carthaginian control over the peninsula probably grew in stages as Phoenician and Carthaginian settlers grew in numbers and productivity. By the end of the 6th Century it seems to have been complete: for the text of Carthage's treaty with the newly-formed Roman Republic, dated by the Greek historian Polybius to 509, bars Roman merchants from sailing down its western coast though allowing them to do business, under strict supervision, 'in Libya' and (it follows) at Carthage herself.

Dominance over the interior of Libya was much slower to develop, but the process is even more obscure. Justin's potted history of events reports that sometime during the 6th Century, the Carthaginians for some years cancelled their yearly stipend to 'the Libyans', only to be coerced eventually, through military action by their landlords, to pay the arrears and, presumably, the regular stipend from then on – this, even though the city was at that time furthering its influence over Sicily and Sardinia. Not till after 480, in his account, did they manage to cease payments. Who these Libyans were can only be surmised: but most likely they were an alliance of several peoples in Carthage's nearer hinterland, since they were able after many years of conflict (Justin states) to enforce their claim. All this may in turn be relevant to the story of Carthage's first known, and historically controversial, leader 'Malchus', as we shall see.

Again, land surveys of the city's immediate hinterland in Libya have found no obvious signs of a Carthaginian presence there until late in that century. As with so much archaeological investigation, the picture is far from complete. Nonetheless, Carthage during her first three to four hundred years may be comparable to medieval Venice, which acquired a maritime empire and Mediterranean-wide power long before it took control in the 15th Century of a large sector of its adjoining mainland.[10]

III

STATE AND GOVERNMENT

CITIZENS AND ARISTOCRATS

Carthage in recorded times was a republic: that is, a state with regularly elected officials accountable to their fellow citizens. This was a political structure that developed well after her foundation. As the example of Tyre shows, her Phoenician forebears were ruled by kings, monarchy being the standard governmental format of the Near and Middle East. It would be natural for the colonies of the Phoenician diaspora to begin in the same style, even if changes came later. In turn, throughout her history Carthage was dominated by a wealthy élite who can conveniently be called aristocrats. This was not a fixed or narrow group, all the same – even more than at Rome, membership of the aristocracy was flexible, open to talent and money, and keenly competed for.

What made a Carthaginian a Carthaginian, socially and legally, is obscure. Presumably anyone who could plausibly trace his (or her) ancestry back to the founders counted. The later Roman poet Silius Italicus, in his lengthy epic on the Second Punic War, claims this pedigree for Hannibal – though in choosing Elissa-Dido's father and brother as the general's forebears and naming them Belus and Barca he is probably drawing on nothing more than a fanciful imagination. We shall see, though, that some Carthaginians down the ages did name several ancestors on inscriptions: obviously they took pride in their genealogy. Of course a mere claim to ancestry would hardly be enough. Citizenship gave rights and benefits as well as imposing duties, so that a legal basis was surely essential. While at Rome the citizen lists were maintained by the five-yearly censors, no official with this stated function is known at Carthage; but the republic had quite a range of magistrates and other administrators, to be introduced shortly, some of whom may well have had census-taking duties.

More debatable is whether there was one Carthaginian citizenship or two. A limited level of citizenship perhaps applied to former slaves of citizen masters, if a number of inscriptions in Punic do refer to such people – for instance one Safot, *'š ṣdn bd* Milkyaton son of Yatonbaal son of Milkyaton, a phrase sometimes interpreted as 'slave freed thanks to' Milkyaton (but, on another interpretation, simply 'slave of' Milkyaton), and a Hannobaal or Hannibal who records himself as willingly re-entering the employ, or service, of a man named Esmunhalos. There seems a slight hint that both men owed a debt to their patrons – moral, legal, perhaps monetary too – rather as Roman freedmen did to their old masters even though they too were now Roman citizens.

Another hint of a superior rank of citizen might be seen in the Greek text of a treaty between Hannibal (in Italy) and King Philip V of Macedon in 215, which in one clause uses a unique term, 'the lord [*or* ruling] Carthaginians' (*kyrious Karchedonious*). Since the Carthaginians are repeatedly mentioned elsewhere in the treaty without the epithet, however, it may simply be a diplomatically ceremonious usage; or perhaps, as has also been suggested, a copying mistake for *Tyrious* with the phrase meaning 'the Carthaginians of (or from) Tyre'. Carthage's bonds with her mother city were famously strong, and there were other cities called *Qart-hadasht* in the western Mediterranean: notably the one on the gulf of Hammamet usually known by the Greek version of its name, Neapolis, and the showpiece capital of Punic Spain (New Carthage to the Romans, and Cartagena today) which had recently been founded by Hannibal's brother-in-law.

A third item sometimes used to back the theory of full and lesser citizens comes from New Carthage. When it was captured by the Roman general Scipio in 209, Polybius reports, his ten thousand prisoners included its citizens and two thousand artisans. Scipio set the citizens and their families free, while promising the artisans that they would eventually be freed too, if they worked faithfully for the Roman war effort. They evidently were not citizens of New Carthage (or presumably of Carthage), but it does not follow that they were half-citizens. If not migrants from other Spanish communities who had come to work in the city, they were probably slaves owned by the citizens. Their case, therefore, does not support the idea that Carthage – any more than New Carthage – had a class of lesser or restricted citizens.[11]

While a Carthaginian citizen probably had the same rights as his fellows, inequalities of wealth, birth, education and opportunity were as present as in democratic Athens or at Rome. Greek writers stressed the importance of wealth as well as ancestry and merit. Effective and sometimes official supremacy remained for lengthy periods in the hands of one or other influential family: Mago's in the later 6th and the 5th Centuries, Hamilcar Barca's two hundred years later. Ordinary Carthaginians could at times play an important or even crucial part in decision-making, as will be shown, but it was invariably under the leadership or instigation of an aristocrat and his equally aristocratic friends.

According to Aristotle, Carthaginians belonged to 'associations' (in Greek, *hetairiai*). These probably were the *mzrḥm* (*mizrehim*) attested on inscriptions both of Carthaginian times and at North African towns later. He mentions them in the context of communal meals (*syssitia*), a social custom that he compares to a similar one that he has been discussing at Sparta in Greece. Regular communal meals often feature in social relations ancient and modern, especially when practised by specific groups – Oxford and Cambridge colleges today come to mind, their Hellenistic equivalent being perhaps the *syssition* of scholars at the Museum of Alexandria. Spartan associations each had a fixed, small number, were governed by strict rules, and all citizens were required to be members partly because the practice was linked to military service.

Whether every Carthaginian citizen had to belong to an 'association' is not known. The 'Marseilles Tariff', a Carthaginian inscription found in the French city, extensively details the payments in cash and in kind due to priests performing sacrifices on people's behalf, then affirms in comprehensive fashion that 'a *mizreh*, or a family' [sometimes translated 'a clan'], 'or a *mizreh* of a god', or indeed 'all persons who shall offer a sacrifice' must pay the amounts set down in the official register. Even on a cautious interpretation, the associations seem to have been quite numerous: some were devoted to the cult of a particular deity (its priests and attendants, most likely), while others were secular – guilds of craftsmen, groups of ex-magistrates, and maybe men who had served closely together in war. For them to share a common meal on particular occasions would be a natural instinct. It would also contribute to social interaction and mutual support if, as in Spartan *hetairiai*, members of a *mizreh* came from a range of economic and family circles.

There are isolated mentions of group dinners which could be *syssitia*: for instance an ambitious and wealthy Hanno in the mid-4th Century was accused of plotting a coup d'état by scheming to poison the entire senate at a banquet in his house on his daughter's wedding day, while distracting the common people with feasts 'in the public colonnades' (see Chapter VIII). In 193 a Tyrian agent of Hannibal's, sent to contact the exiled general's supporters in the city, aroused much comment 'at social gatherings and dinners', Livy reports; these probably included such meals, though obviously not them alone. Beyond this, the role of communal meals and *mizrehim* at Carthage is opaque. No Carthaginian commemorates himself or herself on an inscription as a member of one or as acting in connection with one, or is so described by an ancient writer. If the associations played any specific part in the assembly of the citizens, we are not told of it either.[12]

CARTHAGINIAN NAMES

Family groups and political friendships at Carthage are inadequately known, partly because written sources only occasionally specify them (like the Magonids, and Hannibal's family the 'Barcids'), and partly because Carthaginians bore only single names, like Greeks, and leading historical figures made use of only a narrow range of these. A good five hundred different names, men's and women's, are known from *stelae* and other documentary materials, with nearly all of them derived from the name of one or other deity. So for instance Yadomilk bore a name connected with Melqart, Tyre's city-god, and Pygmalion is based on the (obscure) Pumay, a god commemorated on the ancient Nora stone. Names compounded with Baal, Astarte, Melqart and other divinities were especially common, although the great Carthaginian goddess Tanit seems never to be called on in this way.

In Greek and Roman narratives, many Punic names were modified into forms conventionally used today. Abdmilqart or Habdmilqart (servant of Melqart) became Hamilcar, Abdastart (servant of Astarte) was reduced to Bostar, Bodmilqart (in Melqart's service) to Bomilcar, Gersakun (fear of Sakun, another obscure god) to Gisco and Gesco, Saponibaal (may Baal watch over me) to Sophoniba – the name of the most famous Carthaginian woman after Elissa-Dido – and, as noted earlier, Zakarbaal (Baal, remember me) to Sicherbas and Acherbas. On the other hand the names Hannibal (Baal be gracious to me), Hanno (grace be to him), Himilco (Milkot or Melqart is my brother), Maharbal (hasten, Baal), and Mago (a shortened form of Magonbaal, 'may Baal grant') stayed more or less the same.

Despite the many other names, six hundred or so, that were available to Carthaginians – Baalshillek, Esmunhalos, Hannesmun,

Milkyaton, Mittunbaal, Pumayyehawwiyo, Safot, Salombaal (the origin of the name 'Salammbô'), Yadomilk and Yatonbaal are only some less-known examples – the written historical records offer an often baffling repetition of just a dozen or so borne by leaders, generals, politicians and priests: Adherbal, Bomilcar, Bostar, Carthalo, Gisco, Hamilcar, Hannibal, Hanno, Hasdrubal, Himilco, Mago and Maharbal. On Carthaginian inscriptions too, some of these names are found by the hundred, for instance nearly eight hundred Hamilcars and over six hundred Bomilcars, four hundred-odd Magos, and a relatively spare three hundred or so Hannibals.

Prominent Carthaginians took pride in their ancestry and so must have kept up some form of family records, but nothing remains save for some claims on *stelae*. This makes it hard, or impossible, to work out family connections more closely than across two or occasionally three generations, unless a source expressly gives details. The powerful descendants of the city's 6th-Century leader Mago carried on his dominance of the republic down to the early 4th; but although one of these Magonids was named Hamilcar and his grandson was a Hannibal, no link is known with the family of Hamilcar nicknamed Barca and his sons Hannibal, Hasdrubal and Mago, who with their kinsmen were prominent – and mostly dominant – in Carthaginian affairs for the half-century from 247 on. Wider connections across aristocratic society, such as those which can be worked out for many periods in Roman history, are entirely elusive.

PRAISE FROM GREEKS

In the ancient versions of the foundation of Carthage, as shown earlier, the city's establishment began with a queen, a high priest of Baal (so we may interpret Justin's 'Jupiter'), an admiral (if Livy was correct), and a number of high-ranking other Tyrians. Virgil or, more likely, someone later interpolating a line into the *Aeneid*, depicts Elissa-Dido's people as framing a constitution and choosing magistrates and a senate while Carthage is still being built – in other words, setting up a republican system. This is fanciful yet significant, since it shows the impact made on later memory by that system.

The political structure of the republic is not very satisfactorily known. It is a noteworthy object lesson, in fact, of the difficulties posed by evidence varying in depth, time and language. It has to be pieced together from Aristotle's limited 4th-Century description, and some few statements in other writers from Herodotus to

Justin. It was praised by more than one Greek thinker. Around 368, the political theorist and orator Isocrates called it and the Spartan system the best of any state (he liked their authoritarian aspects). Aristotle in the 340s and 330s praises it in his turn, along with Sparta again and the cities of Crete, as a mainly sound blend of his three basic political schemas – monarchy, aristocracy (rule by the best men, the *aristoi*) and democracy, each one limited by the functions of the other two. Monarchy for him was embodied in the chief magistrates who were elected by citizens for fixed terms; aristocracy in the *gerousia* (body of elders, or senate) who needed the guidance of the magistrates and could be contradicted by the people; and democracy in the shape of the citizen assembly, which was guided by the other two arms of government but could still make up its own mind.

This is an idealised, or at least theorised, portrait of Carthage's political system. Aristotle leaves a great deal out that could help to clarify how it actually worked, and in places is generalised or opaque on what officials and institutional bodies did in practice. Nor does he mention the dominance of the Magonid family in the republic's affairs – from the middle or later 6th Century until only a few decades before he wrote – unless he refers to it when remarking cryptically that Carthage had changed from 'tyranny' (in other words arbitrary autocracy) to aristocracy. On the other hand, this would make his much-admired Carthaginian constitution a coin of very recent minting, an aspect not hinted at in his overall treatment of it. Rather, then, he may be referring to the abolition or neutralisation of the kingship at some much earlier time.[13]

CHIEF MAGISTRATES: THE SUFETES

The chief officials of the republic were an annually elected pair of 'sufetes', a title which Punic inscriptions and some Latin writers attest, although Greeks – and even Carthaginians writing in Greek, as we shall see – invariably use the term 'king' or 'kings' (*basileus, basileis*). Aristotle stresses that wealth and birth were both needed in seeking high office, plainly implying that both were legally required. On the other hand he mentions no details about a minimum requisite level of wealth, for instance, or how distinction of birth was defined. We can infer that Carthaginian ancestry on both parents' sides was not essential, for Hamilcar the 'king' in 480 had a Greek mother; but notable ancestors on at least one side must have been.

Cicero's contemporary Cornelius Nepos mentions that there were two sufetes – he too writes 'kings' – elected each year, and several Carthaginian inscriptions date a year by a pair of sufetes' names. Two yearly sufetes are also recorded, most of them in Roman times, at Libyan and Sardinian cities that retained Carthaginian cultural usages. A passing comment by Plato the philosopher shows him, too, taking for granted that Carthaginian magistrates served annually. A pair a year can thus be accepted as Carthage's historical norm. Evidence for more than two is fragile – for instance Cato the Censor, in the 2nd Century, seeming to write of four sufetes collaborating in some action like levying or paying troops. Unfortunately we have only a very scrappily preserved sentence with no context; Cato may perhaps have been reporting an action taken over two successive years. If more than two a year ever were elected, most likely this happened seldom.[14]

Sufetes as supreme magistrates were a development of the 6th Century or, possibly, the late 7th. A damaged Punic votive *stele* of around 500–450 seems to be dated – though the reading is debated – to 'the twentieth year of the rule of the sufetes in Carthage'. There is no independent evidence to confirm this information, and another reading of the *stele* gives 'in the one hundred and twentieth year' while a third interpretation sees no dating in it at all. If either of the numerals is correct, it implies that the monarchy had lasted at least two or maybe even three hundred years, until 620 or later. If not, the best we can infer is that by the later 4th Century, Aristotle's time, the sufeteship was certainly the supreme office.[15]

In an earlier period of Carthage's history, it is just possible that only one sufete existed: for instance, perhaps 'Malchus' in the 6th Century (if he existed) and perhaps the '*basileus*' Hamilcar who fought the Sicilian Greeks in 480 were sole sufetes as well as generals. One person holding more than one office at a time was common enough at Carthage when Aristotle wrote, and more than likely was a long-established usage. It is just as conceivable, though, that in the first centuries of the republic there were already two sufetes: one could take the field as military commander when necessary, while the other remained at home in charge of civil affairs. Limiting their functions to civil and home affairs would then have occurred later. When they do appear in Greek and Roman accounts, they are running the affairs of the republic in consultation with the senate, and – in later times at least – judging civil lawsuits.

Sufetes is Livy's Latin version of Punic *špṭm* (*shophetim*, *shuphetim* or *softim*), a title often mentioned in inscriptions at Carthage and other Phoenician colonies which had the same office. It is equivalent to the biblical *shophetim*, conventionally translated 'judges'. The difficulty with tracing developments is Greek writers mentioning a Carthaginian 'king' or 'kings' but never a 'sufete'. Herodotus describes Hamilcar, the general who fought the Sicilian Greeks in 480, as 'king of the Carthaginians' – 'because of his valour', he explains – while Diodorus reports how in 410 the city chose its leading man Hannibal, who was 'at that time king by law', as general for another Sicilian offensive. For another Sicilian war in 396 they 'appointed Himilco king by law'; and did so again with Mago in 383, except that this time Diodorus leaves out the term 'by law'. Himilco was already in Sicily as general, so Diodorus' report of his appointment as 'king by law' is best explained as Himilco's being elected sufete for the new year while continuing in the Sicilian command. The other men too, with the possible exception of Hamilcar, can hardly be anything but sufetes: how a sufete could also be a general will be explored later.[16]

Obvious family pride appears in inscriptions that list a dedicator's ancestors going back three or more generations. One document naming the two sufetes together with two generals in an unknown year includes six generations of the forefathers of one general, Abdmilqart, and three for the other, *Abd'rš* (Abdarish). On another, a man named Baalay lists five generations, of whom the earliest had been a sufete and his son perhaps a *rab* (another office, soon to be looked at). Women also commemorated their forebears, as does Arishat daughter of Bodmilqart son of Hannibaal on a votive *stele*. Rather overdoing it, in turn, was one *Pn* 'of the nation of Carthage', dedicator of a *stele* at Olbia in Sardinia, who lists no fewer than sixteen forefathers – a family record going back a good four hundred years. None of these, nor *Pn* himself, held an office, but this vividly illuminates the ancestral claims that ambitious men might parade in their political careers. A candidate who could point to sufetes or at least 'great ones' (senators) among his forebears surely found it an advantage.

When Aristotle describes the 'kings' (*basileis*) as the city's chief magistrates, who act in consultation with the Carthaginian senate, he plainly means elected office-holders. Nor does he suggest anywhere that a titular king still existed too, even though he discusses other official bodies like the senate and the 'pentarchies'. In a famous confrontation with Roman envoys in 218, the Carthaginian spokesman in the senate is termed the *basileus* by Polybius: this must mean a sufete. An inscription in Greek, set up by a

Carthaginian named Himilco ('Iomilkos' in the text) on the Aegean island of Delos in 279, terms him a *basileus* too, so the term was not simply a literary usage. Again, it should mean that Himilco was or had been a sufete.[17]

The sufete is sometimes called a 'praetor' by Latin writers (including Livy once), borrowing the title of Roman magistrates with judicial authority, and once or twice a 'king' as in Greek writers – or even a 'consul', the name of the highest office at Rome. It may be that the sufete or sufetes began under the kings as judicial officers, hence their title; then acquired greater authority over time, until the king was sidelined and eventually not replaced (though some scholars think that the office survived at least in name). His replacement by elected sufetes may well have come about from pressure, if nothing worse, by Carthage's council of elders or senate, whose predecessors at Phoenician cities had always been a powerful makeweight to the monarchs.

ADIRIM: THE SENATE OF CARTHAGE

Phoenician kings always had to collaborate with their city's leading men, who from early times formed a recognised council of advisors as the 'mighty ones' or 'great ones' (*'drm,* approximately pronounced *adirim*). At Carthage this became the senate, as the Romans called it; in Greek terminology the *gerousia*. As just noted, the 'great ones' quite possibly were responsible for the effective end of the monarchy, with the sufeteship as a limited substitute for it – like the consulship at Rome – which at least some leading men could look forward to holding turn by turn. Whether they were always elected by the whole citizen body, or at first by the *'drm* with popular election developing later, is not known. Nor how senators themselves were recruited, or even how many there were at any time, although two or even three hundred is likely as we shall see. The building where they usually met seems to have been close to the great market square (*agora* to Greeks) which was the hub of business and administration, but we do read of two meetings held in the temple of 'Aesculapius', in other words of Eshmun on Byrsa hill.

The senate had varied and broad authority, to judge from our sources. As usual the glimpses are given by writers from Herodotus in the 5th Century to much later ones like Appian and Justin, so that generalisations have to be fairly careful. Again Aristotle gives the fullest sketch. The 'kings' convened and consulted the body on affairs of state; if they unanimously agreed on what action to take, this could be taken without any need to put the issue before the assembled citizens. On the other hand, some decisions taken by sufetes and senate in agreement could still be put before the assembly, which had the power to reject them. Again, if both sufetes – or by implication even one – disagreed with the senate on a matter, the question would go to the assembly. How often this happened, and what questions might be put to the people, the philosopher avoids stating.

What procedures and protocols governed the senate's debates is not known, nor is it clear whether changes in its protocol and range of functions took place over the centuries. Polybius does claim that by the time of the Second Punic War the republic had become 'more democratic' – something he is not enthusiastic about, even hinting that it cost Carthage the war – which would suggest that in earlier ages senate and sufetes had seldom needed to involve the assembly in decision-making. His claim, however, seems overdone. During and after the war the senate can be found directing diplomatic, financial and even military measures, just it had done for centuries. And on the other hand, Aristotle sees fit to describe the Carthage of his own time, a century before Polybius, first as a blend of monarchy, aristocracy and democracy (with aristocracy dominant), and later as 'democratically ruled': perhaps a clumsy generalisation, but a noteworthy one.

The range of functions of the *adirim* was at least as broad as the Roman senate's. They decided on war and peace, though the decision probably needed ratification by the assembly of citizens, as Diodorus mentions happening in 397. They handled foreign relations to the point of deciding on war and peace: for example rejecting the victorious invader Regulus' harsh peace terms in 256, receiving Roman envoys in 218 and accepting their declaration of a Second Punic War, and conversely in 149 themselves declaring war in defiance of the Roman forces surrounding the city. In military affairs, we find the senate in 310 reprimanding (and putting in fear of their lives) the generals who had failed to prevent Agathocles' Syracusan expedition from landing. After Hannibal's victory at Cannae in 216, it authorised fresh forces to go to Sardinia and Spain, and reinforcements with sizeable funds for Hannibal. In 147 it issued (fruitless) criticisms of the savage treatment of Roman prisoners by Hasdrubal, the commanding general in the besieged city.

Some domestic decisions are recorded too. In the mid-4th Century, in a fit of anti-Greek feeling, the *adirim* issued a decree (ultimately repealed) forbidding the study of that language. In 195 after Hannibal left Carthage to avoid victimisation, they were forced to promise to take whatever steps against him might be demanded by envoys just arrived from Rome. No doubt it was a senate decree (even if ratified by the assembly) that proceeded to confiscate his property, raze his house, and formally banish him.[18]

Measures like these would be decreed on the sufetes' proposal, as Aristotle indicates. There must have been sharp debates at times: for example, leading up to the decision in 256 to fight on – for the Carthaginians themselves had earlier asked for terms. Certainly there was some opposition to peace in 202, even after Hannibal lost the battle of Zama, forcing Hannibal himself to exert pressure on his fellow senators and on the citizen assembly too to accept Scipio's terms. Nonetheless, when a powerful faction dominated the state, the sufetes' proposals and the senate's decisions naturally obeyed factional wishes, whatever arguments opponents might put. Livy's and Appian's pictures of the senate's small anti-Barcid group speaking against the Barcids' policies to no avail may be imaginative in detail, but illustrate fairly well what the situation must have been like.

Livy once mentions a smaller senatorial body too. The peace embassy sent to Scipio Africanus in 203 consisted, he says, of thirty senators called 'the more sacred council', termed the dominant element in the senate. No such body appears under this name elsewhere, but now and again other delegations of thirty leading senators do: conceivably this 'more sacred council' again. One delegation persuaded the feuding generals Hamilcar and Hanno to cooperate against the Libyan rebels in 238; one in 202 – surely the same body as the year before, though Livy does not comment – was sent out to ask peace from Scipio after his victory over Hannibal; a third, according to Diodorus, was delegated to learn the invading Romans' demands in 149. All the same, these seem rather demeaning, even if necessary, missions for the supposedly most powerful body in the republic's most powerful institution. Greek writers, including Polybius and Diodorus, do not help clarity by mentioning at various times a Carthaginian *gerousia* ('body of elders'), *synkletos* ('summoned body') and *synedrion* ('sitting body'), without explaining the distinctions. All three terms are applied by Greeks to the Roman senate, which had no inner council. Efforts to treat *synkletos* or else *gerousia* in Carthaginian contexts as indicating the 'more sacred council', and the other two terms as referring to the *adirim*, have no firm evidence to rest on. No Punic inscription describes anyone as member of such an inner body, either.

If the 'more sacred council' did exist, at least in the 3rd and 2nd Centuries, we could see it (given the absence of any specific details) as a largely honorific body of eminent senators – probably ex-sufetes – whose experience and high repute could be called on in difficult situations. They could also have exerted real though unofficial influence in normal affairs. If Livy's term 'more sacred' has any specific validity, it may be that the members also held high-ranking priesthoods, conferring added solemnity on the council.

THE MYSTERIOUS 'PENTARCHIES'

Another arm of government is mentioned, all too succinctly again, by Aristotle and no one else: the 'pentarchies' or five-man commissions. New members were co-opted by existing ones, members served without pay, and the commissions controlled 'many important matters', including judging cases at law. None of these features is described in any fuller detail. Nor is the philosopher very clear in explaining how (or why) commissioners had lengthier tenures of position than other officials: 'they are in power after they have gone out of office and before they have actually entered upon it'. As it stands, this seems to make it pointless for them to have a stated term of office at all, and to imply that there might often be more than five members of a commission in practice.

Carthaginian inscriptions make no mention of anyone belonging to a five-man commission, but do attest a board or commission of ten for sacred places and one of thirty supervising taxes. Were the pentarchies, or some of them, subdivisions of these? Also attested are officials called 'treasurers' or 'accountants' (*mhšbm* sounded as *mehashbim*), whose powers included penalising persons who failed to pay customs dues. If Aristotle is correct that the pentarchies handled many important matters and could try cases, either their tasks clashed with the work of these officials or – much likelier – the *mhšbm* formed one or more of the pentarchies. Carthage's institutions are so opaquely known that these interpretations are a reasonable possibility. Standard public tasks like taxes, sacred places and judicial affairs perhaps seemed to call for lengthier terms of administrative office (three to five years?) for greater continuity. Even so, Aristotle's dictum about pentarchy members holding their positions both before and after they were pentarchy members remains a puzzle.[19]

One official at Carthage is known almost entirely from Punic inscriptions: the *rb* or *rab,* meaning 'chief' or 'head'. A hundred or so men are termed *rab* in the documents without accompanying description, implying an office different from the *rb khnm* (*rab kohanim*, chief of priests) and *rb mḥnt* (*rab mahanet*, 'head of the army' or general). This *rab* seems to have been in charge of state finances, equivalent then to a treasurer. If so, this was the official whom Livy terms 'quaestor', using a Roman title again, who in 196 defied the newly-elected reforming sufete Hannibal until taught a sharp lesson. (At Gades in 206 we read of a quaestor, too, presumably that city's *rab*.) He presumably had the *mḥšbm* as his subordinates, although the inscriptions mentioning these do not refer to him. An inscription mentioning one person, it seems, as *rab* 'for the third time' (*rb šlš*, approximately *rab shelosi*) suggests – along with the large number of *rabim* known – that it was a position with a time-limit. So does Livy's report that the 'quaestor' defied Hannibal because he knew that, after holding office, he would automatically join the powerful and virtually impregnable 'order of judges' (on which more below). The office was probably annual, like a sufete's.

It must have given plenty of opportunities for holders to enrich themselves. Both Aristotle and Polybius tell us that Carthaginians in their day viewed giving bribes as normal in public life, including bribes for election votes. The philosopher comments, in a different context, that it was perfectly normal for Carthaginian officials to practise money-making activities (adding tartly 'and no revolution has yet occurred'). Profiting from public revenues, which he also notices, was a natural extension (rather optimistically, he thinks that wealthy men like Carthaginian officials would be less tempted). In one known period at least, it had become so severe that it was affecting the republic's ability to pay its way: Hannibal was elected sufete partly to deal with it – and his first confrontation was with the chief of finances.

One more feature noted by Aristotle, disapprovingly, is that the same man could hold more than one office at the same time. A votive *stele* interestingly commemorates one Hanno, sufete and chief of priests (*rb khnm*, or *rab kohanim*), son of Abdmilqart (Hamilcar) who again had been sufete and chief of priests. Of course the sufeteship was a one-year office, while the priesthood was permanent. Aristotle no doubt was thinking more of non-religious combinations, like being sufete and *rab* together, or even sufete and general. Though no clear evidence for sufete-*rab* combinations exists, it is possible that occasionally a sufete might indeed become a general too.[20]

THE GENERALS

At some moment in the city's history a further position was created, that of general (*rb mḥnt*, approximately pronounced *rab mahanet;* in Greek, *strategos*). Officially this innovation separated military duties from civil, a contrast with Rome where the consuls regularly and praetors sometimes had to carry out both. The Carthaginians perhaps initiated their generalship in the middle or later 6th Century, when they began sending military forces over to Sicily and Sardinia. Even if they did, it looks as though the office down to the early 4th Century could still, as suggested above, be taken on by a sufete should the situation demand it. That would explain examples mentioned earlier, such as Hamilcar in 480, Himilco in 396, and Mago as late as 383 – 'kings' appointed to commands in Sicily. As mentioned above too, Isocrates in an effusive paean to authoritarian rule matches Carthage and Sparta as two states 'ruled oligarchically at home and monarchically at war'. This is not a sign that Carthage still had real kings active in affairs, for he also praises his contemporary the ruthless tyrant (in modern terms, dictator) of Syracuse, Dionysius I. But it may be a sign that her 'kings' – that is, sufetes – still led armies at least on important campaigns in his time.

All the same, over these centuries there were probably plenty of military tasks not important or enticing enough for a sufete. These could be handled by men who held the generalship alone, whether or not they had been sufetes or later became sufetes. By Aristotle's day (it is clear) a general was not normally a sufete at the same time. But generals too were elected, and the office was enough of a political prize for men to pay perfectly good bribes to obtain it. A century later, effective control of affairs rested with the elected generals of the Barcid family (Hannibal's father and brother-in-law, and Hannibal himself), none of whom is recorded as being sufete along with being general. Instead they were able, it seems, to get kinsmen and supporters elected to sufeteships year after year, not to mention to other generalships as needed.

A general did not serve for a fixed term, for obvious reasons. The appointment seems to have been for the length of a war, or at any rate until another general was chosen to take over command. Then again, more than one *rab mahanet* could be chosen for military operations: most obviously if land operations (in Sicily for instance) needed one commander and naval operations another, or for commitments in different regions. In North Africa itself, during the great revolt by Carthage's mercenary troops and

Libyan subjects from 241 to 237, two generals – Hamilcar Barca and his one-time friend, then rival, Hanno 'the Great' – held equal-ranking generalships, which caused friction. In an effort to improve collaboration, Hanno was replaced for a time by a more cooperative commander who, in practice if not in law, acted as Hamilcar's subordinate.

This is not the only evidence that, at times, one general might be appointed as deputy to another. Two Punic inscriptions have the term *rb šny* (vocalised approximately *rab sheni*), or an abbreviated *hšn'*, each of which seems to mean 'second general'. They imply subordinate commanders and, although details are entirely lacking (save that the *hšn'* was a Hasdrubal), such an arrangement is often reported in narratives of Carthage's later wars. Thus in 397 Himilco, the general in Sicily, had an 'admiral' (*nauarchos* in Diodorus) named Mago leading his fleet, while a century and a half later, in 250, Adherbal in command there had a naval deputy, one Hannibal, whom Polybius terms a 'trierarch'. Hamilcar Barca later appointed his son-in-law Hasdrubal 'trierarch' when operating in Spain in the 230s, even though Hasdrubal's naval tasks were minor by all accounts: the equivalent term in Punic had perhaps become the normal one for a general's immediate deputy, whatever his duties.[21]

Certainly the practice of a supreme general with subordinates became the norm over the nearly four decades of Barcid dominance after 237. Polybius emphasises Hannibal's direction of all military affairs during the Second Punic War, which at its height involved up to seven generals in different theatres. Hannibal commanded in Italy with another officer acting semi-independently under him; three generals – two of them his brothers Hasdrubal and Mago – operated in Spain against the invading Romans; a sixth commanded an expeditionary army in Sicily; and a seventh (apparently another Barcid kinsman, Bomilcar) led out the navy on several rather fruitless sorties. After peace with Rome in 201, with all warfare now effectively banned, what was done with the generals is unknown. Either they became civil (or ornamental) officials, or they lapsed altogether until the Carthaginians unwisely decided to fight Numidia half a century later. In their final war with Rome, they seem to have had two separate and equal generals again: one operating in the countryside, the other defending the besieged city (Chapter XII).

NEMESIS OF GENERALS: THE COURT OF
ONE HUNDRED AND FOUR

The state was notoriously draconian in dealing with its defeated
generals. In later times at least, the penalty for failure was crucifixion, as happened for instance to Hanno, the admiral beaten by
the Romans in 241. We are told that fear of punishment was
always in the mind of Carthaginian commanders, and we read of
one or two who killed themselves to avoid it (the corpse of one
such, Mago in 344 or 343, was itself crucified instead). The process
of judging unsatisfactory military performance must originally
have been carried out by the senate and sufetes (or possibly one of
the pentarchies, but a five-man court for such serious indictments
seems unlikely). A change, though, came in the 5th Century or
early in the 4th, when a special tribunal was created for the purpose
(Chapter VIII).

   This was the body which Aristotle calls the One Hundred and
Four. He also calls it 'the greatest authority' at Carthage, with
members chosen solely on merit: but does not say what it actually
did apart from likening it to the five ephors at Sparta. The comparison looks excessive, for Sparta's ephors not only supervised (and
could prosecute) the Spartan kings but dealt, too, with large areas
of administration both civil and military – areas which at Carthage
were handled by the pentarchies, on Aristotle's own evidence, or
officials like the *rab* and the generals (on evidence from other
sources, inscriptions included). But Justin reports a hundred-strong
senatorial court being set up during Magonid times to scrutinise
generals' actions. This must be the same body. Thus the court of
One Hundred and Four was the authority that convicted and
executed delinquent generals. After a time its supervision may have
widened to generals' subordinates too. An officer was crucified in
264 for giving up the occupied city of Messana in Sicily without a
fight, the same punishment that the court inflicted on unsatisfactory generals, and so perhaps a case of its now judging other
military miscreants. What body had previously dealt with such
officers we do not know – maybe one of the pentarchies. Aristotle's
comparison with the ephors would certainly be more understand-
able if, even in his day, the One Hundred and Four was beginning
to encroach on other bodies' functions.

   Why there were one hundred and four judges is not known; the
figure has been doubted because Aristotle also writes simply of one
hundred, as does Justin. One suggestion, if one hundred and four is

correct (and 'one hundred' just a rounding-down), is that the two sufetes and two other officials (the *rab* and the *rab kohanim*?) could have been members *ex officio*. The ordinary judges were senators selected by the pentarchies, on unknown criteria save for the merit stated by Aristotle, and they served on the court for life.[22]

Supposedly then it was the One Hundred and Four who kept the republic's generals on the straight and narrow in wars, and for the same reason caused them too often to be over-cautious. Yet how impartial its judgements were may be wondered, especially when feelings ran high after a defeat or – worse – a lost war. Generals, and often if not always their lieutenants, were senators themselves: this meant having friends and enemies among the *adirim* and participating in Carthage's vigorous, at times embittered, politics. Such connections could be pivotal to the outcome of a prosecution whatever the merits of the case itself. Punishments or threats of punishment are rarely recorded. Crucifixion did await Hanno, the admiral whose defeat at the Aegates Islands in 241 forced Carthage to sue for peace, yet twenty years earlier a defeated general, another Hanno, not only survived (though heavily fined) but five years later was commanding a section of the navy. Hamilcar Barca, who had to negotiate the invidious peace terms with Rome in 241, was threatened with trial when he returned home, but nothing came of it. Nor was Hannibal prosecuted after the disaster of Zama.

THE ASSEMBLY OF CITIZENS

The citizen assembly was called simply *'m* (*ham*), 'the people'. It most probably met in the city's great marketplace, called the *agora* by Greeks. In later centuries this lay south-east of Byrsa and near the sea; earlier, before the city expanded in that direction, the original *agora* may have been on the low ground between Byrsa and the shore to its east.

The earliest possible mention of the *'m* as a political body is in Justin's story of 'Malchus', thus after 550. Returning from abroad with his army to punish his ungrateful enemies, that general summoned 'the people' to explain his grievances, complain that his fellow-citizens had tolerated his enemies' behaviour, but then grant them – the citizens – his magnanimous forgiveness. He then 'restored the city to its laws', meaning lawful government. If correct, this is a picture of a citizenry which at least was treated with a degree of respect. Whether restoring lawful government implied, among other things, restoring political functions to the '*m* is only a guess, but at some date the assembly gained the power to elect magistrates and – probably as a later development – to vote on policy decisions.

Its normal share in affairs by Aristotle's time involved voting on decisions passed by the senate, resolving a deadlock between the senate and one or both sufetes, and electing sufetes, generals, and other officials like the *rab*. As already noted, Aristotle shows that even some decisions agreed on by senate and sufetes were still put to the assembly. On such occasions the sufetes 'do not merely let the people sit and listen to the decisions that have been taken by their rulers' but allow free discussion (a concession unique to Carthage, he notes), and even then 'the people have the sovereign decision'. This must mean that the assembly could reject the proposals, just as it decided the issue when there was a deadlock. Later on the philosopher remarks that Carthage was a 'democratically ruled' state; rather an exaggeration, but a passing acknowledgement that the assembly's role was both important and, at times, decisive.

These functions seem reasonably robust for a citizen assembly in the ancient world. It is therefore puzzling to read Polybius' disapproving claim that in Hannibal's day 'the people' (meaning the citizen body) had the greatest say. After all we still find the *adirim* making the major decisions then – even in his own account of events, such as going to war with Rome in 218 and discussing peace in 203. No doubt these would in turn be put before the *ham* for ratification, but that was not new. The best surmise must be that by 218 every decision of sufetes and senate, not just some as previously, was formally presented to the assembly, even if merely to be ratified. The dominance of the Barcid generals down to 201, based as much on popular support as on alliance with other leading men, probably gave greater visibility to the assembly, without thereby adding to its real power. This would hardly be a huge democratic advance, but Polybius is really seeking to stress how superior Rome's 'aristocratic' political system was in those days, and he may well be pushing an over-artificial contrast.

No definite information exists about how the assembly functioned. One hypothesis comes from a Latin inscription of AD 48 commemorating a local magnate at the Libyan country town of Thugga, who received an honorary sufeteship from the town's senate and people 'by the votes [*or* the assent] of all the gates (*portae*)'. These 'gates' at Thugga must have been a voting arrangement, perhaps denoting local clans or the residents of different sectors of the town. That the citizens at Carthage likewise voted in separate groups, each called a 'gate' (*š'r*), is speculation all the same. Gates of the usual kind are mentioned on *stelae* or other documents – the New Gate inscription, for example – but never in connection with political or social life.[23]

The citizen assembly perhaps gained its greater prominence under the trauma of the great revolt of 241–237 in Africa. Citizens had to enlist and fight in battle for Carthage's survival, and they settled on Hamilcar Barca as their military and political leader during the revolt and after it. He was followed as general – in effect chief general, whether or not so titled – by his son-in-law Hasdrubal and then his eldest son Hannibal, each elected in turn by the citizen body. The Barcid faction's dominance of affairs clearly included the *adirim*, the magistrates and even the One Hundred and Four, but it always faced some opposition, and the support of the assembly may well have been the Barcids' ultimate strength.

After the peace of 201, the Barcids lost their control and the republic came under the effective (though not official) sway of the court of One Hundred and Four. Their corrupt rule, as we shall see, then brought Hannibal back as sufete a few years later to end the scandals and help set the state back on its feet. For the remaining decades of Carthage's life, politics and government were more vigorous than they had been in a century or more: a vitality which by a tragic irony contributed to the ultimately lethal hostility of her old enemy in Italy.

IV

THE CARTHAGINIAN
'SEA EMPIRE'

CARTHAGE AND NORTH AFRICA

Carthage's trade and influence developed vigorously in her first two or three centuries, although only their outlines are visible. She did continue to pay a tribute to her Libyan neighbours, as mentioned earlier on Justin's evidence, and on trying to end this in the late 6th Century she was forced to back down (Chapter VIII). Along the coasts and across the western seas, on the other hand, her trade and influence made remarkable progress, especially after 600 (Map 3A).

To begin with, it was natural for the city to plant or support settlements along the neighbouring North African coasts, as ports of call for trade and centres for Carthaginian citizens needing fresh opportunities. Some of the many other Phoenician foundations in the region may have had Carthaginian support – colonies like Hadrumetum, Acholla and perhaps Neapolis on the coasts south of the city in the region called Byzacium, Kerkouane near the tip of Cape Bon (which may in fact have been a purely Carthaginian foundation) and Hippacra to the north of Utica.

Carthage likewise came to dominate the coasts far to the east of Byzacium. Oea and Sabratha were other notable Phoenician, or perhaps joint Phoenician and Carthaginian, colonies on the Gulf of Sirte, and beyond them in turn stood Lepcis. Lepcis, whose oldest archaeological remains are 7th-Century, was a Phoenician colony founded by political refugees, according to Sallust, the Roman historian of Julius Caesar's time, who claims to have consulted Punic records. As noted above, the Carthaginians – with wide-ranging commercial interests by then – may have helped the project or at any rate supplied protection, because the area, named Emporia by the Greeks, was very fertile although bordered closely by the African desert. With their Phoenician and perhaps partly Carthaginian origins, Emporia's cities unsurprisingly felt a common interest with their powerful older sister.

By the late 6th Century, if not earlier, Carthage was asserting her dominance over these coasts. Thus around 515 she reacted against Greek colonists trying to settle a day's journey east of Lepcis at a river called the Cinyps, under the leadership of Dorieus, brother of the king of Sparta. With Lepcis still relatively young and undeveloped, the danger of a vigorous stream of Greek migrants taking over the region was real. Significantly, Dorieus had men from the island of Thera as guides, and Thera had been the founder of Cyrene farther east around 630. The new settlement lasted only two to three years before the Carthaginians formed an alliance with the local Libyans, a people called the Macae, to expel its occupants. The Macae were evidently prepared to put up with Lepcis, but not with a Greek colony as well. A show of force may have been all that was needed, for no actual fighting apparently occurred before the Greeks left. All the same, Carthage would meet the indefatigable Dorieus again.

It was perhaps not long after this that Carthage fixed a boundary with Cyrene. Founded in another rich coastland near Pharaonic Egypt, Cyrene quickly prospered, extending its control over its neighbourhood to the west. Given the distance between the two and the desolate nature of the terrain along the southerly reaches of the vast Gulf of Sirte, there would seem little point in territorial clashes, but Sallust had read of a long and inconclusive war over who owned what. His claim of such a war is as implausible, though, as his dramatic tale of how the two cities eventually agreed on a frontier much closer to Cyrenaean territory than Carthaginian, at a site named for two Carthaginian brothers both supposedly called Philaenus (a Greek name, not a Punic one). Supposedly they gave their lives to ensure that this became the border as the 'Altars of the Philaeni', on the coast, almost 700 kilometres east of Lepcis near the modern oil centre of Ra's Lanuf. Polybius, the first writer to mention the place, gives the name as the 'Altars of Philaenus' (singular not plural) – it looks as though the original Carthaginian story of the border-fixing was touched up further by the time Sallust found it. The 'altars' perhaps were on sand dunes, for they had disappeared by the time of Strabo, but the site was remembered.[24]

A similar expansion of influence took place in the western Mediterranean. A number of North African ports west of Hippacra came under Carthaginian control or were founded by her in the course of the 6th and 5th Centuries. Apparently none developed as towns until a later age, but places like Hippo Regius, Icosium, Chullu, Tipasa, Iol and Siga marked out the broadening scope of Carthage's commerce and, inevitably, political influence. Further afield, according to the Greek historian Diodorus she planted a colony on the isle of Ebusus, near the eastern coast of Spain, in 654. Now Phoenician settlement certainly began there around then but, as noted earlier, pottery evidence shows that these settlers arrived from southern Spain. Diodorus' claim probably goes back to Carthaginian tradition, recalling and distorting the fact (again shown by pottery remnants) that some generations later, around 525, the city did establish its authority over the small but prosperous island, perhaps with a fresh body of settlers. Ebusus became the first territory outside Africa to pass under Carthaginian dominance: a milestone in the city's development into a Mediterranean great power.

The *Periplus* of 'Pseudo-Scylax', a Greek sailing guide to the Mediterranean – 4th-Century BC in date but drawing on sources a hundred years older or more – remarks that the entire North African seaboard from the region of Lepcis to the straits of Gibraltar 'all belongs to the Carthaginians'. It was not directly ruled by Carthage. The cities controlled their own territories, had their own laws and institutions (mostly similar to hers, at any rate as time passed), and supplied military and naval personnel, equipment and munitions when called on. They shared some legal rights with Carthaginians, for example of intermarriage. They also had to pay a regular tribute to Carthage, to judge from a report that one talent a day (equivalent to 6000 Greek drachmas or Roman *denarii*) came in from Lepcis early in the 2nd Century. This very large sum more likely represented the tribute from the whole of Emporia in that period – unless it is just a rash over-estimate.[25]

The tribute system was probably in force at least as early as the 4th Century and could well go back still earlier. Like the tribute from subjects of the Athenian empire in the 5th Century, it may originally have been justified as contributions to Carthage's protective military and naval costs, though it was kept going even when she was in no position to protect the tributaries (as after 201, when there was no longer a navy). How the payments were calculated, how comparable Lepcis' or Emporia's was to other regions' dues, and whether these were always paid in money or could be given partly in kind (grain and other produce, for instance), is not known. We may suppose that the 'accountants' (the *mḥšbm*) saw to all these matters, supervised by the *rab*. So too the tribute exacted from the Libyans of Carthage's own hinterland, after they came under her rule.

As mentioned earlier, it was not till after 480, according to Justin's account, that the Carthaginians succeeded in cancelling rental payments to their native neighbours. But from the 5th Century on, they imposed control over much of their immediate hinterland – and in a no doubt satisfying reversal of fortunes, went on to exact tribute from the Libyans (Chapter VIII). How the process unfolded is not known, but Carthage's restraint over expansion overseas, after the failure of Hamilcar's ambitious expedition into Sicily in 480, offers a context. Unwilling or uninterested in further confrontation with the Sicilian Greeks, at any rate for the next seventy years, and maybe deciding that there were still opportunities to exploit in her own continent, she chose – not necessarily right after 480 – to confront the populous but politically disunited Libyans. The 4th-Century Greek author Xenophon, in his reminiscences of Socrates, has his friend describe the Carthaginians as the rulers and the Libyans as the ruled in North Africa, no doubt the view that prevailed in Greece by the year 400. By bringing them under Carthaginian hegemony and taxing them, she must have added significantly to her financial and economic strength. By the year 396, as we shall see, this exploitative hegemony had been in place long enough to exasperate the Libyans into rebellion, unsuccessfully.

Over time, trading relations developed with the African interior too, although we have only glimpses. Trade with the peoples of the Sahara cannot have been as continuous as along the coasts, given the huge distances and sparse populations, but it was valuable: ivory, precious stones like tourmalines and garnets, animals like lions and ostriches (for public shows and sometimes even as pets), and later on elephants for war. Carthaginian merchants may have made journeys into these regions to trade, but the only story recorded is a one-sentence item in the later Greek author Athenaeus, supposedly from a lost essay of Aristotle's – how a Carthaginian named Mago crossed the desert three times living on dried meat and no liquids. Whether he was a merchant we are not told. Equally or more often, the peoples of the south probably brought their goods up to Numidia, Libya or Emporia to do business with locals and Carthaginians. Strabo mentions a south Mauretanian horse-riding tribe, the Pharusii, sometimes travelling as far as Cirta, the capital of Numidia: this can only have been to exchange items of trade. Sabratha on the Emporia coast was, it seems, a Mediterranean destination for other traders coming from and going to the vast expanses of the African interior.[26]

CARTHAGE AND THE ETRUSCANS

Carthaginian trade with the outside world grew busily. Greek pottery finds that are datable to the second quarter of the 8th Century, both Pithecusan and Euboean types, illuminate her dealings with Greek producers: the potteryware will have brought wine, oil and other imports to the city. After around 700 the Etruscans too entered trading relations. At some date a harbour on the Etruscan coast, close to the city of Caere, became the landfall for visiting Carthaginian merchants. In Roman times it still had the name Punicum, the Latin term for 'Phoenician'. A fragment of a late 6th-Century ivory tablet, found in a Ste Monique grave at Carthage, bears a statement in Etruscan, 'I am a Punic man (*puinel*) from Carthage': its owner had probably been a merchant accustomed to travelling to Etruria on business, and proud of his achievements.[27]

Mutually beneficial commerce was not the only tie between Carthaginians and Etruscans. During the mid-6th Century they cooperated against some troublesome newcomers to north-western waters – Greek refugees from Phocaea in Asia Minor, fleeing from Persian conquest, who around 540 joined earlier settlers at Alalia on the east coast of Corsica. Phocaeans were well known in the west, for they had also founded Massilia in southern Gaul around 600 and had additionally developed a regular trade with south-west Spain beyond the straits of Gibraltar. The refugees, on the other hand, raided and plundered their neighbours by land and sea until Carthage joined forces with Caere and other Etruscan cities to confront them at sea, sometime around 535. Though the allies were defeated, the Phocaeans were so badly damaged that they – the refugee newcomers at any rate – thought it better to migrate to southern Italy.

Otherwise Carthaginians and Etruscans got on well with Greeks. Quite apart from trading with the Greek world and responding favourably to Greek cultural forms from early on, Carthage and the Etruscans had no problem around 600 with the Phocaeans who founded Massilia in southern Gaul, a settlement which quickly prospered. Contacts initiated by the mariner Colaeus of Samos with the fabled kingdom of Tartessus in south-western Spain, around 640, were exploited by Phocaean merchants without interference, though equally without encouragement, from the Carthaginians. The Syracusan mother of 'king' Hamilcar, defeated at Himera in 480, has already been mentioned too. Greeks were happily settling in Etruscan cities and marrying locals: like the famous if (perhaps) legendary Demaratus the Corinthian at Tarquinii, whose half-Etruscan son Tarquinius later became king of Rome.

The links between Carthage and Etruria are further and vividly illustrated by a trio of gold sheets found at Pyrgi, Caere's chief port, from around the year 500. Inscribed in both Etruscan and Punic, they commemorate a shrine to Astarte – identified with the Etruscan goddess Uni, Rome's Juno – which was piously dedicated by Thefarie Velianas or Veliiunas, king of Carthage's old ally Caere. Two centuries later, Aristotle noted the trade and trading agreements between Carthaginians and Etruscans as a self-evident example of how such ties did not turn states into a single political entity even when 'they have agreements about imports and covenants as to abstaining from dishonesty and treaties of alliance for mutual defence'. This well fits the treaty made with the newborn Roman Republic, also around 500.[28]

FIRST TREATY WITH ROME

Naturally the Etruscans were not the Carthaginians' only contacts in Italy. Ceramic jars for transport and storage (*amphorae*) of early central Italian types have also been found at Carthage. But her most famous Italian connection is represented not so much by finds as by texts quoted in Greek translation by the historian Polybius. These are two treaties with Rome, the first negotiated – according to him – in the first year of the new Roman Republic (509), and the second generally dated to the mid-4th Century.

Whether he is right about the first date is much debated – some scholars, instead, think it very close to the second – but his reference to the treaty's archaic Latin, the discovery of the Pyrgi gold sheets, and improved knowledge of the economic importance of 6th-Century Rome strengthen the case for an early date. It declares friendship between Rome, Carthage and their allies under specific conditions. Romans or their allies were forbidden to sail beyond the 'Fair Cape', probably Cape Farina (though Cape Bon is another suggestion), unless driven by weather or enemies, and if so could not do business or stay longer than five days. Their merchants coming to 'Libya or Sardinia' were to trade only under supervision by an official, but payment for sales was guaranteed by the state; while a Roman coming to Sicily 'which the Carthaginians govern' would have equal rights with other comers. The Carthaginians promised not to harm various named communities in Latium (the Romans' home region) subject to Rome; to hand over to her any other Latin city which they might capture; and not to establish themselves militarily in Latium. So far as we know, none of these events ever happened.[29]

This treaty implies not only busy commerce between the Romans and Carthage's now extensive areas of dominance (sometimes rather loosely termed her 'empire'), but also a striking inequality between the signatories. The Carthaginians were not regulated by it in how they should do business in Roman territories or where they could sail, whereas Polybius inferred that the ban on passing the Fair Cape was to prevent Romans from gaining knowledge about the Emporia region (a not very persuasive suggestion). If Cape Farina was the 'Fair Cape', the rather more plausible aim would have been to keep Rome's venturesome merchants from intruding into the far western Mediterranean. No ban was needed, meanwhile, against possible Roman descents on Carthaginian-ruled communities or coasts, for Rome was not a major sea-power even though she may have had, or might acquire, a few warships.

Just as significant is that the agreement shows Carthage in control of coastal Libya (its interior was not relevant, nor as yet under her power), coastal Sardinia, and at least some of the Sicilian coasts too – though not of the entire island, despite its literal wording. As outlined above, the North African coastline from Lepcis (or from the Altars of the Philaeni) to the straits of Gibraltar had come under her dominance during the 6th Century. The very limited evidence that survives points to a similar inference for both south-western Sardinia and western Sicily.

PROJECTION OF POWER: SARDINIA

The Phoenician colonies in Sardinia, lying mostly in its south-western third where the broadest and most productive plains lie – but with another at Olbia on a bay in the far north-east – had grown prosperous in the two centuries since their foundation (Map 3B). The settlers collaborated and intermarried with the locals, as native Sardinian burials and goods at or near towns such as Sulcis, Monte Sirai and Tharros showed. Like Carthage and other Phoenician foundations, they traded with the Etruscans and Greeks, as well as the Phoenician homeland and Africa.

Around the middle of the 6th Century this began to change. The dominant pottery in excavations becomes black-figure ware from Attica, and the volume of such imports, it seems, is smaller. Some inhabited sites shrank dramatically, like Monte Sirai and Sulcis, or were abandoned; at others, Phoenician, Punic and also Greek styles in items of art and grave-architecture became common. New settlers, now from North Africa, arrived. Nora and Carales grew in importance during the 5th Century. Carales, the dominant city in Sardinia's most productive region, was perhaps the key base for administration.

This evidence would fit Carthage's implied (if exaggerated) claim in her treaty with Rome that she controlled the island, and Justin's and the late Roman writer Orosius' accounts of interventions there by the Carthaginian general commonly called 'Malchus' – whose real name was more likely Mazeus (or perhaps Mazel) – and his successors. With both authors compressing heavily what they found in earlier works, inconsistencies are no surprise: Justin has 'Malchus' victorious in Sicily but then worsted in Sardinia; in Orosius he is beaten both in Sicily and then, still more severely, in Sardinia (even though Orosius implies that Justin is his source). Still, both point to the same period of time for his activities: in Justin's account they occur about two generations before the Carthaginian defeat at Himera in Sicily in 480, while Orosius dates Mazeus, as he calls him, to the time of Cyrus the Great of Persia who ruled from around 557 to 530.

Mazeus' role in Carthage's domestic history will be looked at later (Chapter VIII). But if there is anything to these claims of 6th-Century wars in Sardinia, they may include dealings with the Phocaean refugees mentioned above. Herodotus, himself a Greek, reports these Greeks behaving like brigands and pirates over several years – harassing Corsican communities by land, no doubt, and Carthaginian and Etruscan shipping at sea (whether they harassed fellow Greeks too, Herodotus does not say). When finally forced into a sea battle against Carthaginian and Etruscan forces, they were victorious despite being outnumbered 120 ships to their own sixty. Yet the allies' tactical loss was offset by strategic gain, for the badly damaged Phocaeans left for southern Italy (although some Greeks, perhaps the original colonists of Alalia, did stay on, according to archaeological finds). The Etruscans recovered security in their own waters, and the Carthaginians were free to intervene or continue intervening in Sardinia.

If Mazeus was a real general, whose political troubles at home resulted from a severe defeat in Sardinia, he probably was not involved in the Alalia naval operation but was active either earlier or, a little more plausibly, afterwards. Alalia rid the region of the

Phocaeans, but Sardinia was a harder challenge. Justin tells of the city's next leaders, Mago and his two sons Hasdrubal and Hamilcar, continuing military operations there one after the other. Carthaginian intervention, as noted just now, was far from uniformly beneficial to the Phoenician cities; so it is possible enough that some had to be subdued by force, along with the neighbouring native Sardinians. It would not be surprising, then, that first Mazeus and later the Magonid generals had long-lasting difficulties – Hasdrubal, in fact, was fatally wounded. But eventually, Justin implies, Hamilcar the Magonid was victorious after many exertions (though later he perished in Sicily).[30]

If the treaty with Rome is a guide, Carthage succeeded in imposing lasting control by about 510, although of course intermittent revolts may well have continued. Thus by the last decade of the 6th Century she was mistress of the most fertile regions of Sardinia. Even if she claimed control over all of it, in practice this did not extend over its vast mountainous interior, though of course trade with the peoples there continued and Sardinian warriors could be hired as mercenaries for other Carthaginian wars, such as Hamilcar's in 480. As in North Africa, the Phoenician towns in the island remained self-governing but probably paid some form of tribute, as would the native Sardinian communities under Carthage's dominance. Part of the island's grain harvest may have been levied for tribute, for we find Hamilcar sending to Sardinia as well as Libya for grain supplies for his Sicilian expedition.

PROJECTION OF POWER: SICILY

Carthaginian hegemony in western Sicily seems to date to the later 6th Century too (Map 3C). The first treaty with Rome, at the century's end, explicitly states that the Carthaginians 'rule' Sicily: a self-serving exaggeration, but in practice the clause covered the parts under Carthaginian hegemony. Unfortunately if unsurprisingly, the evidence for how it happened is literary and fragmented.

Sicily's native peoples, called Elymi, Sicani and Sicels by Greeks, had been joined in recent centuries by Phoenician and Greek settlers who effectively took over most of the coastlands. Greek settlers were particularly enterprising, founding colonies as far west as Selinus on the south-west coast and Himera less than 50 kilometres east of Panormus. According to Diodorus and the later travel author Pausanias, around 580 a Greek adventurer, Pentathlus of Cnidus, tried to found a colony still further west, only to be slain by 'the Phoenicians and Segestans' – Segesta was a vigorous Elymian city in the region, already much influenced by Greek culture – or else by the Segestans alone when he supported Selinus against them. 'Phoenicians' in this context would include the cities of Panormus, Solous and Motya; but not necessarily Carthage.

The next reports, Justin's and Orosius', bring in Mazeus and his successors, with Mazeus fighting in Sicily – successfully or otherwise – before heading for Sardinia and defeat. Mago and then his two sons seem to have operated in Sicily too, though Justin does not say against whom. Sardinia may offer a clue: as mentioned above, the Phoenician colonies there, or some of them, seem to have suffered – not benefited – from Carthage's intervention and may not have welcomed it. Her Sicilian wars, too, may have begun against her Phoenician sister cities to bring them under her hegemony. The wars were probably intermittent, with changing opponents and, it seems, varying fortunes, but Justin does present Mago and his second son Hamilcar – though not Hasdrubal, the elder one – as enjoying notable successes.

Another episode complicates the picture. Around 510, Carthage's old nuisance Dorieus put in another appearance, this time seeking to found a colony in western Sicily. His luck proved still worse than before – he was defeated and slain, with most of his followers, by 'the Phoenicians and Segestans' or simply the Segestans (Herodotus states both versions), or by the Carthaginians (thus Diodorus), or the Segestans again (in Pausanias' brief account). Justin does not mention the episode but, when he writes of Carthage's wars against the Sicilian Greeks in the early 480s, a confused half-memory of Dorieus may help explain why he names Leonidas of Sparta as the Greeks' commander.

With Carthage a power in western Sicily by 509 and fresh from the contretemps with Dorieus, it would be surprising if – this time – Herodotus' 'Phoenicians' did not include the Carthaginians. According to Pausanias, indeed, the Spartan did found a colony named after his ancestor Hercules before he, his expedition and then the fledgling town met their end; but the mere prospect of such a foundation would have prompted the Carthaginians to act. More than one explanation is possible for the variations among our sources. Herodotus may in fact mean the Carthaginians, just as he later describes the expeditionary army of 480 as consisting of 'Phoenicians' (surely not literally), Libyans, Sardinians and others. Rather more likely, the word on both these occasions embraces both

Carthaginians and Sicilian Phoenicians. A third and subtler possibility could be that the Carthaginians commissioned their vassals the local Phoenicians and the Segestans to confront Dorieus; to this might be added the extra possibility that it was Segestan soldiers who actually slew him in battle or claimed to have done so.[31]

The next known period of war in Sicily, between 490 and 480, pitted Carthage against the two powerful Greek cities Acragas and Syracuse, under their rulers Theron and Gelon. It would lead on to the great expedition of 480, the republic's first major military confrontation with Greek states. Even so these struggles seem to have followed on a more or less peaceful period, perhaps as long as two decades, after the defeat of Dorieus. It will have been a period when the Carthaginians confirmed and consolidated their hegemony over the west of Sicily, under Mago's second son Hamilcar. His lengthy career as summed up by Justin – eleven 'dictatorships' (terms as sufete and general combined?), four 'triumphs' (the Roman term for a formal celebration of victory), his eventual death giving Carthage's foes new heart – suggests a momentous leadership at home and abroad, and it need not have been exercised purely in warfare.

Carthaginian Sicily was sometimes called the *epikrateia,* a Greek term for governed territory. It varied at times in extent and was to be challenged repeatedly by enemies in the 4th and 3rd Centuries; but it endured until the later years of the First Punic War with Rome, to end formally only in 241. Again there was no direct control from Carthage over Sicilian lands, except perhaps in dire emergencies like a Greek or Roman invasion. The Phoenician and native cities remained self-governing, but had to contribute forces and supplies for war if Carthage demanded them. These forces were probably not very large. Whenever Carthage launched major operations in the island, she sent over contingents from Africa and other territories – even as early as 480, as just noted. Whether the local communities paid tribute too, how much, and whether in money (which by 500 had been invented) or agricultural and other produce, is not known.

CARTHAGE, SPAIN AND THE ATLANTIC

Pottery remains from Spain may be the earliest of all those at Carthage, for they date to the first half of the 8th Century, even earlier (it seems) than those from Pithecusae and Euboea. Phoenician trade with southern Spain had begun centuries before, notably with the south-western realm along and inland from the Río Tinto on the Atlantic coast, and known to the Greeks as Tartessus, famous for its silver ore. Gades, founded about the same time as Carthage, came to be the main entrepôt for commerce between southern Spain and the rest of the Mediterranean, though the smaller Phoenician trading posts like Malaca and Abdera also took part (Map 3A). The Spanish communities under their princes traded silver, copper, lead, salt, grain and hides for wine, oil, textiles, jewellery and utensils from abroad. These increasingly included items made at Carthage or shipped by Carthaginians from other places, such as oil from Attica. Excavated finds of transport jars (*amphorae*) show that the wine and oil business was very large, while grandees' tombs in the Río Tinto and river Guadalquivir regions were provided with luxury import items like jewellery, lamps, carved ivory, and devotional amulets to accompany the deceased.

Perhaps from the beginning, Carthaginian merchants voyaged into the Atlantic not only to Gades (and perhaps Tartessus) but down the African coast at least as far as the old Phoenician settlements of Lixus and, further south, on the isle of Mogador. They perhaps ventured northwards, too, in search of the fabled tin of the Cassiterides islands, though this may not have happened until later, in the late 6th or the 5th Centuries, as we shall see.

In contrast to Sardinia, Sicily and even Ebusus, Carthage did not intervene militarily in Spain. The only claim that she did is a sentence of Justin's, in a very short account of pre-Roman Spain (mostly legendary) at the very end of his history. He reports that the Gaditanes, soon after their city's foundation, sought help from Carthage against attacks by the native Spaniards, only for the Carthaginians to annex that region to their empire. That one recently-founded Phoenician colony could help – and annex – another, two thousand kilometres away across the seas, is of course a mere fancy, and there is no evidence, archaeological or literary, for any such venture even in the period when Carthage was establishing a hegemony over Sardinia and Sicily. The first treaty with Rome, at the end of the 6th Century, says nothing of Spain (unlike the second, a century and a half later). If the republic did send some help to Gades, it must have been much later and it still did not result in a Spanish *epikrateia*. Trade was naturally a different matter: they followed in the wake of their Phoenician forebears, and contacts with Phoenician Spain were constant and close. Gades, we shall see, may have been the assembly point for the famous Atlantic expedition recorded in the *Periplus* of Hanno, sometime around the year 500.[32]

Carthage traded too with centres like Tingi and Lixus on Africa's Atlantic coast, which have left some remains from Carthaginian times and would prosper down to the Roman era. Trading visits to other parts of Atlantic Morocco were regular, if in places a little bizarre from a Greek viewpoint. With some peoples, according to Herodotus' Carthaginian informers, traders carried out successful deals in a paradoxical silence. Following time-honoured custom they would set their goods out on a deserted beach, return to their ships, and raise a smoke-signal. The local people would come and inspect the wares, leave a quantity of gold on the beach, and depart. The merchants in turn inspected the gold and, if they thought it fair value, took it and sailed away – but if not, would leave everything on the beach and return to shipboard to wait for the locals to add more gold. Traders and natives never met, but 'neither wronged the other' in these dealings. We may surmise that if the locals did not like the goods offered, they would not begin the bartering at all; but experienced merchants would seldom make such a mistake.[33]

HANNO'S PERIPLUS

Carthaginian seafaring on a large scale is vividly illustrated in what may be the most remarkable written document that we have by a Carthaginian. Surviving in a single medieval manuscript, a short but circumstantial Greek text called 'The *Periplus* [coastal voyage] of Hanno *basileus* of the Carthaginians' narrates a naval expedition down the Atlantic coast of North Africa. The work is generally (though not universally) agreed to be a translation, made sometime around 400 BC, of an authentic original. For all that we know, the translator too was a Carthaginian.

The date of the expedition is not known, but is generally taken to be the later 6th or earlier 5th Century. The Greek title *basileus*, 'king', probably translates Punic 'sufete' as shown earlier. This Hanno cannot be more closely identified, but there is one possible clue to his date. Justin mentions a mid-5th-Century war between Carthage and the Mauri (of Mauretania, roughly today's Morocco). He gives no details, but if it did happen it may have been connected in some way with the expedition – for instance, the settlements founded by Hanno perhaps provoked hostility from the locals and had to be sent further help (via Gades?). Or conversely, old Phoenician settlements in Atlantic Mauretania, notably Lixus but also trading-posts like the one at Tangier, first had to be helped against the Mauri and then a decision followed to strengthen Carthaginian interests in the region, by sending Hanno out with new settlers. This might also account for why all his colonies seem to have lain along Mauretania's Atlantic coast. Whether Hanno himself was a member of the then-dominant family of the Magonids – whose leaders in the mid-5th Century included a Hanno, son of Hamilcar the defeated general at Himera in Sicily in 480 – is not known but is a reasonable guess.

Hanno, says the *Periplus*, was sent with 'sixty pentecerters, and men and women to the number of thirty thousand' to found colonies beyond the straits of Gibraltar. Sixty pentecerters would not have had room for anything like so many people, so it is reasonable to infer that their number is a literary conceit, or the translator misread the Punic figure, or else the pentecerters were armed craft escorting transport ships. All the same the number of settlers must have been much smaller, conceivably just a tenth of the supposed total. The narrative records a colony being placed at 'Thymiaterion' and others further down the coast as far as a place called Cerne. 'Thymiaterion' was apparently the town later called Tingi, today Tangier, on the straits, where early tombs dating from around 700 already show Phoenician cultural influences. There is much argument over where the other colonies were placed, but they all seem to have lain along the Moroccan coast.

From Cerne the expedition sailed further south – we are not told why – though it founded no more settlements. The Carthaginians now had some intriguing, not to mention mysterious, encounters that have formed the *Periplus*' main fascination for modern readers. Inland from one anchorage, they heard and were terrified by drumbeats, flutes and cries at night. Over much of the trip they saw fires that lit up the night skies and sometimes came down to the shores, including at one point a blaze 'larger than the rest, which seemed to reach the stars'. On one island just before turning back, they were assailed with stones by the natives but managed to capture three very hairy women 'whom the interpreters [from Lixus] called "Gorillas"'. These fought back so fiercely that their captors killed them, flaying the bodies to take the skins to Carthage. Hanno now turned back because supplies were running short.

Apart from the 'Lixitae' interpreters (the people of Lixus or their Berber neighbours), most of the *Periplus*' names are not easily identifiable, not even those of the colonies. How far south the fleet sailed is regularly debated, and the vivid descriptions of sites and events beyond Cerne have been matched with quite a variety of African places and features. As the *Periplus*, like a ship's log, records the number of sailing-days from one place to the next, identifications depend very much on estimating the fleet's sailing speed, with estimates ranging from a cautious 40 kilometres a day to an optimistic 100 and above. As a result, some interpretations have Hanno sailing around all of west Africa as far as the Cameroon coast; others, in sharp contrast, only as far as the gulf of Agadir in southern Morocco and over to the nearby Canary Islands.

The story of the voyage was placed in the temple of 'Cronus', probably Baal Hammon's. In the 1st Century AD both Mela the Roman geographer and Pliny the Elder knew it, no doubt in its Greek version. Pliny mentions details which he must have found in another source conversant with Hanno's *Periplus*: that the expedition started from Gades, and two skins of the women 'Gorillas' could be seen at Carthage in the temple of 'Juno' – meaning Tanit or (some think) Astarte – until the destruction of the city. He could be right about both, for the *Periplus'* itinerary starts at the straits of Gibraltar, while conceivably the third skin may have been lost or destroyed before the time of his other source.

The *Periplus'* term 'Gorillas' (in Greek, Γορίλλας) has had a strange later life. Some readers supposed that Hanno captured hairy apes, not hairy humans: so a 19th-Century clergyman-scientist, Thomas Savage, applied the word to African apes (and in time it was used of the film hero King Kong). Its real form and sense is another disputed *Periplus* question. Is it a copyist's error for 'Gorgades', the word that Pliny gives to the captive women's tribe (an easy mistake using Greek letters), or for some other term; or a transcription into Greek of a supposed Punic term of disdain, '*oril* or *horil*, 'the uncircumcised ones'? If so, Hanno's interpreters must have meant the whole tribe, as Pliny assumes. Whatever the solution to this ancient puzzle, 'gorilla' is the most lasting, if misapplied, legacy of Hanno's expedition.[34]

In practice, what this famous voyage achieved seems limited. The colonies do not seem to have lasted into Roman times or to have left much trace on the ground. If the stated aim was to plant them, it is not obvious why the fleet sailed on for at least another twenty-seven days after the final one at Cerne. A marked feature in the later half of *Periplus* is the almost constant fright of the travellers at the strange sights and sounds they met, and this second half is sometimes suspected as being mere myth-inspired fiction – or cunning Carthaginian disinformation. If it is genuine, the aim of the further voyage may have been to seek out new places for trading, though plainly none was found.

Even so, Hanno's *Periplus* brings to life the seafaring skills and the (cautious) long-distance enterprise of Carthage in her heyday. His colonising expedition was at least equivalent in size to the Phocaeans' migration to the west after 546. It dates probably to the century of Carthage's widening control over North Africa's coasts, her takeover of Ebusus, the known pacts with Etruria and Rome, and the interventions in Sardinia and Sicily. Nor is it the only travel episode that illustrates her maritime vigour.

HIMILCO'S VOYAGE

Another notable Atlantic expedition, reported by ancient writers though its own record does not survive, was led by one Himilco, who sailed to the north. Avienus, a 4th-Century AD writer whose partly-preserved poem *Ora Maritima* ('the Sea Coast') describes the shores of western lands, claims to summarise items from Himilco's report, which he uses along with other long-past travel accounts. With sources so distant from his own time, and with an unreliable grasp of geography in any case, Avienus is a debatable witness to Himilco's voyage, but at least it is also mentioned by Pliny, who writes that both Himilco and Hanno were sent forth from Carthage at the same time. Himilco's voyage will then date between 500 and 450.

Sailing north from the straits of Gibraltar, he visited the 'Oestrymnides islands' on a voyage that lasted four months from start to end. These islands are another well-debated geographical issue, thanks to Avienus' poetically coloured and often vague language: the Oestrymnians had traded with the Tartessians, he avers, then with 'the colonists of Carthage' and other folk around the straits, and were two days' sail from 'Ierne', which seems to be Ireland. The names 'Oestrymnides' and 'Oestrymnis' (the main island) are not found outside Avienus, but they are generally identified with the famous, if again much-debated, Cassiterides islands whose important trade in tin with southern Spain – *cassiteros* being the Greek for tin – is often mentioned by ancient writers.

Herodotus in the later 5th Century was the earliest to mention the Cassiterides and their reputation as Greece's source of tin, but was dubious about their existence. Later ages acquired fuller though sometimes fanciful details: Strabo describes the islanders in their black cloaks, ankle-length robes and belts circling their chests as 'looking like the vengeance-goddesses in tragedies'; they lived a pastoral life and exchanged tin and lead from their mines for salt and manufactured goods from visiting merchants. The Cassiterides have been variously identified: as the Scilly Islands off Cornwall (or Cornwall itself, supposing that Himilco mistook it for an island), as Brittany or some of the islands off the western Breton coast, or – much more conservatively – as the extensively indented coast of Galicia in north-western Spain.

The tin trade, as noted earlier, was a prized and vital part of Mediterranean commerce. Pliny, while mentioning Himilco, in a brief remark elsewhere calls the first traveller to the tin islands Midacritus, a man otherwise unknown but with a Greek name. Himilco may have been the first Carthaginian official – a sufete like Hanno, perhaps – to explore the route and write an account of his journey, though this is only a surmise. Once they gained a dominant position in western waters, the Carthaginians worked hard at keeping competitors at bay. Strabo tells a story of one later ship-captain who ran his vessel into shoals with the loss of all his crew, rather than let a Roman ship behind him find the route to the tin islands (the authorities at Carthage rewarded him handsomely).[35]

But ancient seas were hard to patrol, and nothing suggests that Carthaginian screening in western waters was foolproof. Colaeus' and the Phocaeans' dealings with Tartessus have been mentioned above. Herodotus, though doubtful whether the Cassiterides – or even an ocean beyond Europe – really existed, does accept that tin, like amber, came 'from the furthest region' of the world but makes no mention of Carthaginian intermediaries. In this as in many other of their dealings with the rest of the Mediterranean world, the Carthaginians had a constant problem over matching their prefer-ences with the realities.

AN EXPANSIONIST POLICY?

Carthage under Mazeus, Mago and their successors looks surprisingly active, indeed assertive. Her size, population and wealth were growing, thanks to busy trade and industry. The area of the city, by the end of the 6th Century or earlier, was over 50 hectares. The 6th-Century troubles of her mother city perhaps brought her some extra advan-tages: Tyre suffered a thirteen-year siege from 585 to 572 by the Babylonian king Nebuchadnezzar, and then had to accept first Babylo-nian and, forty years later, Persian domination, events that did Tyrian prosperity little good. The silver trade from Tartessus seems to have contracted badly or even collapsed. The Carthaginians continued to honour Tyre as their mother city, sending yearly tithes to Melqart's temple there, but at the same time they may have gained some of Tyre's western customers. They may also have received Tyrian and Phoenician migrants seeking a less threatened life.

Establishing her dominant influence over the North African coasts, and over Ebusus, overlapped in time with a similar development in the regions of Sardinia and Sicily that were commercially, agriculturally and culturally aligned with her interests. These activities stretched over many decades, from the middle or later 6th Century (the wars of Mazeus) to the early 5th. Justin's account of them, selective though it is in places – highlighting the clash between Mazeus and his priestly son, ignoring local place-names, studiously vague about chronology – nonetheless transmits what seems a plausible outline, not just a triumphally fictitious one. In fact the wars as he tells them were far from uniform successes, for they included the failed attempt to jettison paying the Libyan tribute, the defeats in Sardinia suffered by Mazeus and Mago's son Hasdrubal, and the practical stalemate against Acragas and Syracuse early in the 480s.

This wide range of military and naval ventures should be seen in perspective, all the same. The armed forces employed were surely much smaller than those in Carthage's later wars. Herodotus gives the Carthaginian and Etruscan fleets 60 penteconters each when fighting the Phocaeans: a penteconter had twenty-five oars on each side, each rowed by one oarsman, who it seems did any necessary hand-to-hand fighting as well. Carthage's expeditionary force would therefore have totalled 3000 men or so, the majority of them oarsmen. It need not have been her entire naval capacity at the time, but clearly was a major effort. The days of hundreds of heavily-manned quinqueremes were far in the future.

The armies campaigning in 6th-Century Sardinia or Sicily probably numbered a few thousand at most, even when supported by allied contingents and mercenaries. They may not always (or even often) have outnumbered their opponents – one reason why operations seem to have been episodic and sometimes adverse. It could also help explain the consternation aroused by the incursion of Dorieus and his followers, who cannot have been much more numerous. Allegedly Hamilcar's great army in Sicily, only thirty years later, did comprise an enormous number of soldiers – three hundred thousand – not to mention 200 warships and 3000 transports, but these figures cannot be taken any more seriously than Herodotus' colossal totals for the Persian forces invading Greece in the same year.

It does not seem likely that these wide-ranging, overlapping and persistent ventures simply happened to coincide, or that their various stages each developed because of separate and *ad hoc* factors. Rather, a conscious plan looks likely: to capitalise on Carthage's growing riches and resources by bringing important nearby territories under firmer influence and exploitation. The republic's concern to clarify and regulate trade relationships is plain from the treaties with the Etruscans and Romans. Trade naturally figured in the dealings by Carthage and her Sicilian Phoenician allies, like Motya, with the island's Greek cities, though whether economic tensions contributed to the wars of the 480s is not certain. According to Herodotus, Gelon of Syracuse in 480 did tell envoys from Greece how he had previously offered – in vain – to cooperate with Athens and other Greek states in 'liberating the trading posts (*emporia*)' which brought these states 'great revenues and benefits', only for them to refuse both his offer and also his appeal for military help against the Carthaginians. Were these trading posts in Sicily, or in a region of more direct interest to mainland Greece such as southern Italy? Gelon's language suggests the latter, which would not make the *emporia* an issue between Carthage and Syracuse, but nothing else is known about them.

The republic's overseas drive for hegemony was partly due as well, perhaps, to political pressures among the Carthaginian élite. It was not just the Barcid generals of the 3rd Century who owed their status and effective dominance to military glory (and carefully distributed booty): so did Mago and then his descendants for a century and more, until their peers combined to dislodge them. Mazeus may have been the first grandee to exploit military success like this, perhaps indeed because it was the first time the resources – in men, ships, munitions and money – were available on the necessary scale. His overthrow cleared the way for the more judicious Mago, but military activities were still desirable, to support the continuing dominance of his family and faction. By 480 their supremacy was secure enough to survive the shock of the defeat at Himera.

By 480, too, Carthage had become the centre of a geopolitical sphere of influence broader than anything previously seen in the western Mediterranean. The tales of Darius of Persia calling for her help in his expedition against Athens in 490, and of his son Xerxes coordinating with Carthage a grand strategy ten years later to attack the Greeks in both the east and the west simultaneously, may be legend but do recognise that now the republic had a status – and potential – which would not have been dreamt of at the end of the 7th Century. It put her on a level, economically, politically and militarily, with just a very few other contemporary powers in the Mediterranean.

V

TRADERS AND
LANDOWNERS:
CARTHAGINIAN SOCIETY

TRADE AND TRADERS

The Carthaginians are often visualised as a nation of seafaring traders, interested only in the bottom line. This supposed obsession is more a feature of modern stereotyping than ancient. True, ancient writers from Herodotus on often mention their trading behaviour, techniques and markets, as already shown. Greeks and Romans often and admiringly stressed Carthage's wealth: the Syracusan leader Hermocrates in 415 described her (according to Thucydides) as richer than all other cities, and two hundred and sixty-five years later, in Polybius' time, the universal view remained that she was the wealthiest city in the world. Cicero makes the entirely specious claim that it was Carthage's passion for trade, and by implication money-making, that eventually brought her down. Nonetheless, ancient sources focus more often on other prime features of the city's life – warfare and politics especially.[36]

A great deal of Carthage's wealth did come from the sea. As noted earlier, the lengthy expeditions of Hanno and Himilco seem basically intent on fostering contacts along Europe's and Africa's Atlantic coasts. The takeover of Ebusus and interventions in Sardinia and Sicily had added to her trade advantages, so there is no surprise in her resolve, obvious in the first treaty with Rome (of 509 or thereabouts) and again in the second (generally dated to 348: Chapter X), to regulate Roman trading contacts with her territories in both islands as well as in North Africa. It would be hard to imagine that her agreements with other commercial states were very different, except perhaps ones made with sister Phoenician colonies that may possibly have given those places easier terms.

From early times on, the usual Carthaginian merchant ships, like others in the Mediterranean, were of two types: a small craft known as a *gaulos* (thought to be a Phoenician word for ship), low in the water with a wide and rounded hull and pointed bow; and the *hippos* (Greek for horse, because of its horsehead prow), narrower and tapering at both bow and stern. In various forms and sizes, such ships and their descendants were the mainstay of the Carthaginian merchant marine down the centuries. It may have been in large merchantmen that Hanno's expeditionary colonists sailed, with his 60 penteconters as escorts. The penteconter itself – the name means fifty-oared ship – was descended from fifty-oared war galleys of more ancient times, and remained the standard ship of Mediterranean warfare until around 500. It could also be used for transport, as for example the Phocaeans did on their migrations; though, as noted earlier, Hanno's expedition would have needed many more than sixty if his colonists went in penteconters too.

Archaeological finds reveal imports to Carthage from all over the Mediterranean, even in early times as was shown above, and also installations for making the famous scarlet dye from the *murex* shellfish. Commerce in tin, iron, lead, silver and other metals continued, although these goods have left fewer physical traces. The remains of *amphorae*, pottery jars used for carrying wine, oil and grain, show continuing imports from Greece, notably Athens and especially prominent during the 5th and 4th Centuries, as well as increasing quantities from southern Italy and Campania, the Iberian peninsula, and later too from Rhodes. Diodorus records a thriving export of olives from Acragas in Sicily to Carthage in the later 5th Century: though he implies that, once olive cultivation became widespread in Libya, the exports fell off.

The Carthaginians in turn exported North African fish, grain, oil (this in later times at least), *murex* dye and other products. In the city's final centuries, after 300, Libyan wine too became an important export, or so suggest the wide-mouthed Punic *amphorae* (suitable for easy pouring) found in many places around the western Mediterranean – Massilia, Corsica and Rome among them – and even further east at Athens.

As well as handling such produce, the city's merchants were also active middlemen, acquiring goods from other producers and selling them on. A sizeable part of the cargoes set out on African beaches for the locals to inspect will have been of this sort, and it is worth noting that (as Herodotus tells it) the Carthaginian traders were paid in gold, not barter items. A 5th-Century shipwreck, just off the islet of Tagomago alongside Ibiza, was carrying a cargo probably of *garum* fish-sauce, in *amphorae* of a type made in the region of Gades and Tingi; while the ship was a western Phoenician type, perhaps even from Carthage. A small Carthaginian ship which sank in the harbour of Lilybaeum (modern Marsala) around the year 250 also carried *garum* along with wine and olives.[37]

What a Carthaginian merchant arriving in a foreign town might have for sale is playfully suggested by the Roman playwright Plautus in *Poenulus*, 'The Little Carthaginian' (or more freely 'Our Carthaginian Friend'), a comedy put on, it seems, not long after the Second Punic War. The 'little Carthaginian' is a rich, elderly merchant named Hanno, searching the Mediterranean for his long-lost daughters and just arrived in a small Greek seaport. For his own reasons he pretends at first to speak only Punic, which allows a self-appointed local interpreter named Milphio to mistranslate him as huckstering a variety of mostly cheap goods: 'African mice' for display at a festival (a joke for panthers?), soup ladles, water- or music-pipes, nuts, lard, spades and mattocks. This miscellany, which is spread over several lines, is plainly meant for humour since the audience knows that Hanno is on a very different mission: but Romans might well expect much this kind of cargo from Carthaginian ships.

Hanno's supposed Punic utterances not only mystified later copyists but modern scholars too until quite recently, the general verdict being that Plautus wrote invented gibberish. Now they are widely treated as genuine – the only specimens of Punic of any length in Greek or Roman literature. Translations of them vary because of the state of the text, but in any version they are unexciting: Hanno prays for help from the local gods, explains that he is seeking the hospitality of an old friend's son who lives in the town, and identifies the young man's house; he then answers Milphio's questions in Punic until the false renditions provoke him into Latin. But his Punic remarks are lengthy enough to suggest that at least some members of his audience could understand him. With Carthaginian–Roman trade going back to the 6th Century or even earlier, this will be no surprise (not to mention that, by Plautus' time, the first and second Punic wars had brought many Carthaginians to Italy as enslaved captives).[38]

It is worth noting that an old street or district on Rome's Esquiline Hill had the name *Vicus Africus*, 'the African quarter': perhaps it was where merchants from North Africa lodged in numbers sizeable enough to give the place its name. A community, small or substantial, of Carthaginians and other North Africans could be found at Rome and other important foreign centres at any time (save during wars), just as resident Greeks are glimpsed at

Carthage in 396 and Italian merchants in 149. Syracuse in 398 had a large body of resident Carthaginians, with plentiful property to plunder when a new war broke out; so did other Sicilian Greek cities, Diodorus tells us (the Carthaginians, by contrast, seem to have left their resident Greeks alone).

Milphio in *Poenulus* describes Hanno as a *gugga*, a joke (it seems) about the merchant's colourful foreign clothing; a modern suggestion is that *gugga* was the Punic name for a purple-hued African bird. The widespread view that it was a word, perhaps derisive, for Carthaginian traders in general is less convincing, for it is not found anywhere else with this sense. Interestingly even so, a Punic-language inscription at Cirta in Numidia – today's Constantine in Algeria – probably from after the destruction of Carthage and thus after Plautus' lifetime, seems to use *hgg'* ('the *gugga*') for the profession of a man coincidentally called Hanno.

Given the importance of trade, within and beyond Africa, to the Carthaginians throughout their history, and the general view that their republic was run by a merchant oligarchy, it is paradoxical that the only rich Carthaginian merchant whom we know in any detail is fictitious. One real merchant may be attested on a mid-4th-Century Greek inscription (now lost) from Thebes: he was 'Nobas son of Axioubos' – probably one Nubo or Nabal (both are rare but attested Carthaginian names), son of a Hasdrubal or Esibaal – who received honours from the Boeotian League of which Thebes was the dominant city. Possibly the men called Aris and Mago whose names – in Greek letters – are stamped on some wide-mouthed *amphorae* found at Carthage were merchants too; but just as possibly or more so, they were the *amphora*-makers or the landowners whose estates produced the wine or oil transported in the jars (as was common practice on Roman-era lamps, *amphorae* and other pottery items). It is surely safe to suppose that most (if not all) of the city's leading men down the ages had links with commerce – directly or through kinsmen or merchant protégés – but this does remain a supposition.[39]

LAND AND LANDOWNING

As mentioned earlier, it was not till after 480, in Justin's account, that the Carthaginians succeeded in cancelling rental payments to their Libyan neighbours. Instead, from then on they imposed control over much of their hinterland – and in a no doubt satisfying reversal of fortunes, went on to exact tribute from it. How the process unfolded is not known, but Carthage's restraint over expansion overseas after the failure in 480 of Hamilcar's ambitious expedition into Sicily offers a context. Unwilling or uninterested in further confrontation with the Sicilian Greeks, at any rate for the next seventy years, and maybe deciding that there were still opportunities to exploit in her own continent, she chose – not necessarily right after 480 – to confront the populous but politically disunited Libyans. By bringing them under Carthaginian hegemony and taxing them she must have added significantly to her financial and economic strength. It was probably during the same period that the North African coastlands, including the other old Phoenician colonies, came under a similar dominance, as noted earlier.

While Carthage's own city-territory (in Greek, her *chora*) remained a separate entity from the subject Libyan territories and the lands of her Libyphoenician allies, nothing banned Carthaginians from owning property in all three. The *chora* consisted of Carthage's immediate environs, probably including Tunes, as well as the Cape Bon peninsula, but its precise limits are not known. Carthaginian citizens very likely owned most of it, apart from any areas directly owned by the state, but there were probably some other property-owners as well – residents from the sister colonies, some Libyans (from the very beginning, according to Justin), even foreigners like Greeks, Tyrians and Etruscans. As mentioned above, there was a Greek community at Carthage early in the 4th Century and no doubt at other times, while property-owning Carthaginians could be found in many Sicilian cities and maybe at Rome.

Polybius, writing of the later 3rd Century, states that the *chora* supplied the Carthaginians' 'individual lifestyle needs' while the tribute from Libya paid the expenses of the state. This should mean that the *chora* provided citizens with their grain, other food and other private goods in a period when the citizen population – male and female, city and *chora* – was probably between six and seven hundred thousand. Its produce may have maintained their slaves and ex-slaves too, for Polybius is probably not being pedantically exact in his phrasing.

Hannibal in 195 owned an estate on the east coast in Byzacium, between Acholla and Thapsus, thus pretty certainly outside the *chora* and in the territory of one of these two Libyphoenician communities. Again in non-Carthaginian territory would be the land grants that Aristotle reports being given to citizens sent out into the Libyan countryside to ease population pressure in the city. He implies that the grants were generous, for they made the grantees 'men of means'. In time, then, Libya was dotted with Carthaginian settlers and their farms and orchards – a continuing factor for major cultural, religious and social impacts.

By Aristotle's day, and probably from early on, the Carthaginians were distinguished for their agricultural expertise. Diodorus, in his account of the Syracusan leader Agathocles' invasion of North Africa in 310, writes a famous description of the marvellous countryside that the invaders found as they marched down the Cape Bon peninsula:

> The intervening country through which it was necessary for them to march was divided into gardens and plantations of every kind, since many streams of water were led in small channels and irrigated every part. There were also country houses one after another, constructed in luxurious fashion and covered in stucco, which gave evidence of the wealth of the people who possessed them. The farm buildings were filled with everything that was needful for enjoyment, seeing that the inhabitants in a long period of peace had stored up an abundant variety of products. Part of the land was planted with vines, and part yielded olives and was also planted thickly with other varieties of fruit-bearing trees. On each side herds of cattle and flocks of sheep pastured on the plain, and the neighbouring meadows were filled with grazing horses. In general there was a manifold prosperity in the region, since the leading Carthaginians had laid out there their private estates and with their wealth had beautified them for their enjoyment. (Diodorus 20.8.3–4)

Diodorus' narrative of this war in Africa reads as though based on a sound, maybe eyewitness source. It also chimes with Polybius' statement about the productivity of the *chora*: for as we have seen, the Cape Bon peninsula had long been an important part of this. When the Romans invaded Punic North Africa in 256, they promptly found quantities of goods to loot in the rich countryside, including no fewer than twenty thousand persons to carry off as slaves. A century later in 153, envoys from Rome – among them the famous, irascible and suspicious Cato the Censor – noted the wealth of the countryside as well as the prosperity of the city. This is echoed by Polybius, who visited North Africa a few years after and stresses both the fertility of the land and how 'the supply of horses, oxen, sheep, and goats in it is beyond anything to be found in any other part of the world'. Strabo rather exaggeratedly claims that even in 150 Carthage still controlled three hundred Libyan towns. Despite the damage done by invasions and local rebellions, Carthaginian and Libyan skills were always able to make the land flourish once more.[40]

As mentioned earlier, archaeological finds suggest that Carthaginians moved out to live in the hinterland not much before the year 400: even within 50 kilometres of the city, recognisably Carthaginian sites are very few down to about the year 300, contrasting with plenty from the next two centuries. Whether this should mean that not many Carthaginians occupied Libyan properties before the final century and a half of the city's existence still needs to be clarified. If correct, Aristotle's report of regular allocations of land in Libya to citizens, good land at that, must be wrong, and we must wonder what made him imagine it. It may well be that earlier citizen settlers lived much like their Libyan neighbours, even if these were in practice their subjects or vassals. Carthaginian domination and exploitation of Libyans and Libya's resources were well under way before 396, to judge by the great rebellion launched – unsuccessfully – by the Libyans in that year.

The development of the countryside beyond the *chora* would be especially notable in its most fruitful areas: the lower Bagradas valley, the so-called 'little Mesopotamia' between this and the Catadas (modern Mellane) river to its east, and also (by the 4th Century) the uplands around the middle Bagradas and its tributaries the Siliana and the Muthul – regions of populous towns like Thugga, Uchi, Thubursicu and Bulla; not to mention the richest region of all, Byzacium. On the island of Meninx, modern Jerba, off the western coast of Emporia, a prosperous countryside with large and small villas existed by the late 3rd Century, apparently untroubled by Roman seaborne raids during the Second Punic War. Thanks to this agricultural prowess, Carthaginian merchants down the ages – and surely too those of smaller but important centres like Hippacra, Utica and Hadrumetum – had their well-stocked cargoes of grain and oil to take to customers abroad.

Agriculture again was the theme of two of the few Carthaginian writers known to us, Hamilcar and Mago – both of them retired generals, according to Pliny and the 1st-Century AD agronomist Columella. When they lived is not known, though Hamilcar seems to have preceded Mago and both almost certainly lived after 400, possibly even after 300. Their works have not survived but Roman authors mention them with respect, especially Mago and his twenty-eight books on estate management, in effect a complete encyclopaedia of farming. Both writers seem to have drawn partly on Greek predecessors, but in turn they powerfully impressed their Greek and Roman readers and later agricultural authors: a striking feat indeed. When Carthage was destroyed in 146 and all the city's libraries were passed on to pro-Roman North African rulers, the Roman senate ordered Mago's work to be reserved for translation into Latin. Sixty years later, a condensed Greek version was brought out by a translator from Utica with the interestingly Roman-Greek name of Cassius Dionysius.

Mago, and no doubt Hamilcar too, wrote for affluent landowners. Hamilcar remains only a name, but a number of passages from Mago and a few from Cassius are quoted or paraphrased by Roman authors (notably Pliny and Columella, as well as Cicero's contemporary Varro). We therefore have welcome glimpses of how wealthy Carthaginians treated their estates.

The beginning of Mago's work was much quoted. An estate buyer, he stressed, should sell his house in the city lest he grow fonder of it than of his country property. In turn, someone especially fond of his town home had no need of a rural estate. Most Carthaginian landowners are not likely to have followed this advice literally (we know that Hannibal had a city house as well as the Byzacium estate), but Mago's real aim was no doubt to emphasise the importance of intelligent and committed farm management. His variegated topics included how to select the best bullocks, site vineyards and prune vines, plant olives, and rear horses and mules. He also supported the less plausible but widespread ancient idea (later taken up poetically by Virgil) that bees could be produced from the carcase and blood of a slaughtered bullock.

Worth noting, too, are some precepts quoted by Varro from Cassius Dionysius, who translated Mago. He recommended judicious treatment of estate slaves, particularly those chosen as supervisors. Slaves should be at least twenty-two years old and knowledgeable; supervisors and ordinary labourers must be given incentives to work well and feel loyalty to the estate and its owner; they should be chastised verbally rather than with blows; and the more alert and committed among them should be further rewarded, including encouraging them to marry fellow slaves and have sons. Such sound advice very probably came from Mago. Again we cannot say how far Carthaginians followed it in practice but, so far as they go, the precepts illustrate a sensibly enlightened attitude to slaves – one rather less forbidding than the strict and utilitarian slave regimen practised by Cato the Censor in 2nd-Century Rome.[41]

WORKERS AND LABOURERS

The potteries, foundries, dockyards and harbours at Carthage needed a sizeable working population. Some would be slaves and some others immigrants from the Libyan hinterland and from abroad, but many Carthaginian men and at least some women will have been breadwinners for their families. Maintaining, and at times extending, the amenities of a prospering city and catering to the needs and interests of its residents called for the normal broad range of occupations, from unskilled labourers such as dockworkers to goldsmiths, architects, doctors and teachers. Of their daily lives and needs not much is known, but the remains of houses excavated at Carthage and at the little Cape Bon town Kerkouane include small-roomed dwellings, some in multi-storeyed blocks at Carthage (in her later centuries), and shops opening onto the streets.

Ordinary city people lived close together, as they did in Phoenician, Greek and Italian towns too. Craftsmen in different trades may well have set up their shops, and therefore homes, along one or more streets, just as Rome had the *vicus Africus* and streets noted for particular trades such as scythemakers, cobblers and booksellers. As noted above, the area south of the walled city and beside the shore of the lake of Tunis seems to have been where the potters, ironworkers and dock labourers dwelt. There is as yet no archaeological evidence of dwelling-places in the sector, but the 'New Gate' inscription mentioned below strengthens the impression. In any case the homes of many of the very poor – Carthaginians and outsiders – must have been flimsy and perishable, leaving no traces.

Votive *stelae* and other inscriptions in Punic, from Carthage and elsewhere, commemorate ordinary folk down the ages: for instance Abdeshmun the scribe, 'Abdmilqart the tax-collector' (*ngš*), Aris a maker of strigils (metal scrapers used in the bath), carpenters named Ariso and Baalyaton, Baalhanno the fisherman, Baalsamor and his son Abdosiri who were each 'chief of the gate-keepers', an interpreter named Baalyaton son of Mago, wheelmakers named Bomilcar and Himilco, Bostar the innkeeper (*Bd'štrt hlyn*), a merchant Halosbaal son of Bostar son of Abdmilkot, a bow-maker named Hanno, and Mago the butcher (*Mgn hṭbḥ*). Another Mago, 'son of Himilco son of Himilco', was a chariot-maker. There were 'the craftsmen who made the female statues for the temple of *Mkl* ' (a little-known deity); goldsmiths – 'the founders of gold objects' – with their foundry; and at a higher social level, the seal-keeper Abdeshmun whose son Baaliyaton became a sufete, and Yehawallon or Yehaw-wielon a road-builder or engineer.

Yehawallon figures in an inscription that is a rarity: a lengthy document in Punic found in the 1960s, attesting not a religious matter but a civic enterprise and dating from the 4th or 3rd Century. This was the building of an important street 'leading to the New Gate'. Just where the gate was is not certain, but the inscription may state – experts' interpretations of the Punic text vary – that it was in the southern wall. If so it would represent further development on that side of Carthage, which fits evidence for her urban growth from the 5th Century on. The inscription, on a block of black limestone, ascribes the project to 'the people of Carthage in the year of the sufetes Safot and Adonibaal' and 'the time of the magistracy of Adonibaal' and at least one other named magistrate, but the stone is damaged, 'and their colleagues'. What Adonibaal's office was is unclear, like so much else; were these men the heads (*rbm*) of the various pentarchies in that period? More interesting still is the range of workers involved in the project: tradesmen, porters and others 'from the plain of the town' (the area south of the city wall?), gold-smelters, furnace workers and, less certainly, 'the weighers of small change', the artisans 'who make vessels' (or 'pots'), and 'the makers of sandals'.

The relations between workers and employers, and levels of wages, are virtually unknown. With coined money not used by the Carthag-inians until the late 5th Century – and even then only in Sicily until the century following – wages would have been paid in goods or valuables. There seems to have been some, probably modest, flexi-bility in employment. Two Punic inscriptions record transactions in which a man 'registered himself back into the employ of his master Esmunhalos of his own free will' and 'without asking for silver'. One is the Hannobaal mentioned earlier, and the other is named Hannibal of Miqne, possibly the same person (though the names are among the commonest at Carthage). In both the man acts – or claims to act – freely, and Hannobaal seals up the transaction with his own seal. Perhaps he and his namesake were freed slaves owning skills that led Eshmunhalos to entice or coerce them to come back and work for him; the denial of coercion may be just a formula. Even so it was an arrangement that earned written commemoration, no doubt for legal reasons.[42]

Other men with Carthaginian names, and of plainly low status, made dedications to Carthage's chief deities, Tanit and Baal Hammon, like the Safot also mentioned earlier, a š ṣdn bd – a slave 'owned by', or freedman 'thanks to', one Milkyaton son of Yaton-baal son of Milkyaton. So did Baalsillek, 'š ṣdn bd his master (*'dnm*) Baalhanno'. Meanwhile *Gry*, a fuller who was slave of, or worker for, a Hanno son of Abdeshmun, had a tomb of his own in Carthage with his name on it. There is no report of Carthaginian citizens becoming enslaved to other Carthaginians, though it may sometimes have happened (for example as a penalty for debt, as could happen in early Rome), but Carthaginian names could well be given to slaves from elsewhere – and very likely to slave children born and raised among Carthaginians.[43]

Why freedmen, if that is what these men were, should each be called 'a man of Sidon' (š ṣdn) can only be surmised. Diodorus' report of the Libyphoenicians having intermarriage rights with Carthaginians may be a clue that migrants to Carthage from kindred cities enjoyed certain privileges (at Rome, citizens of her satellite Latin colonies did). Sidon, second only to Tyre in kinship to Carthage, perhaps gave its name to such a status, limited but still privileged in comparison to resident Libyans, Numidians and the like. That would place a thoroughly Punicised and maybe Carthage-born š ṣdn like Safot, if he was a freedman, on a footing close to but not quite equal with Carthaginian citizens – a situation which these surely regarded as fit and proper.

Whatever their origins, the inscriptions of Hannobaal, Safot, Baalsillek and *Gry* suggest some degree of freedom in their doings. Hannobaal left his master or former master for other (unsuccessful?) activities and then returned. Safot and Baalsillek could make their own dedication (seemingly at their own expense, so it means they could earn money for themselves). *Gry* seems to have run his own fuller's shop, even if he was supervised by his master or patron. There would be equal or greater flexibility for freeborn Carthaginians working for employers, and still wider opportunities if they had independent professions such as scribes, goldsmiths, statute-makers or builders – professions in which they in turn would have employees or slaves.

SLAVES

Slaves worked in the city and the countryside. Their numbers will have grown sizeably with the growth of both the city and the *chora*, and still more as Libya in turn became more prosperous. The Carthaginians built up a significant slave population of which only occasional glimpses emerge. As at Rome, rich citizens no doubt owned large numbers, less wealthy citizens fewer, and probably only quite affluent craftsmen and small farmers could expect to afford even one. Freed slaves surely existed too, as suggested above, but their numbers and the terms on which they might gain their freedom are not known.

Slaves originated from all round the Mediterranean and some no doubt from beyond. Slave-traders were a Mediterranean fixture at all times, and Phoenician slavers had been known even to Homer – one tried to kidnap Odysseus on his wanderings. Cassius Dionysius, says Varro, recommended slaves from Epirus in north-western Greece for their steadiness and loyalty: another piece of advice which may have come from Mago. Others were born to slave parents – as noted earlier, Mago approved of this – while still others may have been persons (perhaps even Carthaginians?) enslaved for debt or other penalties. Others who could become slaves were men, women and children carried off from their coastal homes by raiding pirates, as happened (in reverse) to the daughters of Hanno the 'little Carthaginian'. Some children may have been sold into slavery by poverty-stricken parents who lacked means to raise them, a practice found in other cultures.

Foreign slaves could also be acquired as war-captives, either taken in battle or seized in attacks on enemy territory, especially in the sack of a city. Thanks to the Carthaginian campaigns in Sardinia, many slaves in the later 6th Century must have been natives of that island, while in the late 5th and through much of the 4th Century quite a number will have been Sicilian Greeks. Carthage's off-and-on wars with the Numidians must have brought in many Numidian slaves from time to time, too. The struggles with Rome between 264 and 201 meant that Roman and Italian slaves in their turn could be found in both city and countryside. Their fates were rather happier. The later historian Appian in fact mentions that Scipio, on invading Africa in 204, rescued Roman captives working the fields who had been sent there from Italy, Sicily and Spain. Ransoms, prisoner exchanges and, at the end of each war, enforced repatriations also took home other Roman and maybe Italian slaves.

The glimpses we have of slave numbers are hard to evaluate. Hanno, one of the city's chief men in the 4th Century, armed a supposed twenty thousand slaves when facing arrest for plotting a coup d'état around 350 – a suspect number, though, because he and they in their futile attempt at resistance supposedly shut themselves up in a single 'fort' (which may have been his country mansion). It is fairly improbable too that, grand though he was, Hanno alone owned so many, especially as the narrative requires these to be males only. He very likely gathered slaves from around the countryside and even perhaps from the city, but Justin's figure would be more plausible, even then, if divided by ten.

The same figure of twenty thousand is given, this time by Polybius, for the 'slaves' whom Regulus' army a century later captured on its march through the Cape Bon region towards Tunes. Romans rarely discriminated, all the same, between seizing slaves and seizing freeborn enemy locals as human booty, so it may be that these were country folk both slave and free, who were later sold off into Roman slavery. Appian offers a third figure: towards the end of the second war with Rome and with Scipio's invasion looming, the general in command at Carthage bought 5,000 slaves to serve as rowers on his warships. If this report is true, most of them were probably bought within North Africa or even from owners in Carthage's *chora*, given the urgency of the situation. Since almost no sea-fighting took place and all the warships were burnt by Scipio at war's end, these *ad hoc* oarsmen were perhaps returned to their masters afterwards.

As noted earlier, Mago the agronomist recommended sensibly liberal treatment of farm slaves, but actual practice no doubt varied widely. When in 396 the Libyans launched a great rebellion against Carthage – one of the greatest in their history – they were joined by a large number of slaves in besieging the city. This obviously suggests that many slaves were unhappy with their lot, though their grievances were no doubt different in detail from those of the free Libyans. These must have promised their new allies their freedom at the very least. It could be significant that many slaves in 396 must have been Sicilian Greeks, for a new series of wars which had begun in 409 was marked by wholesale sackings of many important Greek cities, Acragas above all. It was in turn a succession of serious reverses at Greek hands in 398–396 which encouraged Libyans and slaves to revolt. The chief or sole grievance of the slaves who followed Hanno the traitor fifty or so years later was most likely again their enslaved condition. This time, though, the hopes of the rebels were centred on a charismatic Carthaginian, not on crushing Carthage herself. Memories of the failed revolt in 396 no doubt persisted, and not only among the slaves. Hanno at first had support from Libyans and even Numidians, though there are no details and they seem to have dropped him quickly.[44]

On the other hand, the idea that the Carthaginians suffered a constant, destabilising fear of and risk from the slave population has nothing else to go on. The invasion of Agathocles from 310 to 307 caused fresh Libyan unrest, but none is mentioned among slaves. Nor is any heard of during the Roman invasion of 256–255, whereas defections from Carthage by at least some Libyans and Numidians took place. Even more marked is the total silence about slave unrest during the massive rebellion by Carthage's unpaid mercenaries and heavily oppressed Libyan subjects that followed the First Punic War, even though it lasted over three years and is recounted in some detail by Polybius. None, again, is reported during Scipio's invasion late in the Second Punic War, during which he made extensive raids into the Libyan countryside and won a series of major battles. By contrast, as mentioned just now, we read of the Carthaginians buying slaves to row warships of the Carthaginian fleet. Finally, in the crisis of 149 when it was made plain that the Romans encamped outside the city meant to end its existence, the Carthaginian senate offered freedom to the slaves, obviously to recruit them for the resistance. Of course this was a risk, but one that proved to be justified, for everyone in the city fought to the end – in striking contrast to the sister colonies and the Libyan hinterland.

VI

THE CITYSCAPE OF CARTHAGE

THE GROWTH OF THE CITY

By the 4th Century, the roadstead along the shore of the lake of Tunis had been supplemented by an artificial channel extending for nearly a kilometre northward through the marshy lagoons to the area of pottery works and iron foundries next to Carthage's southern walls. Not much of this facility remains, for it was later replaced by the famous and still visible enclosed artificial ports. But wooden docks, for example, have been identified from evidence of post-holes in the soil of the Îlot de l'Amirauté, the little island in the circular port – now a shallow lake – which was built at the northern end of the old lagoon area in the late 3rd or early 2nd Century.

The channel was about two metres deep and some 15 to 20 metres wide – probably wider still where it met the lake – with the earliest datable pottery finds from it dating to the second half of the 4th Century. At the docks in its northern part the Carthaginian shipwrights built their vessels, both commercial and naval, which could then be launched down the channel. Given its width, this may also have received merchant shipping, which would be more sheltered than in the lake and nearer to the city proper.[45]

The defeat at Himera in Sicily in 480, at the hands of Gelon and Theron, prompted the Carthaginians to consolidate and then develop their position in North Africa – to the sorrow, we have seen, of the hitherto independent Libyans. Investigations in the central sectors of the old city have shown that its defences were improved: for although there was peace with the Sicilians and Libya was coming under control, Carthaginians could not help but be conscious of the vulnerability of the site if left unprotected. During the 5th Century powerful fortifications were built along the sea-front east of Byrsa, as shown by the discovery in recent times of the remains of imposing stone walls, over five metres thick, and a mighty double gate opening onto a narrow beach. These fortifications extended along the shore as far as the edge of the lagoons: nor would it make sense if the landward sides of the city were still left open, though so far no traces of land walls have been found (*Illustration 1*).

The city itself was expanding, although the stages can only be partially and tentatively traced. It used to be supposed that Carthage's defeat in Sicily in 480 caused seventy years of reduced trade, limited state activity and general introspection. This was inferred largely from a serious drop in archaeological finds of datable 5th-Century Greek pottery at Carthage, as well as her lack of adventurousness abroad. More recent investigations have not only found new evidence but re-evaluated older finds. It now appears that 5th-Century Attic pottery remains were misdated, or wrongly ascribed to regions like southern Italy (south Italian pottery actually became prominent only in the 4th Century). In addition, substantially more Attic ware has been unearthed in the past few decades at both Carthage and Kerkouane. The continuing business activity thus revealed fits Diodorus' report about Carthage in the later 5th Century importing

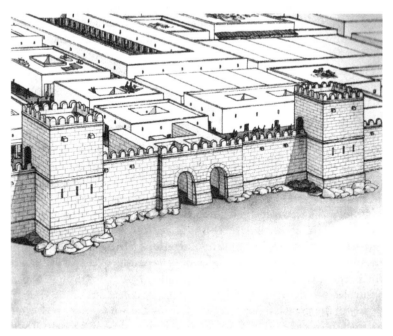

Illustration 1 Sea walls, *c.* 400 BC: artist's reconstruction

olives on a large scale from Acragas. Trade with the Etruscans too did not suffer. These re-evaluations are paralleled by the evidence of the Carthaginians imposing and extending dominance over their Libyan neighbours, and carrying out important building projects in and outside the existing city.

Around the end of the 5th Century or rather later, new structures were built just inside the new sea-walls east of Byrsa but separated from them by open ground some 30 metres or more wide: houses and warehouses. Two centuries later at least some of these were enlarged or replaced to create prosperous city mansions, with the built-up area moving right up to the walls (*Illustration 1*). All this points to a growing urban population, just as it was probably during a stage of vigorous urban development that the New Gate project was launched. This was plainly a large project, for it brought in the (seemingly enthusiastic) participation of a notable range of craftsmen and workers, among them the craftsmen of 'the plain of the town', which (as we saw earlier) probably meant the district around the so-called industrial area south of Byrsa and around the lake of Tunis' harbourage. The New Gate itself, whatever its precise site, could be one stage in the building of land fortifications around the burgeoning city.[46]

Another important, though less traceable, feature of urban expansion was the development of the garden suburb Megara (*M'rt*). Appian almost certainly relies on Polybius, who had been to Carthage, in describing Megara as it was in the mid-2nd Century: a large district next to the city walls, 'planted with gardens and full of fruit-bearing trees divided off by low walls, hedges, and brambles, besides deep ditches full of water running in every direction', with properties belonging to Carthaginian citizens. It seems to have been the broad district north of Byrsa and the necropoleis on the hills overlooking the city: the area today from the resort village of Sidi bou Said along the cliff-edged upland called La Marsa and, though probably not from the start, as far as Cape Gammarth (Map 1B). The archaeological land surveys mentioned earlier have found five sites, dating before 300, in this district; from the period following 300, as many as eleven.

Westward Megara extended, eventually, to the start of the isthmus that bound Carthage's arrowhead to the mainland. In the north this was about a kilometre wide, while from Sidi bou Said the district was up to six kilometres wide, and nearly four beyond the lagoon area and the '*tophet*'. Across that neck of level terrain were built, at some date, the massive triple-wall fortifications described by Appian

– perhaps in the aftermath of Agathocles' invasion but conceivably much earlier, for instance after the great Libyan rebellion in 396 when the city had been put under siege. Such secure defences would have encouraged Carthaginians to develop the area within them still further, even if tracts just beyond the city's hills had quite likely been exploited for orchards and other produce from the earliest times.

Megara in Appian's description was not a district of houses, apart- ment blocks and streets, although lanes and perhaps a few wider roads must have run through it for access. In other words it was not an area of planned urbanisation, but was allowed to continue as a semi-rural district. When the city's great fortifications were built enclosing almost the entire arrowhead of Carthage, from the lake of Tunis to the lake of Ariana and over to Cape Gammarth, the district was at least fifteen times the size of the built-up city (which by then covered roughly 1½ square kilometres).

Megara was probably, too, the 'new city' which figures in Diodorus' telling of the foiled coup of Bomilcar in 308. This over- ambitious general assembled his army 'in what was called the New City, lying a short distance outside Old Carthage', then dismissed all but a picked force and with it marched into the old city to seize the market square (the *agora* in Greek) – only to be driven back with losses through the narrow streets into the 'new city', where he and his surviving followers took refuge on 'a piece of high ground' but were forced to surrender. The details would fit: an area separate from the old city, but next to it and big enough to parade several thousand soldiers, and with a hilltop for a last stand. If it did count as a 'new city', the term suggests that already – during the Agath- oclean invasion – it too had fortifications, though these may not as yet have been the elaborate in-depth structures described by Appian.[47]

TEMPLES AND OTHER SACRED BUILDINGS

Naturally the city held temples of its many gods and goddesses. The most magnificent, the temple of 'Aesculapius' (Asclepius in Greek, and usually identified as Eshmun) as Appian calls it, stood on the top of Byrsa itself and was reached by a great flight of sixty steps from the foot of the hill. Nothing survives even of its foundations because in Roman times the summit of the hill was completely taken off, levelled and replaced by new structures (some broken remnants found on Byrsa's slopes have been tentatively suggested as from the destroyed temple). On the Byrsa side of the marketplace was another grand temple, that of 'Apollo', who seems to have been Reshef, lavishly decorated in gold. It may be that the remains of an early 2nd-Century temple, recently discovered near the suggested site of the *agora* and only a short distance north of the circular port mentioned earlier, was its final version, but this is uncertain.

The other major divinities like Tanit, Baal Hammon, Baal Shamim, Baal Sapon, Melqart and Astarte must have had their own temples, not to mention places of worship for the many lesser deities of the Phoenician and Punic pantheon, but where they lay is not known. We might wonder whether Tanit and Baal Hammon at least, perhaps Melqart too, had their seats on Byrsa with Reshef. At the same time, Tanit and Baal Hammon were the chief deities offered votive *stelae* in the '*tophet*'.

The flat-roofed temples of Phoenician and Egyptian traditions were standard in the Phoenician west, too, including Carthage. This is inferred from carvings on *stelae* and small sculptures. For instance a 6th- or 5th-Century representation from Sulcis in Sardinia and another of similar date from Motya in Sicily present a temple's goddess standing between the two columns of its porch, just as a 5th-Century *stele* from Carthage's '*tophet*' again has a worshipper (or the god) in the entrance porch between columns. Another *stele* found at Motya represents a small temple with the usual two-columned porch, the interior *cella* with a niche for the deity's image at the back, and an Egyptian-style entablature (its lower part adorned with a sun-emblem and a half-moon curving over this) – complete with the dedication to Baal Hammon by one *Mnms* son of *Hqm*. Most notable of all is a fine model or *naiskos* of a handsomely decorated, seemingly square temple or shrine, found at the Libyan town of Thuburbo Maius (some 60 kilometres south-west of Carthage, on the river Mellane) and perhaps 2nd-Century in date. This may represent a small shrine or 'chapel', again with a porch between two fluted columns in front of the interior *cella* of the building.[48]

The entablatures of temple roofs were carved in complex geometric patterns like egg-and-dart moulding and Egyptian-influenced motifs; their fluted columns, round or square, could be adorned with Greek-derived capitals or sometimes with patterns like palm-tree fronds. Within each chapel and temple, there would be an inner room or rooms with an altar, the deity's image and pious offerings, cheap or costly, such as statuettes, jewellery amulets and small carvings. A large sacred precinct would include a courtyard where priests and attendants would gather for ceremonies.

Temples in full Greek form, with a two-sided sloping roof and triangular pediment façade, were few at best and left no recognisable archaeological trace. If any did exist, they would probably have been ones dedicated to Greek divinities adopted by the republic – most famously Demeter and Kore (also called Persephone), adopted in 396 – or ones permitted to the resident Greek community. A pleasing white marble *stele*, now in Turin, depicts Kore or Demeter standing with a horn of plenty in the columned porch of a Greek-style shrine of mixed Doric and Ionian styles, with a crouching lion sculpted in the pediment. The *stele* is generally judged Carthaginian-made from the 2nd Century, though a dissident view sees it as from Sulcis in Sardinia and dating to around 300. Significantly, its dedicatee was 'thy servant Milkyaton the sufete, son of Maharbaal the sufete' – clearly a leading aristocrat, Carthaginian or Sulcitan – and the depicted temple surely stood in his city.

An impressive structure – not at Carthage, but in Carthaginian-influenced Libya – can cast added light on Carthaginian architecture. On the hillside just below Thugga (Dougga, 110 kilometres south-west of Tunis) stands the 21-metre-high tower-like mausoleum of Ataban 'son of Yofamit son of Filaw' (these transliterations are approximate), seemingly the Libyan lord of the region around the late 3rd Century. His inscription, now in the British Museum, is in both Punic and Libyan; one of his stonemasons, along with his own son Zimr, is *'Bd'rš* (perhaps *Abd'rš*, like the Carthaginian sufete mentioned earlier; but interpretations vary) son of Abdastart, while among other specialist workers was an iron-maker named Safot son of Balal or Baalal. These men and their fathers had Carthaginian names, indicating though not proving that they were Carthaginians in Ataban's service. The mausoleum consists of three tiers. The first is cubic in shape resting on a podium of five steps, with a relief sculpture of a *quadriga* (a four-horse chariot) in each vertical face; the second also cubic but of narrower dimensions, with engaged square Ionic columns on each face and on a three-step podium; the third a rectangular, still narrower structure resting on a squared pedestal that originally had a horseman at each corner; and topping the whole a low pyramid on a pedestal with a sea-nymph at each of its corners (*Illustration 2*).

This grandiose erection is unlike anything built by Greeks or Romans (except, perhaps, lighthouses on a much more massive scale) but is strikingly like another monument, this time at Sabratha

Illustration 2 Mausoleum at Thugga (2nd Century BC)

on the coast of Emporia, which can be reconstructed from the ruins that remain: a triangular two-tiered structure, with a pyramid much steeper than Thugga's, on a podium standing on five steps – but with the extra refinement that on both levels all three sides were concave in shape.[49]

The design was popular. There is for instance another, though smaller and much plainer, rectangular two-tier mausoleum, again topped by a pyramid, at Henchir Jaouf near Segermes (south of Carthage and about 25 kilometres inland from the gulf of Hammamet); it has been dated by pottery fragments to around 175–150. A one-metre-high and half-metre-wide rectangular stone marker or *cippus* found in or near Carthage's *'tophet'* has stylised columns carved to frame each of its four faces and is topped by a gabled roof, to resemble a similar structure (*Illustration 3*); on each of the two narrower faces is carved, in skilful style, a gourd or bottle crowned with a triangle – a religious symbol strongly resembling the 'sign of Tanit', to be met below. At Clupea (Kelibia) south of Kerkouane, the stone-cut entrance down to the underground tomb of one Mago has, on its lintel, a plain outline of a pyramid-topped mausoleum; Mago's family perhaps could not afford a real one, which of course would have been hugely expensive.

More striking still are paintings in a tomb in Kerkouane's Jebel Mlezza necropolis, each depicting in some detail a single-tiered and pyramid-topped mausoleum, with a ritual fire burning on an altar alongside. Such monuments were (we should note) well established by the mid-3rd Century, for as noted earlier Kerkouane was

Illustration 3 Stone *cippus* from Carthage: rectangular tower design and 'bottle' symbol on side

destroyed then and never rebuilt. If Carthage's urban terrain was too constrained for similar impressive works, they may have stood in places in the necropoleis on the hillsides of Byrsa, Junon, Dermech and the others, perhaps elsewhere. The 'tower' which the Romans found close to the outer side of Megara's wall in 147, when trying to break into the city, was perhaps one such – not in a necropolis, but neither is Ataban's.[50]

A kilometre south of Byrsa hill and just a few dozen metres east of the shore lagoons was the so-called '*tophet*', an entirely different type of sacred site first discovered in 1922 (*Illustration 4*). A narrow and elongated tract of walled but open-air ground eventually covering some 6000 square metres, it was the place where the cremated remains of very young children were deposited, in pottery urns and often (not always) with an accompanying *stele* and grave-offerings, with dedications to the goddess Tanit and to Baal Hammon. Cremated animal remains also occur, sometimes in the same urn as those of a child. The earliest deposits can be dated to the late 8th Century; over the ensuing centuries, nine levels of deposits built up. On an informed estimate, about twenty thousand such urns were placed there in the two centuries from 400 to 200. The word '*tophet*' is not Punic but has been borrowed by archaeologists from the Hebrew Bible, where it is a valley outside Jerusalem in which

Illustration 4 View of the '*tophet*' at Carthage

Canaanite children were sacrificed to please the Phoenician Baal until the later 7th Century. Carthage was only one of many Phoenician colonies in North Africa, Sardinia and Sicily with a '*tophet*': the site was always outside the settlement, though in her case the city later expanded around it, and hers is by far the largest of them all. What was done in the '*tophet*', or in preparation for the deposit there, is one of the most debated – and perhaps insoluble – questions in Carthaginian studies, as will be outlined later (Chapter VII).

HOUSES AND SHOPS

Secular buildings are not often pictured on *stelae* or in other Punic art, but just enough evidence survives for glimpses of the rest of Carthage's cityscape. In the same well-decorated Jebel Mlezza tomb, one wall shows a neat and naive painting of a walled city open to the shore (*Illustration 5*). The city is painted between a niche with a symbol of the goddess Tanit and, on its own other side, a rooster with sharp spurs (apparently a symbol of the soul), so the wall may depict the 'other-world' city receiving the soul of the deceased. Its semicircular crenellated wall and the square buildings inside would be based on familiar views of coastal towns – maybe, it has been suggested, of Kerkouane itself. Such views would, conceivably enough, be rather like those of many Greek islands' small towns

Illustration 5 Painting of city in Jebel Mlezza tomb VIII

today, although stuccoed instead of whitewashed. Carthage in turn may have resembled an enlarged version of a city like this when viewed from a ship or from the hills on its north side, or – more distantly – from the Cape Bon coast opposite.

Diggings further inland in the old city show evidence of big dwelling-places even in Carthage's early centuries. Similar early houses have been identified at Phoenician sites in south Spain like Toscanos and Cerro del Villar, and later ones at Kerkouane on Cape Bon. They would be flat-roofed, with access by stairs or ladders: cool for sleep in high summer, warm for taking sunshine on winter days. Although there was nothing like standardised floor-plans, many larger houses had interior courtyards reached by narrow corridors from the street and giving access to surrounding rooms, thus letting in light and air. Some large buildings housed apartments, often with the ground-floor rooms let out as shops. On the southern slope of Byrsa hill, diggings have unearthed a sector datable to the early 2nd Century, preserved through being covered over by a deep layer of rubble when the Romans a hundred and fifty years later razed away Byrsa's summit. This is the so-called 'Hannibal quarter', so named because the famous general became sufete in 196 to carry out a number of progressive measures in politics, government and finance which had lasting effects – including perhaps this extensive urban improvement project in what previously was an industrial site (*Illustrations 6 and 7*).

The long-established workshops were replaced with carefully built structures on streets laid out on a grid plan. The streets, 5 to 7 metres wide (wider than in the old city) and of rammed earth, have drainage holes every so often feeding water and other liquids from the buildings lining the streets down into stone-lined wells (soakaways), with the runoff coursing through a basic type of drain made from pottery *amphorae* fitted together. When rain did fall on the streets, it soaked into the ground or ran off. The excavated street which climbs the hillside is fitted at intervals with short flights of steps: the whole sector, and no doubt much of the rest of Carthage's crowded terrain, was a pedestrian (and of course pack-animal) precinct.

The buildings form rectangular blocks, opening on all sides into the streets and subdivided into houses, apartments and shops. In Roman towns they would be called *insulae*, 'islands'. Those excavated measure either some 15½ by 31 metres (a 1:2 ratio), or 15½ by about 10½ (a 3:2 ratio), with the larger buildings lining one side of a street running north to south and the smaller on the opposite side facing them. Each building, small and large, was subdivided into

Illustration 6 View of the 'Hannibal quarter' on Byrsa's southern slope

Illustration 7 Another view of the 'Hannibal quarter'

separate dwellings with walls that are mostly very solid – 50 centi-metres or so. Several are quite narrow at just over 5 metres wide, and while some extend the full depth of their block to the street at the other end, others were subdivided into cramped little units that might serve as lodgings or shops. At least two other dwellings are a contrast: twice as wide as the narrow-fronted ones, and at least one of them handsomely equipped with a stylish entrance of half-columns in white stucco and with stuccoed pillars flanking its marble-mosaic courtyard.

Every subdivided house has its own well-made underground cistern for water, sometimes two, and all of them sizeable. Rain, when it did fall, could be collected in wells, basins, and perhaps from rooftops via downpipes to feed into the cistern, while the relatively high underground water-table could also be reached by wells. In the houses, the only adornments surviving are certain floors with patterned mosaic or terracotta-fragment pavements (decorations that the Romans called *pavimenta Punica*) and pillars covered with white stucco; nor, it seems, have traces turned up of the neat bathrooms fitted with ledge-seats that have been found in some Kerkouane dwellings. The buildings' size and the strong walls capable of carrying upper floors lend support to Appian's mention of buildings being six storeys high in precisely this area. The upper storeys would be reached via wooden stairs; there is evidence at Kerkouane again, for staircases in houses (although of course those storeys must have been many fewer). We may recall Strabo's refer-ence to Tyre's lofty buildings too.

Given the variety of dwelling sizes revealed by the foundations – we have no evidence of how upper floors were divided – it looks as though the population of the quarter must have been quite varied. Its nearness to the crest of Byrsa and its complex of rich shrines surely made it, from the start, an attractive area to many different types of resident. Merchants and priests, scribes, goldsmiths and jewellers (fragments of a jeweller's cutting implements have been identified, such as obsidian and pieces of coral), architects, road-builders, fullers, butchers and bow-makers might all live in the district. Butchers and other shopkeepers, as well as skilled artisans like a bow-maker or statue-carver, could have their shops in rooms opening onto the street while they and their families lived upstairs. Propertyless workers, not to mention visitors to the city, would lodge in rented rooms or whole apartments.

A site excavated near Cape Gammarth, in the Megara district, is a contrast: a semi-rural residence with a section for pressing olives probably from nearby olive groves, along with an unpretentious but affluently adorned house which had stuccoed sandstone columns and floors with Punic-style mosaics. Further investigations in both the city area and Megara will, in time, bring these lively varieties of Carthaginian dwellings and their amenities into sharper focus.[51]

PUBLIC BUILDINGS

Not much is known about Carthage's non-religious public buildings save their names. As noted already, in later centuries there was a marketplace or square (*agora* in Greek) near the shore south-east of Byrsa, for Appian describes it as near the city's famous artificial ports and these occupied the transformed area of the old lagoons sector (*Illustration 8*). Investigators have noted, in fact, that somewhat north of them the terrain shows a marked absence of finds later than the archaic period (thus after the 6th Century): this would of course be typical in a broad open space. Diodorus' account of the coup attempted by Bomilcar in 308 describes the marketplace as surrounded by high buildings while the streets around it were narrow. So does Appian when reporting its final capture by the Romans in 146. Besides its role as a market, it would be the obvious place for magistrates to assemble the citizens for elections and lawmaking. That would explain why Bomilcar's first move was to try to seize it.

Illustration 8 Carthage 1958

In the original colony, the *agora* must have been well to the north, since the urban area included only Byrsa and the level ground eastwards down to the shore (compare Map 1A). Even if replaced as the main square in the 5th or early 4th Century, the earlier one may have remained a subsidiary focal point, for quite likely there were other, smaller marketplaces around the city. Kerkouane has a number of small squares, for example, providing extra space for movement and maybe tradesmen's stalls; in a city of Carthage's size and complexity, lesser market sites would hardly be surprising.

Where in the city the senate, the *adirim*, met is unknown, but there was (it seems) a senate-house – *bouleuterion* in Greek – very near to or even alongside the *agora*. A reference to it by Diodorus seems to put it there, just as in Rome the senate-house opened onto the Forum. Appian, like Diodorus telling of events in 149, writes of returning Carthaginian envoys going to the *bouleuterion* while a massive crowd waited outside: this also sounds like nearness to the *agora*. On the other hand, Livy twice reports the *adirim* holding sessions in the temple of Eshmun (Livy calls him Aesculapius) on Byrsa, in 174 and again in 172 – at night, allegedly for secrecy. Livy's account seems to imply that it was an unusual venue, but it is worth recalling that the Roman senate too could meet in a temple – or a theatre, as on the famous Ides of March. Just possibly Eshmun's temple, or another building within Byrsa's citadel, had been the senate's original meeting-place and continued to be a venue from time to time.[52]

The many administrative functionaries attested on inscriptions – not only the magistrates and the generals, but the accountants (*mḥšbm*), members of the boards of ten and of thirty, and those working in other pentarchies – would have worked in buildings separate or shared. At least one can be identified. When the artificial ports in the old lagoon sector were created sometime around 200, the island in the circular port housed Carthage's naval headquarters, described by Appian as a high building where the admiral in command could survey both the ships and shipyards below and the sea outside. As a result the island is now called the Îlot de l'Amirauté. The admiralty building can be recognised in the excavations of the long and narrow foundations of a six-sided building, about 80 metres long and 25 at its widest, surrounded by the traces of ship-sheds for part of Carthage's fleet. There would similarly be headquarters for the general or generals commanding Carthage's land forces, located (at a guess) further inland for ready access to the outside world. Bomilcar, who in 308 began his coup attempt by marshalling troops in the 'new city' Megara, may have done so at his headquarters, for this would no doubt have a parade-ground alongside or surrounding it.

THE LAND FORTIFICATIONS AND THE PORTS

Some traces of the city's earlier fortifications have been found, as noted earlier, and so have impressive remains of the sea-wall built in the 5th Century (*Illustration 1*). The great walls west of the city, which gave Carthage virtually impregnable security against attack, just possibly were also part of this 5th-Century effort but more likely followed the Libyan revolt and siege in 396: for this was the first great insurrection, and the land walls plainly aimed at guarding the city from just such a threat. Appian's description of them as they stood in the mid-2nd Century is a classic, though it might give the impression that they bounded Carthage just beyond Byrsa and not four kilometres further west. The walls formed a triple line, each 30 cubits (about 13.5 metres) high plus parapets and towers standing at 2-*plethra* intervals (about 30 metres). The towers were four-storeyed and 30 Greek feet high (9 metres), while the walls themselves held two storeys with quarters for elephants, horses and troops.

Some traces of the outer lines were revealed in the mid-20th Century, first through aerial photographs and then by diggings at various points. These revealed a broad trench on the landward side, then a built-up embankment with many post-holes (probably for stockades), and after this a narrower trench. The innermost wall is thought to have stood some metres east of these positions. According to Appian's statistics the walls with their two storeys could accommodate 20,000 infantry and 4000 horsemen, the same number of horses, and 300 elephants – this last almost certainly a notional, or wishful, total since the Carthaginians are never recorded as having so many – as well as fodder and other feed for the animals. At the northern end of the fortifications, where these reached the gulf of Ariana, only a single line of wall seems to have run from there northeastwards to cross the hilly terrain which becomes Cape Gammarth, and down to meet the sea north of that cape. Nonetheless it proved no less hard to breach, as the Romans found during the Third Punic War. It was the south side of the city's defensive enceinte that was less certain. The weak point, Appian remarks, was 'the angle which ran around from this [triple] wall to the harbours, along the tongue of land' forming the shoreline south of the city. He and his source may have been writing from hindsight, for this was the direction from which the Romans launched their final assault in 146. His account of the Roman siege makes it clear that this southern line of wall left an open strand, at least several metres wide, between it and the lake.

The harbours that he mentions were the two artificial ports built in the old lagoon area (Map 1A; *Illustrations 8, 9 and 10*). They continued to be used in Roman times and still survive as shallow lagoons. One was originally rectangular (then changed in Roman

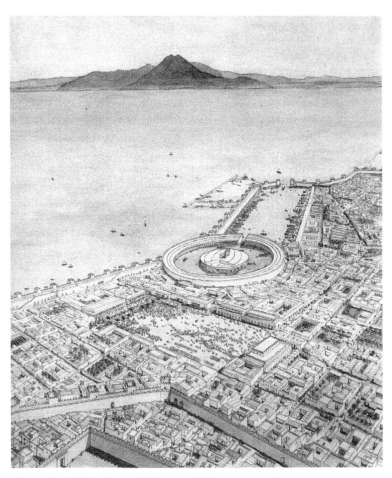

Illustration 9 Carthage *c.* 200 BC: artist's reconstruction

Illustration 10 The artificial ports area *c.* 1922

times to a long hexagon), while just to its north the other is circular, with the man-made and equally circular Îlot de l'Amirauté in its centre. That these were Appian's ports has been confirmed only in recent decades, thanks to excavations on the Îlot (earlier doubts had been due to their distance from the site of the original colony). As noted above, earlier the inlet from the lake of Tunis had been developed as a channel for shipping with dockyards extending into the lagoons area, as shown by finds of timber underlying the later works on the Îlot. It had always had a battle with silt – including effluent from the city – and was finally abandoned in favour of the impressive new constructions, which gave much greater room and safety to shipping and to the war-fleet.

Appian calls the pair of artificial ports the 'Cothon'. The water in them was 2 metres deep (in late Carthaginian times, the sea-level was about one metre lower than today). The rectangular port, originally 300 metres from north to south and 150 east to west, was entered from the Mediterranean via a new channel in a gentle arc, some 250 metres long, which reached the port at its south-eastern corner and could be closed off by iron chains. A millennium later Byzantine Constantinople's Golden Horn would be protected in similar fashion, if on a vaster scale. Some of the south-western side of this entry channel has been found, nicknamed the 'Mur Pistor'. Built of massive blocks of stone cut from the El-Haouaria quarries on the cliffs of Cape Bon – 50 metres of these have been uncovered on its western side – the port was used by merchant shipping and in turn was linked by a shorter channel to the circular naval port about 100 metres away.

This port, 325 metres across, was the secure anchorage for Carthage's navy, quinqueremes each crewed by three hundred oarsmen in groups of five and the dominant battleships of the 3rd and 2nd Centuries. Appian offers a vivid description that must come from an eyewitness, very likely Polybius. The circle of water was surrounded by 'great quays' and a double wall, so that no one even in the outer port could see what was going on, whereas the island's tower overlooked everything. The quays could accommodate 220 ships, with magazines above to hold their sails, masts and other equipment. Every ship's dock had a pair of Ionic columns before it, 'giving a view of both the port and the island like that of a colonnade'.

Excavations have revealed the nature of the docksheds on the Îlot, not mentioned explicitly by Appian but implied in his comment. There were some fifteen built in parallel rows on either side of the central building (the admiralty): each shed 30 to 48 metres long and about 6 metres wide, with a sloping slipway to allow a ship, or even two, to be berthed lengthways. The land circuit of the port has room for only some hundred and fifty or possibly hundred and seventy ship-sheds, not two hundred and twenty as Appian would seem to suggest. They and the island's thirty, however, would be a total nearer to his, and some could receive two warships. His figure for the port's capacity is therefore plausible, though it was no doubt a wartime – or even just a theoretical – maximum.

The cost, effort and skilful engineering of the two ports match the great harbour projects at Rome's port of Ostia under the early emperors. The quantity of groundsoil needing to be removed to create the naval port is reckoned at some 115,000 cubic metres, and for the merchant port about 120,000, while to build up the Îlot de l'Amirauté required about 10,000. When they were built is a question still unresolved. North African and Italian pottery fragments found on the island are of styles ranging from the 4th Century to the 1st, and mostly of the 2nd and 1st. As a result, most opinion favours the early to mid-2nd Century for their construction. This would make them a product of Carthage's recovered prosperity after the Second Punic War – and, more darkly, would make the war harbour a deliberate violation of the peace with Rome, which had ended the war in 201, for this banned any Carthaginian war-fleet larger than ten vessels. Yet, when the Carthaginians surrendered all their existing armaments and munitions to the Roman forces outside the city in 149, Appian's list of the quantities of armour and weapons for soldiers handed over makes no mention of ships or naval stores. Nor did Carthaginian warships (unlike Roman) play a part against the ensuing siege until 147, and then it was a squadron of 50 triremes and smaller craft which that had been built out of old timber.

A more plausible date for the ports would be sixty to seventy years before 149. The bits of 4th- and 3rd-Century pottery are compatible with a time earlier than the Third Punic War, as would be two coins found on site, one Carthaginian, one from Tarentum in Italy, dating to the later 3rd Century. Historical evidence may suggest a particular time. Whereas Carthage had an unimpressive navy when the second war with Rome began in 218 – about 80 ships, many of them unfit for sailing – over the next decade she sent large fleets to sea, while reports got back to Rome of vigorous shipbuilding going on. In fact the largest reported fleet, in 212, was a hundred and thirty ships strong. The degenerate state of the navy in 218 makes it very unlikely that the elaborate Cothon complex was already in being. By contrast, during the war's first decade the Carthaginians had the wealth and manpower for such a project – and the fear, for from the start they not only faced a Roman navy of, as it happens, 220 warships but knew that their enemies planned to invade Africa as well as Spain. Even after Hannibal took the war to Italy, one damaging raid after another was inflicted on Carthage's coastlands by Roman fleets and troops. The need for a secure war harbour, as well as one where merchant shipping could be safe from attacks, was surely acute after 218. After the war, on the other hand, with Carthaginian warships prohibited and prosperity gradually rebuilding, it is conceivable that an overhaul of the circular port was carried out, for instance to make it more suitable for merchant shipping. That could explain why the bulk of the pottery evidence belongs to the earlier part of the 2nd Century, with only a few items from earlier.

The Cothon was not Carthage's only impressive waterside project in her later centuries. Alongside the shore to the south-east of the ports, an exceptionally large platform of stone and rocks also existed. 'Falbe's quadrilateral', now under shallow water and named after the 19th-Century Danish scholar who first studied it, is about 425 metres from north to south and, along its northern side, some 100 wide. There are some remains of walls along its seaward sides, while it narrows southward to project a short way beyond the entrance to the Cothon ports, thus sheltering ships' access to these. Predating adjoining Roman structures, the quadrilateral or trapezoid can be identified as the *choma* or quay 'which', Appian records, 'had long existed as a broad expanse in front of the [city] wall for merchants to unload their cargoes'.

Its date is generally thought to be the same period as the ports. This has to assume that, around the same time as the massive Cothon project, the Carthaginians also built up the quadrilateral's massive structure outside – even though its materials can hardly have come from the sandy and waterlogged ground of the lagoons alongside, but must have originated further afield – and did this for much the same purpose: to improve facilities for shipping. Another possibility, then, could be that the landing platform predates the Cothon. It might have been, for example, an earlier solution to the problematic silting-up of the inlet from the lake of Tunis; while one reason – as just suggested – for the Cothon project could have been to protect the navy and mercantile commerce from enemy attacks, which became a constant menace after the wars with Rome started.[53]

VII

RELIGION AND
CULTURAL LIFE

THE GODS AND GODDESSES

'Before Zeus and Hera and Apollo, before the deity [*daemon*] of the Carthaginians and Heracles and Iolaus, before Ares, Triton, Poseidon, before the gods marching with us [*or* the gods of those marching with us], and the Sun and Moon and Earth, before [the gods of] rivers and harbours [*or* seas] and waters, before all gods who possess Carthage, before all gods who possess Macedon and the rest of Greece, before all gods of those in the army [*or* all gods concerned with warfare]' – this imposing pantheon, in Greek forms, is invoked as the preamble to the oath sworn by Hannibal, his political advisers, and his army when making a treaty with Philip V of Macedon in 215. The historian Polybius quotes it verbatim in its Greek version, a copy of which had been captured by the Romans. Unfortunately it is just an excerpt in a Byzantine collection of texts; if Polybius added any commentary to it (as he did to his translations of Carthage's treaties with Rome), it was not kept. Nonetheless, it is the most wide-ranging list of the divine beings worshipped by Carthaginians, at least in their later centuries. At the same time, its Greek form raises predictable questions: who these divinities were at Carthage, how they related to one another, and whether they had undergone any influences from the Hellenistic Greek culture which was now spreading over the Mediterranean world.[54]

Like every ancient society, the Carthaginians had a very large number of gods and goddesses. Most of their major deities they had brought from Phoenicia. Zakarbaal had been high priest of Astarte at Tyre, Melqart was that city's protecting god, and Baal Hammon was the most prominent aspect of the chief god, Baal, of Phoenicia. In turn Baal Iddir, Baal Marqod, Baal Oz, Baal Qarnem, Baal Sapon and Baal Shamim were other aspects – or in the eyes of many

Carthaginians were other gods, as the word *b'l* essentially means 'lord'. In fact Baal Shamim (*B'l šmm*), 'lord of the skies', had been the leading Baal in early Phoenicia, but at Carthage he held a place less prominent than Baal Hammon.

Other leading deities were Eshmun, Reshef or Rasap (again in several aspects, like Reshef Hes, Reshef *Sprm*, even Reshef-Melqart), and Shadrap or Sadrape. All of these appear on Punic *stelae*, many too in Carthaginians' religiously-based personal names. There were other lesser and fairly obscure ones, largely Phoenician again, such as Semes the sun-goddess, Hudis god of the new moon, Kese god of the full moon, Kusor god of intellect (who could take on a female aspect as Kusarit), Hawot goddess of the dead, Pumay to whom the Nora stone in Sardinia was set up, Sakun and the exceedingly obscure Arish, sometimes Baal *'Rš*) and D*'m* (Dom).

Some other divinities at Carthage had important roles, unlike among the Phoenicians. The chief of these, and in later centuries perhaps the city's paramount deity, was *Tnt*, usually transliterated Tanit (though Tinit may be a more accurate pronunciation). Tanit's origins are disputed: possibly she began in Phoenicia as an aspect, or even servitor, of Astarte; or perhaps instead was a separate divinity, named on a *stele* as 'Tanit of Lebanon' (*wltnt blbnn*); or – least likely but occasionally suggested – a different Phoenician goddess, Anat, who under Libyan influence might have acquired a prefix *ta*. Tanit appears at Carthage quite late, on *stelae* from the 5th or even the early 4th Century, with some noteworthy aspects. She is almost always coupled with Baal, always is mentioned first and Baal next, and bears the name *Tnt pn B'l*, Tanit *pene* Baal (or Phane-Baal) – 'Tanit face of Baal'. She has a distinctive visual symbol or sign, essentially a triangle with a circle at its apex and a line drawn horizontally between the two, so that the 'sign of Tanit' looks like a geometric outline of a woman in a long robe and with arms outstretched. The sign appears in mosaics – a famous one adorns the threshold of a private home in Kerkouane (*Illustration 11*) – and on small items widely used, like figurines and pottery vessels. No other Carthaginian deity had this kind of visual recognition. A further sign of Tanit's eminence is that in 146, as the siege of the city neared its climax, the Roman commander Scipio Aemilianus called on 'Juno', who must be Tanit, in the rite of *evocatio*: the 'summoning out' of an enemy city's protective deity with promises of greater honours at Rome.

Whether Tanit and Baal came to be seen as a married couple is not known, but 'Zeus and Hera' in Hannibal's oath are thought to represent them and were a married couple (as well as being brother

Illustration 11 Entrance to house at Kerkouane, with 'sign of Tanit'

and sister, not a feature ever suggested of the Carthaginian pair). The great majority of *stelae* dedicated to Tanit and Baal were in the '*tophet*', the cremation-cemetery for infants. Even the site of their temple or temples is unknown, though conceivably Byrsa had room for them as well as Eshmun. Temples of many of the other gods are mentioned in inscriptions or literary sources; the city clearly had at least as many sacred places as Rome or Athens, even if the events of 146 and later have left it almost impossible to find any. Hannibal's oath shows, too, that Carthaginians saw a divine presence or immanence in natural features like rivers and other waters, again an instinct of piety shared by Greeks and Romans.

At least two deities at Carthage had no Phoenician background: the Greek Demeter and her daughter Kore, also called Persephone. In 396 the cult of these goddesses was initiated after their temple at Syracuse was destroyed by a Carthaginian army: for a series of disasters had followed, including the great Libyan rebellion mentioned earlier. Priests and priestesses of high-ranking families were assigned to their service (one Hannabaal, *hkhnt š krw'*, 'the priestess of Kore', is attested on a *stele*); leading Greek residents were also brought in to assist, and the proper Greek rituals were practised. The fine early-2nd-Century *stele* mentioned earlier – dedicated, probably at Carthage, by 'thy servant Milkyaton the sufete, son of Maharbaal the sufete' and depicting Kore in her shrine bearing a basket of fruit – vividly illustrates the continuity of the cult. It spread into Libya as well, to flourish in Roman times. The Egyptian goddess Isis also had a temple in the city, though little is known of it: she is best known now for the beautiful Greek-style sarcophagus of one of her priest-esses (see *Illustration 12*).

Illustration 12 The 'Isis priestess' from Ste Monique tomb: marble lid of sarcophagus

Greeks and Romans nearly always avoided using Phoenician and Carthaginian deities' own names, preferring to identify them with deities of their own. Melqart was thus treated as Heracles (Hercules in Latin), Tanit as Hera or, in Latin, Juno – in Roman North Africa she would be named Juno Caelestis – while Eshmun was normally identified with Aesculapius, though occasionally, it seems, with Dionysus or even with Heracles' protégé Iolaus. Other equivalents were again flexible: Reshef is usually thought to have been equated with Apollo, but this is debated; Baal Sapon may have been identified with Poseidon (Neptune) but so too it seems the obscure Baal 'Rš; Shadrap was sometimes seen as Dionysus, occasionally as Apollo. Baal Hammon himself certainly seems meant when Hanno's *Periplus*, Diodorus and some others write of 'Cronus', and in Roman times he was Latinised as Saturn, the Romans' name for that god. But references to Zeus or Jupiter, for instance in Hannibal's treaty, Nepos and Livy, should mean him too – or possibly, but not as convincingly, Baal Shamim despite his less prominent role at Carthage and lack of association with Tanit.[55]

It is often thought that particular families, at least among the aristocracy, paid special reverence to one or another divinity as their protector or patron. This did happen elsewhere – the Fabian family at Rome, for instance, performed strict cult-duties to an unknown god at a site there – so it may equally have featured at Carthage. On the other hand, the examples thought to show it are not compelling. A votive inscription seems to speak of 'Baal of the Magonids' (*b'l mgnm*) in a dedication, along with Baal Shamim, Tanit *pene* Baal, and Baal Hammon. In turn, Hannibal's family is widely supposed to have revered Melqart as their special god. Yet rather than an undisputed reference to the Magonid family, *b'l mgnm* may mean 'Baal of gifts' (the gift-giver) or 'Baal the shield' (the protector) – other senses of *mgn* which are also plausible. In Hannibal's case, his only known connection with Melqart was in offering sacrifice and vows in 218 in the god's temple at Gades, the oldest Phoenician shrine in the western Mediterranean. One or more coins issued by the Barcids in Spain are thought to portray Melqart, but even if that were certain (actually it is very debatable) it would not explain other Barcid coins or, more important, convey anything about the generals' own devotions.

Hannibal and his family really had more to do with Baal Hammon and Tanit. His father made him swear a famous childhood oath, never to be friendly with the Romans, at the altar of 'Jupiter'. When his brother-in-law Hasdrubal founded the city of New Carthage in Spain around 228, its four most conspicuous temples were dedicated to 'Asclepius' (Eshmun), 'Hephaestus' (probably Kusor), 'Aletes' (perhaps a Spanish god) and 'Cronus', but the temple of Melqart – there must have been one – was much less prominent. Livy reports Hannibal sacrificing to 'Jupiter' before his first battle in Italy, and 'Zeus' and 'Hera' head his treaty-oath. Years later he chose the temple of Hera, at Cape Lacinium (Capo Colonna) in Greek southern Italy, to house a bronze inscription with a Punic and Greek account of his great campaigns. No doubt he venerated Melqart too, but scarcely in first place. As the treaty-oath implies, a Carthaginian leader held all his city's deities in religious regard, even if he might feel a special reverence for certain ones.

Disputes will continue about who are mentioned under the Greek names in the treaty's list. Zeus and Hera look like Baal Hammon and Tanit *pene* Baal: if the names mean Melqart and Astarte instead, it is hard to see where else the two dominant deities of 3rd-Century Carthage occur, especially as there is no mention of Cronus. As mentioned earlier, Apollo is commonly viewed as meaning Reshef and Heracles as Melqart, while 'the *daemon* of the Carthaginians' (it has been suggested) was Astarte; her position next to Melqart in the list would certainly fit. Eshmun might be tentatively identified with Iolaus, but who are the gods represented as Ares, Triton and Poseidon, not to mention all the unnamed divinities? The list continues to be open to a range of theories, perhaps insolubly.

What form Carthaginian theology took (if theology is the right term) is not known, save that Melqart, there as well as in Phoenicia, underwent a ritual of death followed by rebirth, either daily or yearly. The priest who performed the rite bore the impressive title of 'awakener of the god [sometimes 'of the dead god'] with the scent of '*štrny*', or perhaps 'the husband of '*štrny*'. The obscure '*štrny* is known only in this context, though she must be divine too and is sometimes thought to be an aspect of Astarte. We have already met one of the Awakeners: 'Hanno, sufete and chief of priests (*rb khnm*, or *rab kohanim*), son of Abdmilqart', whose *stele* lists his priestly role as well. The priesthood was plainly important enough to be taken by leading men in public life. The Awakening rite spread and endured beyond Carthage, for Yazim (*Y'zm*), a great-grandson of Masinissa king of Numidia, held the priesthood in his own country during the last years of the 2nd or early in the 1st Century.

Belief in a mortal person's life after death is suggested by the food and drink utensils often placed in tombs to accompany the dead, and again, though not very specifically, by the tomb-paintings at Kerkouane's Jebel Mlezza. One depicts a bird like a rooster – perhaps the deceased person's soul – in the air next to a mausoleum of the Thugga type, while in another it approaches the walled city which may represent the city of the next world. How a person qualified for a restful afterlife, what rituals were needed to ensure safe passage, or even whether it involved the gods themselves in any way, it would be interesting to know.[56]

THE 'TOPHET' AND CHILD SACRIFICE

The best-known cult practice at Carthage were the urn-burials dedicated to Tanit and Baal in the so-called 'tophet', where the earliest burials in the nine-level site date to the 8th Century and the latest to Carthage's final years. It was noted earlier that 'tophet' is merely a term of convenience: what such cemeteries were called in Punic is not known, whereas tophet (with other transliterations like topet, topheth, tofet) was, according to the Old Testament, the name of a site in the narrow valley of Hinnom outside Jerusalem, in which male children were sacrificed to the Phoenician Baal until the late 7th Century. Crowded with cremation urns which are often, though not always, accompanied by dedicatory stelae, the Punic site has stirred debate ever since urns taken for scientific investigation revealed the ashes and bones of very young children: chiefly infants, stillbirths and some foetuses, in some cases accompanied by bones of animals (mostly young sheep and goats). Similar human and animal remains, though on nothing like the same scale, had previously been found at Nora, Tharros and Motya. Again, a well-known stele from the 'tophet' of Carthage depicts a priest in a flat-topped cap, with his right hand raised in a gesture of respect or supplication, and a baby borne in the crook of his left arm – supposedly on the point of being put into Baal's red-hot embrace. All this fuels the linked questions of child sacrifice and human sacrifice at Carthage and her dependencies.

Greek and Roman writers often claim that the Carthaginians practised a rite of sacrificing chosen Carthaginian children to the gods – more specifically, to their chief god 'Cronus', Baal Hammon. Cleitarchus, an early commentator on Plato, and then Diodorus both give a pathetic description of infants being placed on the arms of a bronze statue of 'Cronus' over a blazing fire, so that they would fall still living into the flames. Plutarch writes that rich parents without children bought children of poor families to sacrifice them; the grieving mother must look on without shedding a tear or the payment was forfeited, while the children's screams (he adds) were drowned out by ritual flutes and cymbals.

The most famous episode of sacrificed children is reported by Diodorus for the year 310. Facing defeat from the invading forces of Agathocles, the Carthaginians realised that they had brought disaster on themselves through their cavalier attitude towards the gods, especially Cronus who – instead of receiving the sacrifice of the noblest children – had long been fobbed off with substitutes purchased and then nurtured for the rite. So now two hundred noble children were sacrificed to him by the state, and three hundred others voluntarily by families anxious to clear themselves of suspicion.

Other source items, varying in relevance, have been adduced in support, including the children 'passing through fire' in the Jerusalem '*tophet*' and several Biblical reports of kings sacrificing their first-born sons to placate their gods. In Justin, Herodotus and Diodorus respectively, there are accounts of Carthage's 6th-Century leader Mazeus putting to death his son Carthalo for disrespect, of Hamilcar during the battle of Himera in 480 burning 'entire bodies' (of humans, or animals?) and then leaping into the sacrificial fire himself on losing the battle, and of Himilco, the general campaigning in Sicily in 406, seeking to appease Cronus by sacrificing a boy to the god as an epidemic raged in his army.

Diodorus later reports a Carthaginian army in 307 sacrificing chosen victim-prisoners by fire after a great victory over the invader Agathocles – only to suffer suitable punishment when their own camp caught alight, killing many. When plague struck the Carthaginians, Justin asserts, they would appease the gods by immolating – that is, sacrificing by fire – both grown men and immature boys. Alexander the Great's biographer Curtius Rufus states that the Carthaginians persisted in sacrificing a freeborn boy down to the destruction of the city, implying that this happened at moments of crisis (in contrast to their mother city Tyre when besieged by Alexander). Then, imaginatively if quite fictitiously, the epic poet Silius Italicus transports envoys from Carthage to the victorious Hannibal in Italy with an order that he hand over his son for that year's sacrifice; Hannibal refuses, promising instead to shed Roman blood to please the gods. More noteworthy is a remark by the Christian writer Tertullian, himself a Roman Carthaginian, that in his own day around AD 200 the rite of infanticide was still performed in secret, even though banned by the Roman authorities.

What most of these writers have in common is the claim that Carthaginians carried out child sacrifice. In detail, though, there are disagreements and contradictions among themselves and with the archaeological evidence. Mazeus' son is an adult – in fact is the priest of Melqart at Carthage; Hamilcar at Himera is a suicide and there is no claim about him acting out a rite; both the sacrifice in Sicily in 406 and the mass killings in 310 were to appease an angry god in a crisis, whereas Curtius and Silius make child sacrifice a regular yearly rite and Diodorus implies that regular sacrificings had been the norm. Plutarch describes the children bought from poor mothers as having their throats cut, not as being cast into fire; he is also the only one to include childless couples among the sacrificers, contradicting the other sources who insist that the sacrificed victims had to be the parents' own. Still more strikingly, it is older children and even grown men who are given to the god or gods by Biblical sacrificers, by the Carthaginians in 409 and 310, and in Curtius', Silius' and Justin's reports – not infants. In 307, supposedly, it was foreign prisoners after a victory, in other words adult men: a unique event, and a suspect one since (as Diodorus takes care to stress) it promptly brought condign catastrophe down on the perpetrators, whose own camp burnt down with heavy loss of life.

None of this incoherent variety makes the written reports look especially reliable. The evidence from the '*tophet*' presents difficulties in turn. The bones of animals, especially lambs, accompany human bones in some of the urns studied, but most urns contain only human or animal remains respectively. Animal bones are found in larger percentages from earlier periods, like 30 per cent in the 7th and 6th Centuries, than in deposits of the 4th to 2nd Centuries (10 per cent). Analyses of the human bones from urns at Carthage and elsewhere – Motya and Tharros, for instance – show that the great majority are of infants, including some stillborn, or foetuses; the very few exceptions included children between two and four years old, and (at Carthage) a single older child aged between six and twelve. In some urns, the remains of a stillborn child and of an older child were placed together; and on current evidence this other child was normally only a few months older. There is also forensic evidence suggesting that many or most of the infants had died before being cremated. Nor (another noteworthy point) are children's remains at all common in ordinary necropoleis. It should be added that there is no sign, so far at least, of a mass cremation of many hundred victims like the one that Diodorus reports for the year 310.[57]

Some *stelae* from various '*tophets*', including ones later than the year 146, state that a named person dedicated a *mlk*, a *mlk 'dm*, a *mlk 'mr*, or a *mlk b'l* to Baal Hammon (or Baal Hammon and Tanit), often with the pious formula 'because he heard his voice'. The meaning of the phrases with *mlk*, itself pronounced *molk* or *mulk* and meaning 'sacrifice', is disputed. Some interpretations make *mlk* '*dm* the sacrifice 'of a male (victim)' and *mlk* '*mr* that 'of a lamb', while *mlk b'l* is taken to mean a sacrifice 'to Baal'. In other views, *mlk b'l* is taken neutrally to mean 'sacrifice of a victim' or, rather surprisingly, 'sacrifice of a citizen'; some reject the meaning 'lamb' for '*mr* (indeed by itself '*mr* can mean 'word'); and a *mlk* '*dm* could mean, not 'sacrifice of a man' – an odd term if a baby was meant – but one 'of reddening [*or* rouging]' – a rite, that is, for which the priest put on red-ochre colouring for ritual purposes.

With scholarly investigations still being made, a definite answer to the question of child sacrifice is not possible yet. Even so, some comments can be made. First, the normal urn-deposit in the '*tophet*', especially at Carthage, was usually one of newly-deceased or still-born infants, or foetuses. Second, very few features of the '*tophet*' burials match the descriptions in Greek and Roman writers, who claim to be describing the normal rites for human sacrifice at Carthage (above all, the writers depict the victims as older children and sometimes grown men). Third, the presence sometimes in one urn of two babies, unequal in age but close, is inexplicable if the Carthaginians were supposed to be sacrificing one child at a time, and nonsensical if the sacrificed one was supposed to be just the first-born. It would, though, make reasonable sense if both had died of natural causes in the same period, especially as it is not necessary to suppose that both were always from the same family. Fourth, the inconsistencies among the written sources, and between them and the archaeological evidence, make it virtually impossible to use either to reinforce the other. The sources, incidentally, never mention the '*tophet*' under any name or say anything about what happened to the sacrificed remains.

A Latin inscription of the 2nd or 3rd Century BC, from the town of Nicivibus in Numidia (today Ain N'gaous in Algeria), records parents sacrificing a lamb in gratitude to Saturn – the Latin name for Baal Hammon – for the life of their daughter Concessa. They call the lamb a 'substitute' (*pro vikario*) and the rite a *molchomor*, which seems to be their transliterated version of *mlk* '*mr*, and use the telling phrases 'breath for breath, blood for blood, life for life'. While this is often viewed as sacrificing a lamb in order to avoid sacrificing their Concessa, it looks just as likely that the lamb was given to Baal because the god had not taken Concessa's life – in other words, that she had recovered from a serious illness or accident. The animal bones in separate '*tophet*' urns may have a similar explanation while, conceivably, those in the same urn as an infant's remains may be a sacrificial thanksgiving to Tanit and Baal for not taking a second child as well.

The *stele* of the priest and baby, and Tertullian's statement about baby-sacrifices still being done secretly in his day, need to be considered. The *stele* does not in itself depict a sacrifice: interpreting it as doing so is based on assuming that it matches the descriptions in Diodorus and other sources. Strictly speaking, the male figure holding the baby is simply making a gesture of prayer, blessing or greeting: equally likely, then, he may be giving thanks for the baby or offering a blessing on its behalf. Tertullian's statement should carry particular weight, if we can be sure that he is reporting fact; at the same time, it needs to be noted that he is writing as an assertive defender of Christianity against allegations of secret Christian lusts and crimes (including infanticide), while making no claim of having seen the sacrifice rite himself or even of relying on an eyewitness.

Regular and widespread sacrifice of one's children would be remarkable, though not literally unthinkable, in societies where many children died at birth or before reaching the age of one. Although there are no figures for Carthaginian society, it is generally estimated that in the Roman world of the first three centuries AD (the period of ancient history with the fullest evidence) one in every four babies – or even one in every three – died as infants from natural causes. Small children were again more vulnerable than most adults in epidemics and times of scarcity. If the Carthaginians, and other Phoenician settlers in North Africa, Sicily and Sardinia, were sacrificing still other children of theirs, they were regularly jeopardising their own communal survival.[58]

The contradictions in the written sources and the near-disconnection between them and the archaeological evidence (itself open to other explanations) make it hard to believe that this did happen. If Tertullian can be trusted, together with Diodorus' reports of the boy sacrificed in Sicily in 409 and of the child-holocaust of 310, it may be deduced that at certain moments of stress, public or private, the killing of a child was done as an appeasement of the god; and further, that a state sacrifice was rare and, if it did occur, involved an older child or children. Just possibly the child six to twelve years old, whose remains have been found in the '*tophet*', was a deliberately sacrificed victim (in some assessments, he was a negro boy and so perhaps a slave). On the evidence too, it looks as though a victim was not always kin to the sacrificers, or an infant. The '*tophet*' itself, almost entirely devoted to infants, foetuses and animals, will have had minimal connection to such acts.

LITERATURE AT CARTHAGE: DID IT EXIST?

When Carthage was sacked in 146, its libraries were handed over to 'the minor kings of Africa' (so Pliny the Elder writes), save for Mago's agricultural encyclopaedia. The minor kings must have been the royal family of Numidia, Carthage's close neighbour and enemy; perhaps the king of Mauretania received some books too. What was in the libraries is debated, since few Carthaginian authors are known, but along with Mago's work that of his fellow-agronomist Hamilcar no doubt was in them, together with Hanno's *Periplus* and any similar records (one by Himilco, for instance).

Other works in the libraries perhaps included the sources used for 'the Punic books [*or* books in Punic: *Punici libri*] that were said to be King Hiempsal's', mentioned by the Roman historian Sallust. Hiempsal II of Numidia, a descendant of its unifier Masinissa, reigned from about 88 to 50 BC. Sallust cites Hiempsal's work for a compressed, and fairly fanciful, account of how the North African peoples originated and how the Phoenicians settled there; perhaps too for his description of Lepcis Magna and the heroism of the Philaeni brothers. As inscriptions and buildings from Numidia show, by Hiempsal's time and even earlier the kingdom – and especially its capital Cirta, modern Constantine – had extensively assimilated Carthage's language and culture, so it would be natural to write works in Punic (Sallust needed an interpreter). He seems to suspect that the king was author only in name: whoever did compose the work probably drew on at least some Carthaginian materials as well as Greek ones. The late-Roman historian Ammianus in turn reports that Hiempsal's grandson Juba II, an unusually bookish monarch and author, drew on *Punici libri* for the dictum that the Nile rises in a Mauretanian mountain near the Atlantic: maybe those books were his ancestor's, or else Carthaginian treatises – plainly very speculative – like the ones that Hiempsal too had looked up.

Some works in Punic survived into much later times. Ammianus' younger contemporary St Augustine, a self-consciously proud North African, comments ironically to a fellow African that, if disdainful of their old tongue, the friend then ought to deny the recognised value of the wisdom in 'Punic books'. He thus implies that not only did such books still exist but they survived in their original language, and though he does not explicitly say that they were written in Carthaginian times, there is no good reason to doubt it. Incidentally, a tradition that sacred books survived the catastrophe of 146 BC through being hidden away is mentioned by Plutarch in a mystic-philosophical discussion – very Greek in content – about souls after death; but the claim may be a mere fancy to enliven his essay.

It is also hard to tell whether Polybius', Diodorus', Justin's and other authors' sporadic but sometimes detailed reports of events in Carthaginian history go back to Carthaginian accounts (in Punic or in Greek). Hannibal certainly wrote of his own campaigns in seeming detail, originally as a temple inscription in Hera's temple at Cape Lacinium (Capo Colonna) near Croton in southern Italy; but he no doubt published it at home too. Twenty years later he issued a pamphlet in Greek about a booty-hunting Roman general's recent actions in central Asia Minor, no doubt taking a critical view of them and him.

While he is the only Carthaginian known as writing on historical events, one or two other items may offer glimpses of a narrative tradition. A Punic inscription set up two centuries before his time briefly reports military actions in Sicily by 'the *rbm* Adnibaal [Hannibal] son of Gisco the *rb* and Himilco son of Hanno the *rb*', including the sack of Acragas and other measures. The events date to 406, for the two generals and the sack are recorded by Diodorus. More indirect glimpses come in from much later times, such as two verse inscriptions of perhaps the 1st Century BC, at Mactar about 180 kilometres south-west of Carthage. In Neo-Punic, the later form of the language, they were set up by the *mzrh* or citizens' association there (or one of them) to praise two leaders who had defeated serious attacks on the town and its territory, maybe at different periods – one a revolt and one an incursion from outside – and restored prosperity to Mactar's landowners. Further away and later still (the mid-4th Century AD or perhaps the later 3rd) Julius Nasif, a Roman-ised Libyan officer at a rural centre far to the south of Lepcis Magna, had a Neo-Punic poem incised on his burial *stele*, using the Latin alphabet, to commemorate what must have been the high point of his career: defeating a marauding tribe that had attacked the area and capturing its chieftain.[59]

It is interesting that all these accounts deal with military matters, even the verse inscriptions. Military verse is not a genre found in Roman inscriptions. Nor has the rhythmic structure of the poems anything to do with Greek or Latin versification: instead they show features of a distant ancestry in ancient Canaanite and Biblical poetry, as does some of their vocabulary. The biographical and autobiographical aspects of the accounts, both prose and verse, are also worth noting. A *stele* at Carthage records that the family of a citizen named Milkpilles honoured his memory with an inscriptional biography set up in the temple of Isis – which reminds us of Hanni-bal's personal record in the temple of Hera, and indeed of how Hanno the navigator placed the original of his *Periplus* in Baal Hammon's. Milkpilles need not have been a military man, even if his biography too was in verse: for Mactar is the origin of another verse autobiography of Roman times – this one in Latin – telling, in endearingly unsophisticated fashion, how a humbly-born farm labourer there advanced through hard work and enterprise to wealth and local honours. While poetic, or would-be poetic, life stories in Latin inscriptions are not unique to North Africa, the 'rime of the ancient Mactarian' looks like a civilian match for the Neo-Punic martial paeans.

It seems likely enough, then, that at least military-historical and biographical writing was well established at Carthage at any rate from the 5th Century on. The traditions may have gone back much further, for her close relations with Tyre should mean that educated Carthaginians knew their mother city's ancient 'annals' if nothing else. We saw earlier that there is enough plausible detail in the story of Elissa to suggest that the foundation-account had some basis in fact, while the Carthaginians' interest in family history is clear from the sometimes lengthy ancestral lists lovingly recorded by *stele*-dedicators. If written works in these fields have not survived to any extent, probably it is because Greeks and Romans were uninterested in reading or preserving Punic-language literature, not because literary composition was rare at Carthage.

Greeks and Romans did pay attention to authors who wrote on Carthaginian affairs in those languages. Some of them were surely read at Carthage too, for instance Philinus of Acragas, the 3rd-Century historian of the First Punic War, and Hannibal's friends and biographers Silenus (another Sicilian) and Sosylus of Sparta. Even philosophical works found readers. A young Carthaginian philosopher, Hasdrubal, son of one Diognetus (a Greek migrant to Carthage, or a Carthaginian who took a Greek name), lectured at home on the subject, in his own language, till he left for Athens around 163 aged twenty-four. There he adopted the name Cleitoma-chus on becoming an Athenian citizen, enjoying a distinguished career until his death in 110/109. He became head of the Platonic academy after his teacher Carneades, and wrote a reported four hundred books – probably in the sense of rolled *volumina* – to make a lasting impact on philosophy. One of them was a treatise of consolation to his surviving countrymen after the destruction of the city. It was in Greek (Cicero read it) and is yet another pointer to Carthaginians' familiarity with that language and culture. It would be interesting to know how many, if any, other Carthaginians made the same journey for philosophy's sake.[60]

VISUAL ART, INCLUDING COINAGE

Works of art at Carthage go back to the city's earliest centuries, though what remains of them is regrettably limited, consisting chiefly of finds in graves and tombs and, perhaps for this reason, mainly religious in their import. It was noted earlier that various offerings and mementoes could be placed in tombs, including figurines, lamps, ornaments and jewellery, as well as jars and bowls with food and drink to nourish the dead person's spirit journey to the next world. Yadomilk's pendant is one such item. From the start, artworks reflected many different cultures or were pieces imported from these, the earliest influence being of course Phoenicia's and, almost equally early, Egypt's. Thus from a 7th-Century grave on Byrsa comes a finely-worked ivory piece, the tiny remnant (less than five centimetres high) of an ornamental carving, showing a goat with head turned back, standing on a sacred tree – a long-established motif of plenty in eastern Mediterranean art. From a Douimès necropolis of about the same period there survives a cylindrical ivory handle, about 13 centimetres long, for a bronze mirror: it depicts a woman (probably a goddess) with Egyptian hairstyle and long robe, and hands clasped over her breasts (*Illustration 13*).

It is hard to say whether either of these was an import or was made at Carthage. A terracotta statuette in a more unsophisticated style, dated to the 7th or 6th Century, does look locally made: an abstractly stylised, flat-topped head and roughly cylindrical torso, complete with what seem to be nipples, depicting perhaps a protective goddess (*Illustration 14*). Perhaps later in date is a tiny terracotta sculpture – again from a necropolis, this time on Borj-el-Jedid – of a mother, in long robe and with a shawl covering her head, who kneels over an open-top bake-oven (or maybe a well) while her child, abstractly rendered with no features, peers over the top to see what is happening (*Illustration 15*). This simple piece has a

Illustration 13 Ivory mirror-handle depicting a goddess(?), *c.* 7th Century

Illustration 14 Terracotta statuette of a goddess, 7th–6th Century

Illustration 15 Mother and child at baking oven

particular appeal in its little scene of domestic life, something rare in surviving Carthaginian art. A contrast to its peaceful image is offered by a splendid tondo or disc in terracotta, only some nine centimetres in diameter and well preserved, from the 6th-Century necropolis on Douimès: it depicts a fully-armed cavalry warrior at full gallop, with crested helmet and round shield, his faithful dog racing alongside, while behind the warrior appears the sacred disc-and-crescent symbol of the sun and moon (*Illustration 16*). The image occurs elsewhere at western Phoenician sites like Utica and Ebusus, but the energy and sharply-drawn quality of the figures on the work from Douimès suggest that fine artistic activity was already going on at Carthage in that early period.

The mother and child theme, this time in firmly religious terms, recurs in a terracotta statuette of later date (perhaps as late as the 3rd Century) that represents a robed goddess wearing a tall, fez-like headpiece and bearing on her shoulder a daughter with similar headgear and an elaborate necklace. The pair may represent Astarte and Tanit, who are sometimes linked together in Phoenician art, or even Demeter and Kore. Other distinctive home-made pieces include many votive masks from graves, notably ones with negro features or with stylised aspects like ferocious grins or staring eyes: their aim

110

Illustration 16 Terracotta tondo: cavalryman and his hound

was to ward off unfriendly spirits. Wide-open eyes are notable, too, in a full-length statue of a robed male dedicator from Utica, perhaps of the 3rd Century, and 4th- or 3rd-Century ornamental trinkets like glass pearl-shaped pendants with huge painted eyes and intricately-fashioned glass spirals for hair and beard.

Eastern Mediterranean art forms survived more or less to the end: the so-called 'Hannibal quarter' on Byrsa's slope yielded a small terracotta god – it may be Melqart – enthroned, wearing a conical cap, and with right hand raised in a gesture of blessing. Egyptian themes remained popular down the centuries. There is a fine gold amulet-case with engraved Egyptian motifs of 7th–6th Century date; Egyptian divinities like the distinctively ugly Bes and the maternal Isis are represented on amulets; *stelae* and small sculpted models (like the famous ones from Thuburbo Maius) depict the façades of Egyptian-style temples; and many of the terracotta votive masks placed in graves are Egyptian in style. Some items were probably brought to Carthage from the eastern lands, but others must have been made locally.

Other cultures beside Phoenicia's and Egypt's contributed to the artistic variety at Carthage. Etruscan objects and styles were always attractive, as shown for instance by a bronze figurine of a goddess or maiden found at Sidi bou Said and thought to have come over in the 6th Century if not earlier; by painted bowls with Etruscan-style motifs of the 4th Century; and by a small terracotta of a chubbily nude seated boy, found at Kerkouane (a 4th- or 3rd-Century version of a widely-spread Phoenician religious image, the 'temple boy').[61]

111

From around the 5th Century, however, the most pervasive influence was the Greek world.

With the Carthaginians carrying on trade with Greeks, warring with the Greeks of Sicily (and before them, the Phocaeans in Corsica) and intermarrying with Greeks even at the highest social levels – like the Greek mother of 'king' Hamilcar – this influence was predictable. It never supplanted all others, but its attractions grew as trade expanded, Greek culture flourished and, from Alexander the Great's day onward, Greek and Macedonian dominance was imposed over more and more of the eastern Mediterranean, including Carthage's motherland Phoenicia.

Apart from the pottery goods imported from the city's earliest days, the Carthaginians' interest in things Greek was no doubt partly stimulated, ironically enough, by the artworks looted from Sicilian cities in the 5th and 4th Centuries' wars. A notorious prize acquired in 406 was the hollow bronze bull made for Phalaris, tyrant of Acragas in the 560s (allegedly for roasting his political enemies alive). Other carefully kept booty included portrait busts, statues – Cicero describes a splendid one of Artemis the huntress, which the Romans restored to Segesta in 146 – and sacred objects of gold and silver. Another stimulus must have been coinage, which Carthage began to produce only late in the 5th Century, to pay her military forces in Sicily: from the start, Carthaginian coins were under Greek influence. Her adoption of Demeter and Kore in 396 gave further impetus.

An early example of Greek or Greek-influenced art in a western Phoenician setting was found in quite recent times, not at Carthage but at Motya: the marble statue of a curly-haired youth or 'ephebe' wearing a close-fitting cap and standing in a full-length robe of realistically chiselled folds, intended to represent fine cloth – so fine that the viewer is no doubt about his sex – while one hand rests on his hip and the other was perhaps raised in blessing or greeting (the arms do not survive). A remarkable sculpture of early 5th-Century classical style, this represents a young god receiving (or maybe a young priest making) an offering. Motya was of course much nearer and much more exposed to the appeal of Greek Sicily's art and aesthetics, but it is entirely believable that Carthage too would import similar pieces, or commission resident Greek sculptors and designers to make them – and that eventually there would be Carthaginian workers skilled in the same arts.

One such artist was Boethus 'the Carthaginian': his and his father Apollodorus' names are Greek, but on a statue-base at Ephesus bearing their names he terms himself a Carthaginian. The later Greek

travel writer Pausanias saw a gilded statue by 'Boethus the Carthaginian' at Olympia, surely the same man. His father may well have
been an immigrant to Carthage from Sicily or Greece, while it looks
as though Boethus in turn left his native city to seek his fortune in
that world. Not every Greek migrant or Carthaginian craftsman
skilled in Greek methods need have done the same.[62]

From around the year 400 art in Greek forms proliferated at
Carthage and in the Carthaginian world. Remnants of buildings
show Greek types of ornament, like the surviving upper part of an
Ionic sandstone pillar in the '*tophet*' intricately carved with intertwined palm fronds and acanthus leaves in its capital, reminiscent of
3rd-Century Greek decoration, and the remains of an Ionic column
from the 'Hannibal quarter' on the slopes of Byrsa. Ataban's
Carthaginian-descended mausoleum at Thugga makes use of Ionic
columns, just as the ships' docks in the naval port, as Appian
describes them, were each marked out by a pair of them.

Elements or wholesale borrowing of Greek styles characterise
votive figurines, *stelae* and other objects: thus a 4th-Century terracotta statuette, found at Kerkouane, depicts a woman musician in
Greek garments, their folds realistically rendered (*chiton* robe, and a
himation cloak drawn up over the back of her head), one leg bent
slightly forward as she beats her tambourine drum. A grave at
Carthage produced another 4th-Century statuette still more in Greek
style, of an attractive young woman playing a double flute, swathed
in flowing robes and this time with one leg bent slightly back (*Illustration 17*). Both wear decorated high caps. These make a sharp
contrast with another tambourine-player of much the same period: a
formal Phoenician-style sacred image, the face abstractly rendered,
with ringleted hair and flat painted robe, both hands clasping the
tambourine to her breast. This is a valuable reminder that Greek
influence did not push aside other forms.

Much Greek and Greek-influenced work at Carthage is of
memorable quality. On the back of a small bronze mirror there
survives a masterful profile, done in high relief, of a goddess with an
elaborate coiffure, a silver-inlay earring, and a rather engaging half-
smile: again a work of the 4th Century or perhaps the 3rd, and fully
Greek in style even though it must represent a Carthaginian goddess
(*Illustration 18*). Ivory intaglios – ornaments with incised figures or
busts, as usual found in graves – of the same period or a little later
depict rather sedately dancing maenads (women practising the
frenzied ritual worship of Dionysus) and a sensitively realised one of
Dionysus himself. The carefully-wrought head of Demeter, or else

Illustration 17 Fluteplayer from Carthage: terracotta statuette, 4th Century

Illustration 18 Bronze mirror (back), profile of a goddess

another goddess, figures on well-made terracotta incense burners, each around 30 centimetres high, with coiffured hair topped by the incense bowl, while a beautifully designed head of Medusa in terracotta – her curling hair intertwined with snakes identifies her – with staring eyes and slightly parted lips, again fully Greek in style, was an offering in a shrine near the *'tophet'* (*Illustration 19*). Just as elaborate, with mixed Ionic and Doric features, is the *stele* dedicated by Milkyaton the sufete described earlier, representing Kore or Demeter in her temple and dated to the 2nd Century – not long, therefore, before the fall of the city.

Illustration 19 Terracotta head of Medusa

Works of art (and architecture) in different styles, as well as works combining different traditions, coexisted easily throughout Carthage's history. A *stele* set up around 250 in Hadrumetum's '*tophet*', and very well preserved, presents a full-frontal winged sphinx standing on a handsome Ionic column, with its dedicator's inscription above and, over this, a gable-like top (recalling those of grand mausolea like Ataban's at Thugga) decorated with a series of stylised palm fronds: an impressively executed combination of Egyptian, Greek and Carthaginian elements (*Illustration 20*). Another *stele*, probably 3rd-Century, shows the face and shoulders of a young man again entirely Greek in appearance – head turned to one side with a troubled or questioning expression, shoulders covered by a cloak with loose folds and a brooch (*Illustration 21*).

Illustration 20 Cippus from Hadrumetum

Illustration 21 Stele of a youth, from Hadrumetum

A small stone ossuary or box for a deceased person's preserved bones, from the necropolis of Ste Monique on Borj-el-Jedid, has a lid sculpted as a full-length and three-dimensional portrait of a priest with curled hair and beard framing a strikingly lifelike face, its features rather like those traditionally given to Zeus (*Illustration 22*). Wearing a long robe with intricate folds and a long panel of cloth draped down from his left shoulder, he offers a blessing or prayer with his right hand and clasps an incense bowl in his left. Ossuaries, several of which have been found in necropoleis at Carthage, were common in the Near East including Judaea, less so in

Illustration 22 Ossuary of a priest from Ste Monique tomb, 4th–3rd Centuries

Greece or at Rome. Another from the same necropolis and of much the same era (the 4th or 3rd Century) also depicts a priest named Baalshillek, similarly robed and bearded, with raised right hand and vessel in his left, around whose figure the stone has been chiselled away to raise him above the rest of the lid. Although so much like the other sculpture in these details, Baalshillek's figure is flat, the details incised into the surface and in a far plainer style, recalling Phoenician forms rather than Greek.

Two full-sized sarcophagi, recovered from the Ste Monique necropolis and dating to the later 4th Century, can complete these examples. One corresponds to the unnamed priest's ossuary: an elderly bearded man with the same robe (including the ceremonial cloth panel draped down from the shoulder) and in the same stance. The other is one of the most remarkable pieces of sculpture found at Carthage. Again it shows a blend of influences: made of Pentelic marble (1.93 metres long and 48 centimetres deep), its gabled lid is carved as a beautiful priestess or goddess, standing upright like the priests (*Illustration 12*). She wears a veil which falls over the back of her head to her shoulders and is topped by a hawk-shaped crest – a symbol of the Egyptian goddess Isis – while around her neck is a broad Egyptian-style collar hiding the top of her robe. This in turn is a Greek *peplos*, gathered above the waist to let a fold fall over either hip, then reaching down to just above her sandal-shod toes. Below the waist, the *peplos* is sheathed in two great folded wings that touch the ground beside her feet: another Egyptian aspect, recalling both Isis and Horus. In her uplifted left hand the girl holds a scentbox or phial but, in contrast to the raised gesture of each priest's empty right hand, her right hand wears a wrist bracelet and remains at her side clasping a dove.

The statue was brilliantly painted, although only traces survive. While incorporating so many Egyptian hieratic features, its presentation of the girl's face, figure and robe is altogether Greek of the Hellenistic era, just as similar statues do in Ptolemaic Egypt of the same period. Again there is a sharp contrast in another Isis icon from Carthage (*Illustration 23*): this one a terracotta statuette of the 4th

Illustration 23 Another Isis effigy: terracotta statuette

or 3rd Century in much more classic Egyptian style, with long plaited hair falling to the shoulders, hands apparently clasped behind the back, and the body below the waist completely clasped by the deity's feathered but non-naturalistic wings.[63]

Greek-style works of art, particularly if large, highly decorated and made of costly materials like marble or ivory, would be expensive to commission or even to buy in a market. Nor need they have appealed to every Carthaginian. Religious and even aesthetic traditions would also help to ensure that other long-established forms were continued too. The same range can be seen in the genre of tomb-razors unique to Carthage, Punic North Africa, Sardinia and Ebusus: copper or bronze pieces shaped like a hatchet-head with a projecting spur as the handle. Buried with the dead for ritual use in the afterlife, from about 500 on these were incised with pictures of a god of the next world, sometimes with Egyptian themes like Horus or a pharaoh figure, often with a Carthaginian god (especially Melqart), and from the 4th Century on often with Greek deities – not only Melqart's equivalent Heracles, but Asclepius (Eshmun) and Hermes (perhaps Sakun) among others.

Carthaginian coins were not meant to be artworks, but often have impressive artistic quality. They were a relatively late development for the city, which like other Mediterranean cultures had normally used barter, exchange and weighed pieces of precious and semi-precious metals in trade. Late in the 5th Century, a time when coinage was in widespread use in Greek lands including Sicily, the Carthaginians and their Sicilian allies started to strike their own in the west of the island – very likely in preparation for the major offensives which they mounted between 409 and 405 and which needed large and expensive mercenary forces. The first issues were in silver and bronze, based on the tetradrachm (four-drachma coin) of Athens and its fractions. Then, during the first half of the next century, they also struck gold coins to the standard of the Greek gold stater (worth 20 drachmas), obviously in much less quantity, and ones of electrum – a blend of gold and silver.

The coins often though not always bear legends, for instance the name of the issuing city (Ṣys, the Punic name of Panormus, or Qart-ḥadasht), sometimes also words like mḥnt (mahanet, the army) or 'm mḥnt (ham mahanet, the people of the army), mḥšbm (mehashbim, the accountants, or paymasters), or b'ršt (which seems to mean 'in the territories'). From the late 4th Century coins were struck at Carthage too, in gold and electrum, again for state payments – most are found in Sicily again – but along with small bronze coins for local use. Not many decades later a new silver standard was adopted, now for convenience called the shekel, which was slightly lighter than the stater. Larger values, two and three shekels, were also issued at times, as well as fractions of the shekel. This gave a considerable flexibility to the city's monetary system in an age of growing diplomatic and military commitments.

The motifs on the coins were limited. A horse or a horse's head, a palm tree, and the profile of a goddess or god account for most types, though of course each could have many variations: the horse may be standing still, galloping, or standing with its head turned back, for instance; some coins show only the forepart of the horse; sometimes behind it there is a palm tree, or above it a star or moon. The goddess almost invariably is Tanit – including on coins struck by Hannibal in Italy during the Second Punic War – usually wearing earrings and very often crowned with a cornstalk garland. Occasionally it is Astarte or, in another suggestion, Elissa-Dido in a distinctive Phrygian cap (a soft head-covering with long flaps at back and sides); or still more occasionally Isis. The god is normally Melqart, adorned with a lionskin helm that typifies his Greek equivalent Heracles. In the later 3rd Century a few other types appeared: occasionally a lion (*Illustration 24c, d*), and the Barcid generals in Spain struck some fine-quality coins with an elephant or a warship's prow on the reverse as well as Melqart portraits without the lionskin but with a distinctive Herculean club, and with a war-elephant (*Illustration 24i*). Both striking and pathetic is a small number of 2nd-Century coins discovered only in 1994 – half-melted or worse, they are survivals of the destructive fires set by the Romans once they took the city in 146.[64]

In most cases and from the start, the artistic quality of the precious metal issues is good to excellent, the bronzes (cheaper in value and larger in quantity) much less so. The styles are virtually all Greek and largely under the influence of Sicilian Greek issues, especially Syracuse's, but the deities and the types on the reverse are distinctively Carthaginian. The Carthaginians' ability to adopt, adapt and develop what they wanted from other cultural worlds is no less evident in their coinage.

a

b

c

d

e

f

g

h

i

j

Illustration 24 A selection of Carthaginian coins from Sicily and North Africa:

(a) silver tetradrachm: obverse, front body of galloping horse, crowned by winged Victory, and corn-symbol, legend *Qart-hadasht*; reverse, palm-tree with *mḥnt* ('the army'): Sicily, early 4th Century, *17.1 grams*

(b) silver tetradrachm: obv., Tanit or Kore with dolphins; rev., horse's head with palm-tree, legend *'m mḥnt* ('the people of the army'): Sicily, late 4th Century, *16.8 gr.*

(c) silver tetradrachm: obv., head of Elissa-Dido(?) with Phrygian cap; rev., lion with palm-tree and *s'm mḥnt*: Sicily, 4th Century, *17.05 gr.*

(d) silver tetradrachm: obv., head of Elissa-Dido(?) with Phrygian cap; rev., lion and palm-tree, with legend *s 'mmḥnt* ('of the people of the army'): Sicily, late 4th Century, *16.9 gr.*

(e) gold tridrachm: obv., Tanit wearing necklace and earring; rev., standing horse; *c.* 260 BC, *12.4 gr.*

(f) silver trishekel: obv., head of Tanit; rev., horse's head: Carthage, *c.* 260 BC, *22.3 gr.*

(g) silver six-shekel : obv., head of Tanit; rev., leaping horse: Carthage(?), *c.* 260 BC, *44.3 gr.*

(h) billon: obv., head of Melqart in style of Hercules, with lionskin; rev., lion with Greek legend *Libyon* ('of the Libyans') below, and Punic letter *m* (*mem*) above: overstruck on a Carthaginian coin by the rebels in the Truceless War, 241–237 BC, *7.3 gr.*

(i) silver 1.5 shekel: obv., head of Melqart in style of Hercules, with war-club; rev., war-elephant: Spain, before 218 BC, *10.8 gr.*

(j) bronze: obv., head of Tanit; rev., standing horse: Carthage, early 2nd Century, *95.1 gr.*

VIII

CARTHAGE IN AFRICA

POLITICS AND RIVALRIES:
MAZEUS-'MALCHUS'

The rich élite who ran Carthage's affairs were pretty certainly not just a merchant oligarchy but a more complex blend. Merchants of course bought property, in Carthage and outside, with some of their profits: this was a reliably safe investment. Meanwhile some wealthy Carthaginians no doubt held most of their wealth in land, and their opportunities for acquiring more land would grow as the city's control over Libya did. Mago the agronomist's command, to sell your town house if you wished to be a serious estate owner, implies that such people did exist. It need not be doubted, all the same, that they would often invest in trading ventures.

Such families and more strongly mercantile ones surely had close relations (marriage included). Equally they must often have undergone changes in circumstances – some dying out, some deciding to give up the risks of overseas trading in favour of landowning, some the other way round. All the while, newly enriched men would be doing their best to become accepted members of the dominant élite in their turn, which meant above all gaining (and according to Aristotle often buying) public office and joining the *adirim* (the senate). These factors, competitive and cooperative, were permanent elements in Carthaginian politics and government. It would be unsafe, though, to imagine a sharp difference between 'merchant' and 'landed' families in society, and still more unsafe to suppose that Carthaginian politics and policies involved tensions between commercial and landed interests.

On the other hand, it can be cautiously inferred that most or all of Carthage's dominant figures down the ages belonged primarily to landowning families. Quite notably, the affairs of the republic from the mid-5th to at least the early 2nd Century were very often directed by military men: from 'Malchus' and then Mago until Hannibal, himself the last in a long series of such *rabim mahanet*. Perhaps they were all from wealthy merchant families; but wealthy and prominent merchants did not become Carthage's dominant figures. In spite of Carthage's maritime reputation, none of her historical leaders was a naval commander, unless Hanno of *Periplus* fame counts as one (which is uncertain). Nor did her projection of power involve many sea battles: we know only of Alalia, and that was at least tactically a defeat. Much if not most of Carthage's leadership in historical times consisted, then, of generals.

We have already met the charismatic 'Malchus', as moderns usually call him, who was both Carthage's first recorded leader after Elissa and the first of these military men. His doings are told by Justin and by Orosius, the 5th-Century AD compiler of a Christianised world history, but 'Malchus' is not his proper name. The manuscripts have Mazeus, Maceus, or Maleus; in these a 17th-Century editor thought that he could recognise the Phoenician *mlk*, and so printed 'Malchus'. But *mlk* applied to a person means king or ruler (Melqart, *Mlqrt*, literally means 'king of the city'), and did not become a name until much later, even in the eastern Mediterranean. In any case it is never advisable to amend textual readings unless all the existing ones are unacceptable, which does not apply here. Just possibly the real name should be *Mzl* or something similar, for in Punic *mzl* means 'good fortune'. For convenience, though, Mazeus – the commonest form in both sources – will do.[65]

In Justin's telling, he warred successfully in Africa, then conquered part of Sicily – only to suffer a bloody defeat in Sardinia and be ordered into exile along with his surviving soldiers; Orosius' much shorter account makes him suffer repeated defeats in Sicily as well as Sardinia. When a petition for pardon from his men to Carthage was rejected, the troops sailed with him to the city and laid siege to it, forcing the authorities to capitulate. Mazeus used his victory to put ten senators, his chief enemies, to death, but it was a brief supremacy: accused soon after of aiming at monarchy and of the crime of executing his own son, he was tried and himself put to death. Both writers are rather more interested in the clash between him and his son. While besieging Carthage, Mazeus was snubbed by his son Carthalo, the priest of 'Hercules' (thus Melqart): for, returning from Tyre after delivering there Melqart's share of Mazeus' Sicilian booty, Carthalo ignored his father's summons and went into the city to fulfil his religious duties. On coming forth a few days later in priestly garb, he suffered first a stern lecture on filial duty from Mazeus and then public execution on a cross in his regalia, as a warning to others.

The story of Mazeus is about equally accepted and rejected by moderns. Justin's rather loosely organised account has problematic features – Mazeus' entire army sentenced to exile, and his surprisingly harsh treatment of his son for putting religious duties first – not to mention the question of whether Trogus found the episode in any reliable previous historian. The Carthaginians, as already noted, probably did have their own historical traditions. Trogus could have drawn on these, even if indirectly – for instance using a Carthaginian or pro-Carthaginian author writing in Greek – as the detail about the tithe-offering to Melqart of Tyre suggests (such offerings were made yearly). The clash between father and son is obviously rhetorically embroidered, especially Mazeus' harangue to Carthalo, whereas the rest of the account is quite plain in style. If Carthaginian tradition did include Mazeus' story, that of course does not prove it did happen, but equally does not prove it to be fiction. Some other points suggest that an element of fact underlies it.

It was noted earlier that the period assigned to Mazeus' activities – in Justin, two generations before the battle of Himera in 480; the reign of Cyrus the Great, according to Orosius – would be compatible with evidence for Carthage's initial 6th-Century intervention in both Sicily and Sardinia. This was a time of tense relations, too, with the Libyans, when the city stopped its stipend to them for several years but was then forced to resume paying it, arrears included. As a tentative hypothesis, Mazeus' successes against 'the Africans', as Justin calls them, marked the start of the Carthaginians' refusal to pay, a stance which lasted some years – perhaps decades. With that feather in his cap he might well be reappointed general to further the city's interests overseas.

It would be no surprise, in turn, if successes abroad strengthened his position – as his son's priesthood of Melqart and his army's devotion both suggest – and at the same time created jealous enemies. The attack on him which led to his armed return may not have been the first (for a comparison, there was more than one against Julius Caesar in Gaul before he staged his own military return in 49 BC), but once he suffered a severe defeat in Sardinia with losses heavy enough to weaken his army, his enemies could act effectively. If he and his rebellious troops then sailed to Carthage, they must have been overseas, most probably in Sardinia. The exile decree could have been, in practice, an order bidding them to stay there indefinitely.

None of this looks impossible to believe, even if Trogus or Justin coloured it up for impact. Nor need it be assumed that the disgraced army consisted solely, or even mostly, of Carthaginians. There would be a cadre of Carthaginian officers and maybe a citizen contingent, but even in the 6th Century the city may have been hiring mercenaries, Libyans among them, just as it was to do for Hamilcar's expedition to Sicily some decades later. Despite the defeat, the survivors stayed loyal to their general: not just because of his charismatic leadership but because his enemies at Carthage made the mistake of tying the men's fate to Mazeus'. Their armed return obviously took his opponents by surprise, but the political struggle was between aristocratic cliques manipulating a largely passive citizen body, as their quick capitulation and his ensuing fall confirm. Plainly Mazeus had no soldiers at hand to save him in the end, which again suggests that most of them had been non-citizens and that he, willingly or not, had paid them out and disbanded them.

The clash between father and son, which interests Justin and Orosius quite as much as the political events, may be a moralistic fiction as sometimes suggested; or on another interpretation, dramatises symbolically a conflict at Carthage between rival power sources on the old Phoenician model, palace versus temple. This interpretation in effect keeps the name 'Malchus' and views him as a genuine king, while not explaining why the rivals should be father and son. If the story is fiction of any type, another puzzle would be why it is made an intrusion into a separate political affair. The report of the son being crucified, in his priestly garb and in sight of the city, is lurid but not inevitably suspect: if such an event occurred, it would remain vivid in people's memory for a long time.

A more prosaic explanation of the clash could be that Carthalo, once appointed priest of Melqart, did put religion ahead of filial duty (just as Thomas à Becket would put religious before royal duty seventeen centuries later). Instead of defending his absent father's interests, he left for Tyre at a critical moment, so enabling Mazeus' enemies to gain the upper hand; then made the further mistake of seeming to join them when he returned. If he next emerged in full priestly regalia to see his father, he may just possibly have been trying to act as a religious peace-broker – a final mistake. For a powerful and resentful father to put his son to death is not impossible to believe: other cultures have similar and better-recorded examples, like the emperor Constantine and tsar Peter the Great. Whether Mazeus' enemies had also tried to harness Melqart in their support – thus compromising Carthalo – can only be guessed, though that might explain why Mazeus crucified the god's priest with his symbols of sanctity.

Even if shorn of these details, in outline Mazeus' story is of a leader becoming pre-eminent through military achievements in Libya and the islands, provoking opposition at home and crushing it, then being himself crushed in a political turnaround. Carthage's increasing prosperity, and her growing influence over her sister Phoenician colonies along North Africa's coasts, would almost certainly lead to sharper differences in riches and political strengths among her leading families, and so to greater competitiveness. Was Mazeus the first leader to enjoy a lengthy dominance over her affairs? This cannot be known, but his rise was, more likely than not, the product of some decades (if not generations) of social and political jousting among the élite. He may have been also the prime mover of the vigorous projection of the city's power which developed during the 6th Century, and which was popular enough with all Carthaginians to be carried on long after he was gone, by the next dominant group.

THE MAGONID ASCENDANCY

That group (Justin records) was led by Mago and then his two sons Hasdrubal and Hamilcar. Hamilcar's mother, and so probably Hasdrubal's too, was a Syracusan, just one of the many intermarriages known in Carthaginian society. (Herodotus calls Hamilcar's father Hanno and knows nothing of a Magonid family; his 'Hanno' looks like a mistake.) It is not certain that Mago's political dominance followed directly on Mazeus' fall, but there was probably no great interval, especially if Mazeus' end dates to the 530s. That in turn would give about half a century for the first two generations of Magonid leaders, as Hasdrubal died before Hamilcar, and the latter then perished at the battle of Himera in 480. Mago and his sons succeeded in consolidating a family ascendancy which was to last more than a century. It was based partly on astutely handling political relationships at home – more astutely than Mazeus had done – and partly on skilful, even though not always prosperous, military leadership.

The struggle between Mazeus and his enemies had been politically disruptive, for it had climaxed with them trying to unseat an appointed general (who may also have been sufete) and with him then seizing the city by military means though not by actual violence.

It would be interesting to know whether Mago was part of the opposition, though he was not one of the leaders executed by Mazeus. The dominance that he in his turn enjoyed until his death was due, Justin stresses, to hard work and personal merit as well as military ability, all qualities which created prosperity and territorial expansion for Carthage.

Mago's only specific measure to earn mention was 'regulating military discipline' or, rather differently translated, 'setting in order the military system' (*ordinata militari disciplina*) – the first Carthaginian leader to do so, says Justin. Since Carthage had been waging wars before his time, it is not clear what the regulation would amount to, but a good possibility is that he brought military service more firmly under the regular authorities' control. That Mazeus' army had been more loyal to their leader than to the republic, even to the point of insurrection, suggests that the business of recruiting and maintaining soldiers (citizen and foreign) had been left to a general's unfettered discretion. If Mago curbed this, he did so probably more in principle than practice, for he and then his sons effectively controlled the state in any case as generals, sufetes or both. The city's arrangements for recruiting and paying off soldiers, perhaps too for their training and equipment, are other matters that he may have regulated. Certainly one suggestion, unfortunately unprovable, has been that he introduced the Greek-style formation called the hoplite phalanx, a line or successive lines of well-drilled, heavily-armed and closely-ranked infantry.

Nothing is said about Mago regulating the Carthaginian navy – ancient writers tell us very little, in fact, about Carthaginian naval organisation and equipment in any period – but it is at least conceivable that Mago or his successors kept the city's war fleet up to date. The trireme was invented in their time in the eastern Mediterranean: a sleek, manoeuvrable warship armed with a powerful bronze ram and rowed by up to 170 oarsmen seated in three levels one above the other. A fleet that went on relying on the smaller penteconter would invite disaster; but on the other hand triremes were more expensive. Carthage therefore needed to add to her resources if she was to update both her navy and her land forces.

This would account for the Magonids' continuing wars which, Justin says, were waged by all three leaders. As shown earlier, the Carthaginians in their first treaty with Rome, around 509, implicitly claimed control over Sardinia and Sicily, with archaeological evidence pointing to their dominating at any rate Sardinia's most productive regions. These advances were not easily won. Concise though he is, Justin records Mago's son Hasdrubal dying in battle in Sardinia, and Hamilcar later perishing in Sicily (though he does not mention the defeat at Himera itself). There was a setback in Africa, too. During the brothers' shared rule the Libyans confronted Carthage in arms with a demand for the arrears of annual tribute, and after at least one battle – which the Libyans seem to have won – the city (as noted earlier) agreed to pay up rather than fight on. This decision made sense if Hasdrubal and Hamilcar reckoned that the proceeds from annexing resources overseas outweighed the cost (and indignity) of paying the tribute to their Libyan neighbours, not to mention the risk of a war and more defeats.

What official positions they and their father held are not clearly reported. Justin summarily says that 'they carried out and at the same time decided all business themselves'. Greek and Latin authors' habit of turning Carthaginian magistracies into what they thought or guessed were the Greek and Roman equivalents leads him to describe both Mazeus and the Magonids simply as *imperatores*, generals, although he does add that Hamilcar held eleven 'dictator-ships' (*dictaturae*, at Rome a short-term emergency office with sweeping powers) and celebrated four *triumphi* (at Rome, victory parades with sacred rituals). But even if Pompeius Trogus perhaps explained what Carthaginian institutions these were, his abbreviator does not. Eleven repeated 'dictatorships' hardly look like emergency appointments; on the other hand Justin later writes of Hannibal the Barcid being 'consul' at Carthage, meaning sufete. If he is being consistent in terminology (not that this is certain), Hamilcar the Magonid's 'dictatorships' may be the best that Trogus and he could offer as the name for a combined sufeteship and generalship. The word does not have to imply a deliberate contrast with the term *imperator*. Hamilcar is the only Magonid whose official position Justin records, even in this Romanised form, whereas he terms all these leaders *imperatores*. The word, then, describes their effective dominance, which was based on military leadership – a quality that Justin stresses for Mago and implies for the rest.[66]

Hamilcar's triumphal parades would probably be ritual proces-sions through the streets, perhaps from the *agora* up to Byrsa and the temple of Eshmun with its sixty-step stairway, to show off to citizens and to the gods the booty and chief captives from his campaigns – a practice common enough in eastern lands like Assyria and Egypt, and indeed not unlike the Roman triumph. As it happens, Polybius mentions a similar parade – which he calls a *thriambos*, Greek for *triumphus* – staged at the end of another great African revolt, two and half centuries later in 237, when the victorious Hamilcar Barca had the captured rebel leader led through the city by young Carthaginians 'inflicting every torment' on him. A story is told by Polyaenus about Gisco, a Carthaginian leader recalled from exile in 341, who humiliated his defeated political enemies by placing his foot on their necks as they lay prostrate in chains: a gesture perhaps imitated from Pharaonic Egypt. But the idea that this was also what a general did during his victory procession is just a guess. Gisco, Polyaenus adds, then forgave his foes (pharaohs usually had theirs flayed).[67]

The Magonids must often have been absent from the city; yet despite this and their intermittent, but sometimes serious, military defeats, they remained in control for decade after decade. The family obviously had strength in numbers. Mago had his two sons, each of whom had three of their own, and after them came further descendants. Other kinsmen, like the relatives of their wives and the husbands of any daughters, and non-kin supporters – especially among the *adirim* – can be supposed. Interlocking relationships of blood, wealth and political benefits would help explain the strength of the dynasty and its ability to recover from setbacks. Both Hamilcar, who perished in 480, and his brother Hasdrubal who had died earlier left three sons each, all of whom (Justin tells us) together ran the affairs of Carthage from then on. If Justin does not exaggerate, this may have been achieved through sharing out, and taking turns in, the available appointments – as sufetes, generals, priests and heads of pentarchies (if these existed by then). In practice only five of them must have done so, for Diodorus mentions that one of Hamilcar's three, another Gisco, was exiled as a punishment after Himera. Even so it was a remarkable achievement for the others to collaborate in seeming harmony over some decades, while at the same time placating the rest of the city's leading families whose share of effective power was held back.

The next generation of Magonid ascendancy was when Carthage finally cut off the yearly tribute to her Libyan neighbours and set about imposing a steadily growing hegemony over them instead. Justin claims a wide, and not entirely plausible, range of conflicts in Africa: the 'Africans' forced to give up receiving tribute, war waged with the Numidians, and hostilities even against the *Mauri* or Mauretanians (who dwelt in Morocco). Trouble with the lords and minor kings of eastern Numidia's peoples was probably inevitable as Carthaginian dominance spread westward, for there was no firm or sharp border, ethnic or physical, between Libya and Numidia. By contrast, the only clashes feasible with any Mauri would be by sea, in defence of Carthaginian trading-posts or colonies. No other evidence exists for clashes, but it was noted earlier how Justin's claim may connect with the expedition recorded in Hanno's *Periplus*. Meanwhile conflict in Sicily was very sensibly avoided, whereas trade prospered. When Syracuse under Gelon's brother and successor Hieron joined the Italian Greek city of Cumae, near Naples, in war against the Carthaginians' old allies the Etruscans and beat them soundly in 474 in a sea battle off Cumae, Carthage stayed neutral.

Magonid rule during the 5th Century thus developed Carthage's strengths at home and over areas that she could dominate. It was pointed out above that the older view of stagnation and economic regress during the century has had to be revised. Indeed by 415, when Syracuse was menaced by Athens, one proposal put to the Syracusans was to seek help from the Carthaginians because 'they have acquired great amounts of gold and silver' – though the suggestion got nowhere and the Carthaginians not long after proved more than happy to enrich themselves some more with Sicilian plunder, on a massive scale.

Inevitably there would be critics and opponents, led by men or families who failed to win the share of offices and other appointments (to priesthoods, pentarchies and military commands) that they felt they deserved. After Himera, even though the dead Hamilcar's memory was revered, his son Gisco was exiled in punishment for the defeat, dying at Selinus in western Sicily, a city with strong Carthaginian connections at the time. All the same, with brothers and cousins at the head of affairs, Gisco's fate seems puzzling. Perhaps he was the only other Magonid with Hamilcar at the defeat and was singled out to be the scapegoat, whom his kinsmen could reject so as to retain the family's grip on the state. Certainly his son Hannibal did not suffer lasting damage: in the later part of the 5th Century first he and then his cousin Himilco (whose father Hanno 'the *rb*' was, it seems, Gisco's brother) became the dominant figures leading the state and commanding its armies.

THE END OF THE MAGONIDS

What prompted the renewed aggressiveness in Sicily from 409 on is not clear. Diodorus puts it down to Hannibal son of Gisco's thirst for revenge against the Greeks who had defeated his grandfather at Himera – a rather limited motive, even if shared by his fellow citizens.

The damage recently inflicted on Syracuse by the disastrous Athenian invasion of 415–413 may have made eastern Sicily look attractively weak. Still, Acragas, which had a thriving trade with Carthage, was mercilessly sacked and razed in 406 (Acragas' tyrant too had fought at Himera). The inscription about the sack has already been quoted (Chapter VII). Possibly too Hannibal and Himilco, descendants of three generations of military high achievers, had as yet no military successes of their own, a problem for a dynasty much of whose claim to leadership relied on distinction in warfare.

The Sicilian wars of 409–405 and 397–396 were the last led by Magonids, though only the first in a long series fought against Syracuse and her allies over a century and a half. The victories won by the cousins had their costs – the most notable and ironic of them being the end of Magonid power itself. Hannibal, after unusually ferocious campaigns that included destroying temples and tombs, perished of the plague in 406. Similar sacrileges a decade later supposedly brought about the ruin of Himilco's expedition against Syracuse and its allies, forcing him to make a shameful peace, abandon his non-citizen troops, and return to Carthage with the citizen remnants of his disease-stricken army. There, shunned by all, he starved himself to death.

It was most likely after his spectacular downfall that the court of One Hundred and Four was established (cf. Chapter III). An earlier start is just possible; since its purpose was to discipline generals who had misbehaved on campaign, the court could conceivably date to the 470s following Himera. Gisco's exile as punishment for his father's debacle at Himera might seem to support this; but his brothers and cousins were still in power then. Arguably they might feel they had to accept the creation of the One Hundred and Four to placate their fellow citizens, but Gisco could be exiled by other methods (as Mazeus had been), whereas such a court would have remained a standing threat to the family. It is hard to see them agreeing to it, and in fact it would have had nothing much to do for the next eighty years.

Although Justin announces the court before Himilco's catastrophe, his epitome is oddly wilful at this stage. He does not report how the Sicilian Greeks defeated Gisco's father in 480 but merely that he was killed in battle, then claims that 'Himilco' succeeded him in Sicily. Having thus got Himilco's time wrong, Justin entirely ignores his and Hannibal's campaigns from 409 to 405 even though their most notable act was the sack of the greatest city in Greek Sicily apart from Syracuse. He is equally mute about the resulting rise to power of Dionysius I at Syracuse, a tyrant who proved to be one of Carthage's most enduring adversaries. Later on he claims that Dionysius was finally murdered by his own supporters – confusing him with his son-in-law Dion, who later ended the tyranny of Diony-sius' son but fell victim to treacherous friends.

These errors and omissions are Justin's own doing. A separately surviving contents list of the books of Trogus' history shows that Trogus did narrate the sack of Acragas and other cities, followed by Dionysius' rise. Justin's erratic presentation here is a warning that his seemingly early start for the new court does not prove such a date. Carthage's avoidance of overseas wars for decades after 480, and her successful imposition of hegemony over her Libyan neigh-bours, would hardly account for a court being established to try failed generals. Even the disgraced Himilco was not prosecuted in 396, though he would have been a prime candidate and he lived some miserable weeks, even months, at home before taking his own life. It seems likeliest that the court of One Hundred and Four was set up at some point after this, but still long enough before Aristo-tle's time for the philosopher to be impressed by its status, powers and range.[68]

THE ASCENDANCY OF HANNO
'THE GREAT'

Himilco's successor Mago in Sicily had been his fleet commander (presumably his 'second' or subordinate general, *rb šny*: cf. Chapter III), who is not described as a relative. Vigorous and resourceful, Mago quelled the great Libyan rebellion of 396, then returned to Sicily in 393 to carry on the war with Dionysius and reach a peace the following year which left Carthage dominant over the western half of the island. When a new war was provoked by Dionysius in 383, Mago was killed in battle – the date is uncertain, but most likely in 382 or 381 – to be replaced as general by his son. (A story told by Polyaenus about a 'Himilco' may, but more likely does not, involve this son whose name is not known.) The new general defeated the Syracusans and made a favourable peace with Dionysius, only to disappear from the record afterwards. By mid-century the leading men at Carthage were certainly not of the old dominant family. Carthaginian politics had entered a new and more fluid state.

These new leaders were Hanno – already mentioned as the man eventually accused of plotting a coup – and his enemy 'Suniatus', a

Latin form of *'Šmnytn,* Eshmuniaton. This was not the first time that political rivalries had erupted at Carthage (Mazeus and his opponents being the most obvious predecessors), but for the first time both men were virtual equals in status and influence. Hanno was appointed 'war leader', which must mean general, against the ageing Dionysius in 368, which indicates a high military reputation. But Eshmuniaton, according to Justin at any rate, was 'the most powerful of the Carthaginians at that time'. In due course, having got rid of his rival, Hanno is called by Justin 'the foremost (*princeps*) of the Carthaginians'.

He had first proved his military capacities in the late 370s, when the Libyans took advantage of a severe epidemic afflicting their Carthaginian overlords to rebel again: Hanno repressed them. This looks, too, like what the contents list of Trogus' history sums up as 'the campaigns of Hanno the Great in Africa', in the context of Dionysius' last years – campaigns which Justin leaves out. Their date must be earlier than 368 when Hanno was given military command against the tyrant of Syracuse. In this short-lived Sicilian war he showed dash and resourcefulness enough to impel Dionysius to accept an armistice. That effectively ended matters, as the tyrant then died, although a formal peace took longer to arrange.

The contents list of Trogus' history calls this Hanno *magnus,* 'the great'. No other source does, but as it happens two other Hannos – in the later 3rd and mid-2nd Centuries – have the same term applied to them in Greek (*megas*) by Appian and by Zonaras (a Byzantine whose work abbreviates the Roman historian Cassius Dio). It is usually interpreted as a translation of *rab,* the 'chief' of an official body or an army. Yet so many Carthaginians are styled *rab* on inscriptions down the centuries that it would be strange to find it applied by foreign writers to just these three, and by only a few writers at that. Moreover the father of Himilco the Magonid, another Hanno, is officially termed 'the *rab*' on the Punic inscription recording Himilco's and Hannibal's sack of Acragas, yet no ancient author calls him *megas* or *magnus.*

Besides this, the term is ignored by, or is not known to, most Greek and Roman sources: not only Justin but also Aristotle, Polybius, Diodorus, Livy and Polyaenus (who mentions quite a few Hannos). It looks, then, as though the writers who bestow the epithet on the three Hannos drew it indirectly from a separate historical tradition. Quite possibly this was a biographical record, for as mentioned earlier, Carthaginian aristocrats paid attention to family ties and genealogies. This could suggest too that all three belonged to the same family. Whether *megas* and *magnus* do translate *rab*, or an inherited family sobriquet of some sort, can hardly be decided.

This first Hanno 'the Great' had a brilliant yet ultimately disastrous career. After his success in Africa and his appointment as general in Sicily, he destroyed his powerful rival Eshmuniaton by having him convicted of treasonable contacts with Dionysius. Eshmuniaton was no doubt put to death, as Hanno himself would later be. Justin claims that because 'Suniatus' had written to Dionysius in Greek, the senate decreed a ban on studying or speaking Greek. This is exaggerated at best, and a fiction at worst, for Carthage's dealings with the Greek world went on as normal. There is no report of her Greek residents being expelled, for instance; and Dion of Syracuse kept up his friendships with various Carthaginians – at one point being criticised for writing privately to the city authorities there (no doubt to the sufetes, and probably in Greek). If there is anything behind the story, it may be that by 368 some Carthaginians did feel bitter towards Sicilian Greeks and their ways after forty years of repeated wars. This one, the fifth since 409, was an unprovoked aggression by Syracuse. So at any rate Diodorus states, and so it must have looked from Carthage. The sense of outrage, even if short-lived, might be strong enough for Hanno to manipulate it to his political advantage.

Eshmuniaton's ruin may have been achieved through the senate or, more likely, by arraignment before a sufete (the *adirim* had no judicial authority that we know of, and his case does not look like one which the court of One Hundred and Four would judge). With him gone, Hanno and his supporters now had the upper hand. Their opponents continued to be strong, all the same, while Hanno's grandiosely showy way of life probably turned other Carthaginians against him. Two stories told about an arrogant Hanno seem to mean him: first, Pliny the Elder writes that a Hanno, 'one of the most distinguished Carthaginians', so skilfully tamed a lion as a pet that his persuasive powers were judged a threat to the city's freedom and he was put to death for treason. A later Greek author, Aelian, offers a still more imaginative story of a Hanno training birds to chant 'Hanno is a god', only to find that, when set free to spread this message, they went back to their usual cries instead. Both stories look made up, but the import of both is that this Hanno was rich and arrogant and his fellow citizens thought him dangerously ambitious.

Hanno 'the Great' certainly was brought down by them when convicted of plotting a coup d'état. The account in Justin is detailed though not wholly satisfactory (Trogus' original probably did better). Some time around 350, Hanno allegedly plotted to seize power by murdering all the *adirim* at his daughter's wedding banquet. The scheme was discovered but, too powerful to be prosecuted, he was foiled instead by a decree banning all such public feasts. Undeterred, he tried to bring on a slave revolt; he was foiled again. Now he retired with twenty thousand slave supporters to a 'fort' – it was shown earlier that Justin probably means his country estate – but failed to attract help from the Libyans and a Numidian king (Justin writes a king of the 'Mauri', but they were impossibly distant). He was captured, mutilated gruesomely, and crucified, while Justin claims that his entire family was executed too. This is exaggerated, for at least one son, Gisco, was simply exiled.[69]

As usual with a résumé, especially one by Justin, much is left unexplained: what prompted Hanno to try a coup if he was already so powerful, why he seems in the story to have no citizen supporters outside his own family, how he organised the slave revolt – which, despite being foiled, still raised thousands of followers for his last stand – and how the successful resistance against him was organised. The account is obviously a version coloured to absolve the rest of Carthage's élite from any association with the miscreant. An attempted coup by a Hanno did occur before the 330s, for Aristotle mentions it. He implies, too, that there was indeed a faction backing it. He does not date the event, but his Hanno must be Hanno 'the Great', for otherwise we would have to suppose two separate Hannos in two different periods, both of them powerful men, who each tried and failed to make himself master of the city.

It looks as though Hanno and his supporters overreached themselves – perhaps through trying to monopolise the sufeteship and other offices while prosecuting opponents like Eshmuniaton, and courting popularity with lavish displays and gifts – and as a consequence the resulting tensions finally broke out into conflict. Whether or not Hanno did plot a mass murder of his senatorial enemies, he could readily be accused of it (just as more than one alleged enemy of Rome would be accused of scheming to slaughter the entire Roman senate). In turn he perhaps did flee to his country estate with a body of supporters, not necessarily just slaves, while Justin's twenty thousand should be estimated downwards to a couple of thousand at most. By force or intimidation, he was captured and the movement collapsed. Whichever faction won this round – Eshmuniaton's or another – the upheaval unveils further the levels of competitive tension in Carthaginian public life as the century advanced. Nor would it be the last such drama.

The competition and tensions must have been connected, partly at least, to the city's increasing power and wealth, together with the stresses of repeated, large-scale and costly wars with Syracuse (now a major power too) and from the restive Libyans. In the 370s Carthage even intervened briefly in southern Italy, while in 348 she made a second, updated treaty with the Roman republic, also increasingly powerful in the central Mediterranean (Chapter X). In 344 the internal wars convulsing the Sicilian Greeks encouraged her to make a vigorous new effort to extend her dominance over the island (Chapter IX). The rewards, risks and enticements of political success would sharpen the conflicts among ambitious aristocrats, occasionally even to the point of violence as in Hanno's case. Not that violence was inevitable: when military setbacks in Sicily led to the exiled Gisco being recalled in 341 and elected general, reportedly he celebrated his victory over his family's foes only in the symbolic way mentioned earlier, by placing his foot on their prostrate necks in public.

The renewed warfare launched in 344 looks like the work of Hanno the Great's victorious opponents. They would certainly have a need for military success to bolster their position. Defeats undid them instead. One general, Mago, killed himself to avoid being prosecuted (his resentful fellow citizens crucified his corpse). His successors were completely beaten at the river Crimisus in 341, a disaster where no fewer than 3000 citizen soldiers were lost – all of them, we are told, from aristocratic families. It was this debacle that brought Gisco back, and the necks which he symbolically trod on may have included those of the disgraced generals. Whether so or not, his recall marked a triumph over the opposing faction or factions.

POLITICS AND WAR IN THE LATE
4TH CENTURY: BOMILCAR'S PUTSCH

Gisco was able to make a fairly good peace with the Sicilians, which will have confirmed his effective supremacy in the republic. As time passed, however, the competition between factions or individuals became more evenly balanced, to judge from Aristotle's view in the 330s that Carthage's political system was mostly admirable. Gisco's conciliatory attitude seems to have lasted, while at the same time his family remained prominent. This pleasing state of affairs lasted some twenty years, encouraged no doubt by concern over the momentous developments in the east: Alexander the Great's extraordinarily fast conquest of the Persian empire, his sacking of Carthage's mother city Tyre – an ordeal witnessed by Carthaginian envoys to the sacred rites of Melqart there – and the annexation of Egypt, with whom Carthage shared the centuries-old frontier set by the brothers Philaenus.

The Carthaginians watched these events carefully, avoiding domestic discord if only because new civil dissensions would make them look an easy further target for Alexander. As Phoenician descendants and off-and-on foes of Greek Sicily they might count as extra prey. Besides, they welcomed Tyrian women and children sent to them for safety. Reportedly they sent an agent named Hamilcar to pose as an exile and win entry to Alexander's entourage so as to keep Carthage informed on his doings – but it was the king himself who told their envoys at Tyre to take home the warning that he had plans to march in Carthage's direction eventually. His death in 323 and the disruption of his empire eased their worries. Several generations of in-fighting among the empire's successor states followed, including Egypt under its new Greek pharaohs, the Ptolemies. (Incidentally, the suspicious Carthaginians put their agent to death on his return, claiming that he had intended to betray the city to Alexander.) By then, Carthage was concerned at developments in Sicily that, in the end, would bring down a near-catastrophe on her in Africa.[70]

Ironically the republic played a part in the revived truculence of Syracuse, now the most powerful state in the island, by first opposing and then helping the unscrupulous populist leader Agathocles to become its effective ruler – ironically, because Carthage's dominant faction more than once showed itself anxious not to fight a new war in Sicily. No fewer than four times – around 325, in 319, 315 and then 314 – she intervened in the Syracusan and Sicilian Greeks' squabbles to persuade the antagonists to patch up agreements. None was lasting, yet there seems to have been no serious opposition to this sensible approach to Sicilian affairs. Only when Agathocles in 312 went back on the spirit of the third agreement did frustration affect Carthaginian politics. The general commanding in Sicily since at least 319, another Hamilcar, was then accused by both his fellow citizens and also Carthage's Sicilian allies of betraying his city's interests – even of seeking Agathocles' help to make himself master of Carthage. Resentment plainly ran high. Hamilcar was convicted in a secret hearing without his knowledge and only then recalled, but died before he could be punished. Justin claims that the senate found him guilty, but this is probably a mistake for the court of One Hundred and Four (which consisted of senators).

His replacement was Hamilcar son of Gisco, 'one of the most distinguished' Carthaginians according to Diodorus. The two men might seem political rivals, given that the first Hamilcar's shabby treatment benefited the second. But it is possible instead that the first Hamilcar lost the trust even of his own faction when the policy of restraint in Sicily backfired, for an item in Justin suggests that the two Hamilcars were connected by blood or else had been allies. One of the generals commanding in Libya three years later, the Bomilcar who afterwards attempted a coup but failed, died on the cross denouncing his fellow citizens for repeated injustices towards past leaders – allegedly false charges against Hanno 'the Great', Gisco's exile, and the secret verdict on 'his uncle Hamilcar'. The second Hamilcar, son of Gisco, had recently been killed at Syracuse and did not form part of this litany. But for Bomilcar to link himself and his uncle with Hanno and Gisco suggests at least a political association between them all, and maybe kinship too, while the second Hamilcar was Gisco's son and Hanno's grandson.

By contrast, the other general appointed with Bomilcar against the Syracusan invasion was a family enemy, Hanno – because, says Diodorus, the Carthaginians saw such rivalry as a guarantee against either man becoming a danger to the state. With the city on the verge of disaster at Agathocles' hands, this reasoning seems more of a recipe for state suicide than for survival; nor was it ever tested, since Hanno was soon killed in battle. It seems just as likely that Carthage's two main factions or rival families joined forces to present a united front in the crisis, but that Bomilcar's failed coup after Hanno's death prompted a later notion that they had been jointly appointed to prevent precisely such an attempt. But the fact that family reasons made the two men political rivals shows that factional politics had indeed endured down the decades, even if on the whole Hanno the Great's family and their friends kept the upper hand.

What tempted Bomilcar to his putsch? Perhaps he feared that his political group was losing its pre-eminence in the city's affairs, or at least in its military affairs – with his uncle secretly convicted and recalled, the other Hamilcar defeated, captured and shamefully killed at Syracuse, and he himself required to join hands with his long-standing opponent. More personally, he may well have feared being prosecuted over the defeat which had cost Hanno his life, while at the same time being encouraged by the acquisition of power recently won by so many generals overseas: not only Agathocles in

Sicily but Alexander the Great's marshals in the east, including Ptolemy I over in Egypt. Incidentally, both Diodorus and Justin claim (with slightly differing details) that he had ideas even of joining forces with Agathocles. It may be that Bomilcar, like his uncle, thought that Carthage should try to live at peace, so far as possible, with Syracuse rather than carry on wars which either ended in stalemate or, as at present, threatened disaster; and that he was the best person to bring this about.

The putsch failed, all the same, because he lacked enough support. Although the military situation gave him the excuse for mustering his forces in Megara, he could rely on a mere 500 citizen soldiers and 1000 mercenaries for the attempt to seize the *agora*, no doubt along with the senate house and other key buildings. Diodorus says that he 'proclaimed himself tyrant', which of course corresponds to no Punic word. It may mean that Bomilcar declared himself sole sufete and general (or chief general), or even perhaps borrowed the Greek term *strategos autokrator*, 'supreme general' – the standard title taken by Sicilian Greek leaders bent on tyranny. If he hoped to overawe his fellow citizens he was badly mistaken. Their reaction proved his lack of wide support. After initial panic, 'the young men gathered and, forming up in ranks, attacked the tyrant', who was driven out of the old city back into the new. Then with 'all the citizens coming together under arms', the putschists, cornered on a Megara hilltop, capitulated under promise of amnesty. Bomilcar alone was tortured to death in the middle of the *agora*, no doubt in ways reminiscent of the execution of Hanno 'the Great'. It was there, in Justin's telling, that he denounced the Carthaginians for how they had treated Hanno and the others.

Three generals were next appointed, all it seems of equal rank: Himilco, Adherbal and another Hanno, and during 307 the Greek invasion – which had for a time mastered virtually the entire Libyan interior and even taken Utica and Hippacra – ignominiously collapsed. It is not at all probable that the new generals came from the faction, still less the family, of Hanno the Great and Gisco, unless somehow its survivors managed with amazing speed to shake off any association with Bomilcar and keep out the friends and supporters of Bomilcar's late colleague and foe Hanno. More likely it was this Hanno's group that benefited from the abortive coup, while whatever was left of Hanno the Great's and Gisco's was badly hurt at least.[71]

Disappointingly, political life at Carthage falls into virtual darkness for most of the next six decades, as our already limited

Greek and Latin sources turn their attention to other states. It can be surmised that powerful families – including ones newly risen to prominence – and their circles of supporters continued competing for office at every level. If, as suggested earlier, the supposed nickname *magnus* or *megas* misunderstands some kind of Punic family epithet, then Hanno the Great's family was not obliterated or barred forever from public life, for during the 240s one of the city's leading figures was another Hanno the Great, according to Appian. All the same, the lengthy parade of Carthaginian generals and admirals again recorded from the 280s to the early 240s – bearing the usual handful of personal names – are bereft of known political links. It is more likely than not that by the time of the first war with Rome, the ruling élite included not only long-established factional groups but more recently-arrived ones. In the politics of the years that followed, while the second Hanno the Great would play a major part, at some stage before 250 the family of another Hamilcar, nicknamed Barca, came to prominence too.

THE LIBYANS AND NUMIDIANS

In the 4th and early 3rd Centuries Carthaginian rule over inland Libya extended a good distance up the Bagradas valley, to judge from the invading Greeks' capture of Thugga in 307 ('Tocae' in Diodorus), a hundred and twenty kilometres west of Carthage. Diodorus names quite a number of towns in the hinterlands of Libya and Numidia affected by the operations of Agathocles and his lieutenants in 309–307, but in contrast to identifiable places on the coast – like Utica, Hippacra and Hadrumetum – all except Thugga are in Greek forms otherwise unknown: Phelline, Meschela, Miltine, Acris and a few others. It is pretty certain, though, that the lands lying between the Bagradas and Byzacium were equally under Carthage's power, and so too the territory north of the Bagradas: the highlands of the Monts de la Méjerda (or Kroumirie) and of Mogod near Hippacra. On the other hand, Sicca 175 kilometres south-west of Carthage, Theveste south-west of Sicca and 260 kilometres from Carthage, and districts in between like the territories of Mactar and Zama, were not brought under her hegemony, it seems, until the mid-3rd Century (Chapter X).

There was little if any ethnic difference between the Libyans, meaning the communities ruled by Carthage, and the Numidians to their west. The Greek notion that Numidians were so named because they were nomads was a fancy, for the name was indigenous (a community called the Nemadi still lives in Mauritania). Both Libyans and Numidians were a mixture of small settled communities and pastoral rural dwellers, though pastoral and semi-nomadic life was more prevalent than the settled form the farther west one travelled from Carthage. Libya was dotted with villages and rather larger fortified centres separated by pastures, cultivated tracts and woodlands which spread across hills, plateaux, valleys and the Méjerda range, the Téboursouk range (the southern side of the Bagradas valley) and the Zaghouan range (separating the gulf of Hammamet from the interior). From the edges of Libya to the river Muluccha (today the Moulouya, just east of the port of Melilla) were the Numidian lands, with Mauretania beyond them. The Libyan mountains are spurs of the great Atlas complex that extends westwards across Numidia and Mauretania, forming a series of parallel ranges separated by high plateaux and valleys, while the Sahara lies to their south.

Carthage's Libyan territories were not much larger than the island of Sicily and, it seems, were equally well populated. The Libyans were hard-working and productive, while the Carthaginians' inter-mittent practice of settling citizens in the countryside with substan-tial land grants probably furthered the territories' economic development (and perhaps population). It seems that they consisted of a number of regions, each termed an *'rst* (approximately pronounced *ereset*). A Neo-Punic inscription of 128 BC near Mactar, a region seized by the Numidian king Masinissa before 150, commemorates a kinsman of his, *Wlbh*, who was 'governor (or administrator: *'š 'l*) of the *'rst* of *Tšk't* ' or Thusca, while Appian mentions that this region covered fifty towns. Thusca and some other Libyan areas in Roman times were termed *pagi* ('rural districts' in Latin), for a dedication in the 50s BC at Utica mentions three named Muxsi, Gususi and Zeugei, while in AD 113 the emperor Trajan was honoured by 'the 64 communities of *pagus* Thusca and Gunzuzi [no doubt another spelling of Gususi]'. As it happens, some Carthaginian coins struck for use in Sicily during the First Punic War bear the legend *b'rst*, 'for the region' or, on another view, 'for the lands', meaning the Sicilian territories dominated by Carthage.

Thusca's region, Gunzuzi's, and the others mentioned are usually seen as the main administrative subdivisions of Carthaginian-ruled Libya, along with the Cape Bon peninsula, Byzacium, and sometimes the 'Great Plains' around Bulla in the west, even though these are not recorded as *'rst* or *pagi*. On the other hand, still more *pagi* are found in Libya and Numidia in Roman times, including much smaller ones. There were, for example, 'the *pagus* and *civitas* [district and civic community] of Thugga'; one at Uchi, 10 kilometres from Thugga; a *pagus Gurzensis* in 12 BC with many *civitates* near Hadrumetum and thus within Byzacium; a *pagus Minervius* near Hippacra, and others in the territory of Sicca far to the west of Carthage.

The *'rṣt* of Thusca, Gunzuzi, Muxsi and Zeugei were perhaps traditional Libyan regions, and so too *pagus Gurzensis*. Not all the names can be explained, though 'Gurzensis' was named from a town called Gurza near Hadrumetum, and Zeugei possibly from the town of Ziqua (Zaghouan). In Roman times, at least, their communities could act together for ceremonial purposes. They perhaps shared local religious rites and events. But that they were administrative units, even if just for tax purposes, should be doubted. A Numidian royal could be appointed to govern one (hardly anything less would suit his rank) without this offering firm evidence for Carthaginian practice. Nor does a Roman law of 111 BC, regulating among other things the tax and other financial arrangements for the recently-annexed *provincia Africa*, mention any large administrative units. Once Libya became a province, however, followed a century later by Numidia, the Latin *pagus* could come into use for a wide range of territorial districts, large and small, in both.

Carthage's administrative districts in Libya were more likely smaller, with several in each of the *'rṣt*, to judge from the Thusca--Gunzuzi and *pagus Gurzensis* inscriptions. Each district would embrace various towns and villages and each, perhaps, had an administrator called an *'š 'l* or *ishal* – a Phoenician term, though not found in Carthaginian documents. These officials need not always have been Carthaginians, for as time passed there would be a growing élite of Punicised Libyans too. They would report to the treasurers (*mḥšbm*) at Carthage, or to a general commanding in Libya when there was one. Carthaginian tax-collecting was often harsh: the 3rd-Century Hanno the Great earned a grim reputation for his methods, no doubt loyally imitated by the putative *'š 'l* in every Libyan district.[72]

By the mid-3rd Century, as mentioned earlier on Polybius' evidence, Libyan taxes and produce enabled the city to maintain her armaments and wage wars. The Libyans also furnished recruits, willing or conscripted, for Carthage's armies. Herodotus includes Libyan troops, presumably paid recruits, as early as 480 in the army defeated at Himera, while by the Barcid Hannibal's time Libyan conscripts formed one of the most reliable corps in his army. The one indicator of what Libya paid in taxes is that, as the stressful First Punic War of 264–241 wore on, the Carthaginians took half of all rural produce and doubled the money taxes of the towns. If the agricultural tribute too was doubled over its pre-war level, that earlier level would have been one-quarter, but this is not certain. A widespread level of taxation on produce in ancient and later times was the tithe, a 10 per cent levy: this was applied in the territories of Syracuse in the 3rd Century, was extended to the rest of Sicily by the island's Roman rulers, and was generally viewed as a fair level which did not obstruct prosperity. The normal tax on Libyan agriculture must have been higher, since it aroused so much repeated resentment – Diodorus writes that Agathocles in 310 expected support from the Libyans for this reason – and may be estimated at around 15 per cent. No doubt it rose further whenever Carthage needed more revenues, nor would the first war with Rome be the sole, or the earliest, time that it rose to fully half the yearly output.

It need not follow, either, that the towns' pre-war taxes had been a quarter of townsmen's overall incomes, for it is very unlikely that these now had to give up half their entire income. Such a proportion in the ancient world (and of course even today) would be an unsustainable burden on most of the population. The taxes levied on towns could range between 10 and 15 per cent without wrecking their local economies – but could rocket to twice that when their overlord was hard pressed for funds.

The Carthaginians' often high-handed treatment of their Libyan subjects repeatedly provoked rebellion. It happened in 396 after the disastrous campaign in Sicily, when much of the army perished from plague and its commander Himilco abandoned the rest to bring home his surviving citizen soldiers. A fresh rebellion followed in the 370s, again a time when the Carthaginians were weakened by a severe epidemic. Two generations later Agathocles' invasion of North Africa from 309 to 307 encouraged a new revolt (just as he hoped) because, as Diodorus puts it, the Libyans 'hated the Carthaginians with a special bitterness because of the weight of their overlordship'.

Libya did grow in prosperity in spite of this treatment. The other major factor enticing Agathocles to invade North Africa was the wealth of its countryside: a feature confirmed by the amount of plunder garnered both near the coast and in the interior. Sixty-six years later, when the Libyans rebelled yet one more time against the extortionate treatment meted out to them in the First Punic War, enthusiasm was so great (writes Polybius) that women too contributed all that they could, even their jewellery. Jewellery would come only from more affluent levels of Libyan society. There is no way of reckoning what that proportion of the population was, but all the Libyans' contributions together put enough funds into the rebel leaders' hands for them to finance a major war against Carthage.

After putting down this revolt (it took three harrowing years: Chapter X), the Carthaginians seem at last to have improved their relations with their subjects. When the Romans invaded Libyan territory three and a half decades later, plundering and ravaging much in the style of Agathocles, no defections to them are reported. Similarly, Carthage's sister colony Utica joined the great rebellion in 238, yet remained stubbornly loyal under a long Roman siege from 204 to 202. If the tax regime and conscription burden was now lighter, one reason could be that the Carthaginians realised they needed to conciliate their Libyphoenician allies and Libyan subjects. Another would be the conquest of southern Spain from 237 on, which created a new and rich source of revenues – rich enough to sustain Carthage's great-power ambitions and a new war with Rome without a renewed crushing burden on Libya. In 149 too, when the Romans went to war to destroy Carthage, most Libyans were more loyal than some of the Libyphoenicians like Utica, Hadrumetum and certain other coastal towns, which defected to the invaders. The rest of the Libyans and Libyphoenicians surrendered only three years later, when the city faced the final Roman assault (Chapter XII).[73]

Over the centuries, Carthaginian influences did leave an imprint on Libya. No doubt too there were Libyan influences on Carthaginian culture, even if the evidence is now sparse. The Carthaginians who periodically settled among them, the Libyans' own dealings with the city and – no doubt another important factor – so many Libyan soldiers' service with Carthaginian armies over three centuries, would all contribute to these outcomes.

The evidence for Carthage's impact dates mostly from after the fall of the city. For example, Neo-Punic and Latin inscriptions commmemorate local sufetes at many places in both Libya and eastern Numidia. At Carthage herself, votive inscriptions were set up by sufetes from unknown towns called *Glmt* and *Phls* (one of them Kerkouane, perhaps?). An inscription of 139 at Thugga, honouring the late Numidian king Masinissa, terms his Numidian grandfather Zilalsan 'the sufete': so if Zilalsan had been elected – maybe as an honour – to the sufeteship there, Thugga must have adopted the Carthaginian magistracy for itself by the mid-3rd Century at latest. This is only a possibility, all the same, for the grandee Zilalsan may (just possibly) have been accorded a sufeteship or its honorary title at Carthage herself, rather than at up-country Thugga. Sufetes are, however, attested after the fall of Carthage at quite a number of places, such as Thinissut, Curubis and Siagu in or near the Cape Bon region. The citizens, *b'lm*, of towns sometimes earn mention too. The inscription at Thugga, for example, records a temple being set up by them to Masinissa, who had annexed the region decades earlier and whose son Micipsa now ruled them. To a degree, therefore, official institutions from Carthage were imitated at many centres across Libya and, in time, further west too.[74]

Carthaginian names became common among Libyans and Numidians: one of Masinissa's sons was named Mastanabal (he was father of Rome's later enemy Jugurtha), one of Micipsa's an Adherbal, while the officials of *pagus Gurzensis* in Byzacium all bear Carthaginian names – Hamilcar son of Milkyaton, 'Boncar' (Bomilcar) son of Hasdrubal, Muttunbal son of Safon. Carthaginian gods and goddesses, notably Baal Hammon, Tanit (often with her visual 'sign'), Astarte and also Isis, Demeter and Kore, had numerous shrines and offerings. Most strikingly of all, the Punic language flourished in both Libya and Numidia for centuries after 146, with St Augustine mentioning its use among rural folk even in the last half-century of Roman Africa.

Numidia's many peoples had had dealings with the Phoenicians and Carthaginians from very old times. Carthaginian trade-settlements like Hippo Regius, Rusicade, Icosium and Iol dotted the coast not only as entrepôts for Numidian trade but as way-stations for ships en route to or from the far west. The Numidian people formed two broad tribal groups, the Masaesyli dwelling in the west and centre, the Massyli in the east, each with district and clan sub-groups. Until the 4th or even 3rd Century, most Numidians lived in rural settlements and were proverbial for their itinerant way of life, with movable huts (Latinised as *mapalia*) of brushwood, twigs and leaves. They pastured flocks, and also their famous small horses which made Numidian cavalry the best in the western Mediterranean. A few more substantial centres came into being perhaps in the 4th Century: notably Cirta in a commanding position over a deep gorge of the river Ampsaga, which became the Massylians' capital, and Siga the Masaesylians', just inland from the coast 900 kilometres to the west.

Carthage never subdued the Numidians, despite fighting plenty of wars against them as well as regularly recruiting them for overseas campaigns. Carthaginian culture, on the other hand, began to exert influence there in the 3rd Century at latest, most notably on Numidian chieftains and their retinues. Not only did the Massylian prince Zilalsan bear the title of sufete, in whatever connection, but his grandson Masinissa spent his boyhood being educated at Carthage. During his fifty-five-year reign, from 203 to 148, Masinissa made Punic the language of government, introduced Carthaginian methods of administration, gave some of his sons Carthaginian names as just noted, and adopted features of Carthaginian religion – one of his great-grandsons is found with the priestly title of 'awakener of the god' (of Melqart, that is) in a late-2nd-Century Neo-Punic inscription. As we have seen, more than one marriage between Numidian princes and the daughters of aristocratic Carthaginians is known. Indeed even one of the city's last generals, Hasdrubal, was a grandson on his mother's side of the prolific Masinissa. It has already been noted, too, that the Numidian royal family were given Carthage's libraries by Scipio Aemilianus. Ironically enough, the expanded Numidian kingdom after 146 inherited, and propagated, the culture of the city whose destruction Masinissa played a major part in procuring.

IX

CARTHAGE AT WAR: SICILY

THE CARTHAGINIAN WAR MACHINE: THE NAVY

It was firmly held by Greeks and Romans, and is still widely believed, that throughout her military history Carthage focused her own energies on seamanship and hired foreign professionals to man her armies. Polybius reflects this conviction when comparing Carthaginian and Roman war-making:

> Whereas for a naval expedition the Carthaginians are the better trained and prepared – as it is only natural with a people with whom it has been hereditary for many generations to practise this craft, and to follow the seaman's trade above all nations in the world – yet, in regard to military service on land, the Romans train themselves to a much higher pitch than the Carthaginians. The former bestow their whole attention upon this department: whereas the Carthaginians wholly neglect their infantry, though they do take some slight interest in the cavalry. The reason of this is that they employ foreign mercenaries, the Romans native and citizen levies. [...] The result is that even if the Romans have suffered a defeat at first, they renew the war to the fullest, which the Carthaginians cannot do.

This is Greek generalised theorising and nothing more. Polybius' own narrative of the First Punic War proves that the Carthaginians were as tenacious as the Romans; and since he was interested in Agathocles, he should have known something of their earlier wars in

Sicily, in which they showed the same qualities, and deployed citizen troops as well as others.[75]

Carthage's fleets were certainly crewed by citizens, as ancient sources insist. All the same, the very large ship numbers reported at various times – for instance 100 triremes and 300 other craft during Himilco's operations in the early 390s, 200 in 340 during the war with the Greek liberator Timoleon, 300 or more quinqueremes in 256 when the Romans threatened Libya – needed tens of thousands of oarsmen. As noted earlier, a trireme properly required 170 of these and a quinquereme no fewer than 300. Even a fleet of 100 triremes, then, would call for 17,000 crewmen – to say nothing of officers and any shipboard soldiers – while 220 quinqueremes (the total accommodated in the circular naval port of later times) required no fewer than 60,000. It is rather hard to see Carthage alone being able to provide them all, even supposing that inhabitants of the city's *chora* were liable to serve as well as the city-dwellers. Moreover, her Libyphoenician allies such as Utica, Hippacra and Lepcis are never mentioned as providing ships for her fleets (a contrast with Rome's maritime allies in Italy). In fact, when Scipio arrived in 203 and put Utica under siege, the only Carthaginian naval movements reported were made by ships coming from Carthage. It does look likely, therefore, that the Libyphoenicians (and maybe Libyan coastal communities too) contributed only manpower to her navy.

The republic always had warships available, but the details of naval administration are not recorded. The forested mountains of Libya would provide plenty of wood, such as oak from the Mogod and Monts de la Méjerda uplands north of the Bagradas river. Numidia's forests may have been an extra resource. Carthaginian shipbuilding is vividly illustrated by the remnants of two warships found in 1969 on the sandy shallow seabed off Marsala (ancient Lilybaeum). They probably sank, or rather were sunk, in some battle or storm of the First Punic War; whether they were biremes, triremes or even quinqueremes is debated. The ram of one survives, while there is enough of the other's wooden hull to reveal that it was built by a standard ancient method: once a spine of keel, stern-post and bow-stem was put together, horizontal courses of interlocking planks were fixed to it to form the shell of the craft; then the internal timber ribs were fixed to these. The shell was constructed using mortise-and-tenon joints (as in skilled joinery), with carefully cut tongues projecting from one plank to fit into matching slots in the next. In turn, a wooden dowel was driven at right-angles through each of these joins for added strength, while other dowels and nails fastened the vertical internal timbers to the shell. The deck or decks were finally built into this completed frame.

Such hulls were not only strong but required remarkable skill to construct. The skills of the workforce are further illustrated by the Punic lettering – in several differing hands – on the keel and planks of the 'Marsala wreck', for their purpose was to identify the positions of the timbers in precisely the pattern needed. Ships could be built to a virtual blueprint under the supervision of literate overseers; the ordinary workmen may have been literate too as sometimes thought, but in fact they needed only to learn and recognise the standard letters. With forests readily accessible, a large number of ships could be built very quickly. Diodorus, as it happens, mentions that fire destroyed the dockyards in 368 – fire was an ever-present risk in such places – yet the Carthaginians were soon able to launch 200 ships to crush a rash naval offensive by Dionysius of Syracuse.[76]

Carthaginian ships must originally have been built beside the roadsteads on the eastern shore, but later in the dockyards south of the old city, using the channel from the lake of Tunis. When the circular artificial port was built, probably in Hannibal's day, this became the headquarters of the navy (Map 1A), but its dimensions and Appian's description suggest that the shipbuilding yards lay elsewhere. The Carthaginians did use the port in 149 for building 50 hasty warships, but this was because the city was surrounded by besiegers. Where the navy was housed during the winter and between expeditions, before the ports were built, is unknown (moorings in the lake of Tunis might be guessed). To build, maintain, refurbish and eventually replace these hundreds of warships demanded not only crewmen aboard ship, but also craftsmen ashore with every kind of skill, from sailmakers and joiners to potters, bronze-smiths and armourers. Not all, perhaps, worked full-time for the navy alone, for in peacetime – which was fairly frequent – and in winter it would make fewer calls on craftsmen and suppliers. On the eve of a major expedition, contrastingly, there would be heavy demand for them.

Carthage's earliest recorded sea battle was the clash against the Phocaeans around 535 with a fleet of 60 penteconters; though a tactical defeat, it was a success in the longer run. Towards the end of the same century, the trireme became the dominant ship of the line: so the 200 warships which Diodorus reports for the expedition to Sicily in 480 will have been mostly or entirely triremes. This was an attack craft with sleek hull, narrow width and bronze-clad ram. Each oarsman pulled his own oar, with the rowing-benches along each side of the hull arranged vertically in threes. Space even for water was minimal, which meant that like penteconters it could not spend more than one or two days at sea before having to put in to land for fresh water (and cleaning out). If supply ships accompanied the fleet, longer continuous trips may have been feasible, but resupplying like this is rarely recorded. A larger warship called a quadrireme, claimed by Aristotle to be a Carthaginian invention, came into use around 400 (others credited it to Dionysius of Syracuse). It must have had oarsmen grouped in fours, perhaps two per oar, but quadriremes played smaller recorded roles in warfare than triremes or the later quinqueremes.

The next sea battle reported in Carthage's history was not fought until 406, off Mt Eryx on the west coast of Sicily, against the Syracusans – again a defeat, though this time only of a squadron. Over the following century, naval honours were about even between the Carthaginians and the Sicilian Greeks: there were defeats and setbacks (like storm damage) in 396, 311 and 307, but victories in 396 again, 368 and 309. It proved impossible to stop Agathocles invading North Africa in 310, but by 307 Carthaginian control of her own waters cut off the abandoned remnants of his army from escaping abroad (they sensibly changed sides instead). These seesaws of fortune may surprise, for the predominant view is that Carthage enjoyed clear naval superiority over every other state in the western Mediterranean at least until she fought Rome. The Carthaginians themselves may well have believed the stereotype. A general in Sicily in 264 warned the Romans not to involve themselves there, lest Carthage prevent them even from washing their hands in the sea. The war that followed was to destroy this over-confidence.

The era after Alexander the Great's death brought incessant wars to the eastern Mediterranean both on land and at sea, which in turn made the quinquereme (in Greek, *penteres*, supposedly invented by Dionysius of Syracuse) the main naval warship. The quinquereme did not become dominant in the west until later, it seems, for as late as 307 Diodorus still records triremes as the standard warship in clashes between Carthaginians and Sicilians. The design and mechanics of a quinquereme remain debated. Its oarage probably consisted of rowers grouped vertically in fives along the hull – two on a top bench pulling one oar, two more beneath them pulling another, and the fifth man pulling a third on the lowest bench – for a total of three hundred men, with room on deck for soldiers too. It was obviously heavier and more difficult to manoeuvre than a trireme, but it had a massive ram: the main tactic was, it seems, to try for a head-on blow against an enemy ship to hole it, then back off and turn against another while the first one sank. As well as soldiers the quinquereme could carry archers and even catapults, making it a formidable war machine. Styles could vary, for an improved version was owned (and perhaps designed) by one Hannibal the Rhodian around 250. When he and it fell into the Romans' hands, they used it as the prototype of a new fleet which they launched in 242 to win the First Punic War.[77]

Carthage's late adoption of the quinquereme may have unexpected extra significance for history. After Agathocles' final defeat, she fought only one more war in Sicily before 264 – against Pyrrhus of Epirus in 278–276 – which involved little sea-fighting. When war with Rome broke out, therefore, the quinquereme navy had not had serious combat experience, nor indeed had that generation of crews. As a result, the gigantic naval battles of the First Punic War may not have been fought by opponents who were as dissimilar as usually thought (historic sea-warriors versus venturesome landlubbers).

CARTHAGE'S ARMIES

Another of Carthage's naval paradoxes is that the sea was not normally the dominant or chief element in her wars. After the Carthaginian and Etruscan expedition against the Phocaeans around 535 and before the first war with Rome in 264, her fleets generally operated in support of land campaigns. This was inevitable, since campaigns took place as a rule in Sicily or Sardinia – and occasionally in Libya when an enemy invaded. In the Second Punic War the navy played an even more secondary role to the great military operations of Hannibal and other generals.

Carthage's wars were primarily waged on land, to take and control territory or to repel attackers. It was noted earlier that down to the 6th Century her armies were probably small and already included hired contingents (Chapter IV). Citizen soldiers, all the same, were regularly involved too. They may be the 'Phoenicians' in the army sent to Sicily in 480, or some of that contingent. For the great expeditions from 409 on, citizen troops were recruited along with Libyans and mercenaries at least until the last years of the 4th Century. We meet other evidence too: Carthaginians arming themselves and sallying from their homes during a false alarm that Libyan rebels had broken into the city (this was around 379), and their descendants doing the same in 308 to defeat Bomilcar's coup.

Aristotle had been told that Carthage encouraged military valour by allowing citizens to wear decorative armbands to show how many campaigns they had fought; he plainly found no surprise in the report. Polybius' dismissive claim about Carthaginians neglecting military service, except perhaps as cavalry, would apply at most to the 3rd Century, when their armies did consist largely of subjects and mercenaries. Yet even in his own account, citizen troops still appear from time to time: notably when the city's mercenaries and Libyan subjects together revolted in 241, nearly forty years later when Hannibal recruited citizens as well as others to enlarge the army which he led to Zama, and in the city's last wars when her forces were formed, of necessity, chiefly from Carthaginians defending their homeland.

Just how many Carthaginian citizens served in an army is seldom reported, but we have a few indications. When the humiliated Himilco was forced to terms in 396 and sailed home with only his surviving citizen soldiers, 40 triremes were enough to carry them. Even if the decks were packed to danger point, not more than forty to fifty men can have travelled aboard each besides the oarsmen. Since a disastrous plague had killed thousands of the original expedition, both military and naval personnel, maybe some of the surviving Carthaginian soldiers plied the oars as well, but hardly more than 8–9000 citizens in all (seamen and soldiers) can have sailed for home. The original contingent of soldiers probably totalled between 5000 and 10,000.

This would match the other figures recorded. Ten thousand Carthaginian citizen infantry, distinctively equipped with white shields, were part of the army defeated at the river Crimisus by Timoleon in 341, with 2500 of them forming a body called the Sacred Battalion (in Greek *hieros lochos*), recruited from wealthy aristocrats and expensively and showily accoutred. In the disaster, out of 10,000 dead from the Carthaginian army no fewer than 3000 were citizens. How many more were among Timoleon's 15,000 prisoners is not known.

When war with Agathocles broke out thirty years later, Hamilcar son of Gisco's expeditionary army of 14,000 included 2000 citizen troops, 'among whom' (writes Diodorus) 'were many of the aristocracy'. Agathocles' arrival on Carthage's doorstep the following year brought forth a uniquely large army of citizen troops, if Diodorus can be believed: 40,000 foot including once more the Sacred Battalion, along with 1000 horse and 2000 chariots (a war vehicle sometimes used by Carthaginian armies in this century). This meant perhaps some 45,000 men altogether, all of them citizens because 'they did not wait for the soldiers from the countryside (*chora*) and the allied cities'. Such numbers, if closely or even roughly accurate, must have accounted for most Carthaginians of military age available in the city. (They suffered a humiliating defeat, partly through the treachery of the plotter Bomilcar.) In turn, 'the soldiers from the *chora*' may mean not solely, or mainly, rural citizens but also Libyan levies, while those from 'the allied cities' would be Libyphoenician contingents. Three years later three separate armies, totalling 30,000, were again 'sent out from the city' against the invaders, who had vulnerably split up their own forces. Many in these three armies must have been citizens again, but Diodorus specifically notes that Carthage was now so crowded with refugees from the countryside that sending out so many men relieved the pressure there. The armies probably then included Libyan and Libyphoenician soldiers as well, and maybe even mercenaries brought in from overseas, so the citizen elements cannot be estimated.

Sixty years were to pass before another mention occurs of citizen forces. Even though the Romans' first invasion of Libya in 256 almost brought Carthage to her knees, citizen combatants are not reported at any stage. Quite likely they were fully involved in the very large fleets of the time – up to 350 ships fought at Cape Ecnomus against the Roman invasion fleet, and 200 a year later off Cape Bon (the *Hermaea Acra* to Polybius) trying vainly to repel another. But in 240, with the city blockaded from Tunes by some rebel mercenaries and Libyans, while a small army operated rather fruitlessly in the countryside against others, Hamilcar Barca was elected general to lead out a second force of about 10,000 troops, made up of citizens, loyal mercenaries and even some deserters. Since he cannot have left Carthage herself undefended and there was still a navy of sorts in being, his citizen contingent (perhaps 6–7000 strong) would not represent anything like the total number of military-age Carthaginians at the time, but what that was cannot be guessed.

The final appearance of citizen troops – before the special conditions of the Third Punic War – was in Hannibal's army at Zama in 202. There they formed its second line together with Libyan infantry, while a corps of recently recruited foreign mercenaries stood in front of them and Hannibal's own veterans from Italy behind. One wing of the army, too, consisted of Carthaginian (apparently citizen) cavalry. Unfortunately, and even though Hannibal had spent nearly a year training them, all these compatriots proved to be poor fighters against Scipio's veterans.[78]

Until the Punic Wars, or the later 4th Century at earliest, the total strengths reported for armies are not very plausible. Hamilcar's expedition in 480 supposedly involved nearly one-third of a million troops – half of whom, the victors claimed equally implausibly, were killed at Himera. His grandson Hannibal's army in 409 was reckoned at 200,000 foot and 4000 horse by Ephorus, one of Diodorus' sources; by another, the Sicilian Timaeus of Tauromenium, at the more modest but not much more convincing total of 120,000. Diodorus then claims a death toll of 150,000 in Himilco's plague-stricken army in 396 (no doubt the fanciful guess of Ephorus or Timaeus again). Half a century later, in 344, Mago the general in Sicily had a rather more credible 50-60,000 troops, with 300 war chariots, while three years later at the river Crimisus the army, including the Sacred Battalion and other citizen troops, supposedly numbered 70,000 foot and several thousand cavalry.

If these mid-4th-Century army figures represent not just the troops operating in the field but an estimate of all Carthaginian forces in the island – field army and garrisons together – they may be rather more realistic than the colossal totals alleged for the 5th Century. Even so the estimates look more than a little exaggerated. There are, in fact, hints that the army at the Crimisus was smaller than claimed. Timoleon with at most 11,000 troops first crushed the Sacred Battalion and the other citizen infantry – 10,000 Carthaginians in all – as they forded the fast-flowing river; then the ensuing rout of the rest of the army would be easier to understand if originally it numbered fewer than 60,000 (though it is possible that even 60,000 Libyan conscripts and foreign mercenaries might dissolve into simple panic when the citizen forces were smashed). Again, after losing 10,000 dead and 15,000 captured, the army ceased so completely to be a fighting force that at Carthage there were fears of an immediate Greek invasion.

The forces reportedly ranged against Agathocles in Libya thirty years later – 40,000 in 310, 30,000 in 307 – look rather more reliable, facing invaders who never numbered more than 20,000. Over in Sicily in the same period, Hamilcar son of Gisco started operations with 2000 citizen troops, 10,000 Libyans, and 2000 Balearic and Etruscan mercenaries (the only appearance, incidentally, of Etruscans in Carthaginian service). On the other hand, his supposed 120,000-strong army later besieging Syracuse unsuccessfully is plainly another ludicrous exaggeration.

The wars with Rome in turn involved armies rarely more than 60,000 or 70,000 strong, at any rate according to our chief sources.

For instance, the army sent in 262 to relieve Acragas is given as 50,000 foot and 6000 horse, while two decades later the strains of the war reduced Hamilcar Barca's to barely 20,000. His son Hannibal at Cannae in 216, on the other hand, commanded 40,000 foot and 10,000 horse, and at Zama fourteen years later an army rather smaller. Whether the Carthaginian army that Scipio defeated at Ilipa in Spain in 206 really numbered 74,000 (as Polybius states), or 54,500 (as Livy writes), or neither, is a moot question.

As Polybius' remarks show, the Carthaginians were famous – or notorious – for using mercenaries in their armies, whereas citizen and Libyphoenician soldiers and Libyan conscripts were forgotten in the stereotype. It was noted earlier that conscripts and foreign professionals are recorded at least from 480 on, when Hamilcar the Magonid recruited not only Carthaginians and Libyans but also Iberians (that is, Spaniards), Ligurians (from northern Italy), Gauls, Sardinians and Corsicans. His grandson Hannibal's forces seventy years later consisted of Carthaginian citizens, Libyans and Iberians; then Diodorus reports the enrolment three years after that, in 407, of Libyphoenicians, Numidians, Mauri, and Campanians from Italy to serve alongside the citizen and Libyan divisions.[79]

Different regions furnished different types of soldier. Libyans, Iberians and Gauls were primarily infantry, the Iberians often armed with a distinctive curved sword, Gauls with long swords for slashing. The Numidians were most famous for their formidable cavalry but could also arm infantry, at any rate for fighting within North Africa. Balearic islanders were limited in number but were light infantry wielding dangerously accurate leather slingshots with stone or iron balls to soften up enemy forces at the start of battle or harass them during and after it. Campanians, from the region of Italy south of Rome, were primarily armoured infantry but also provided some cavalrymen; enterprising and often ruthless, they were used from the late 5th down to the 3rd Century – and by Sicilian Greek states too – though their availability may have lessened as Rome increased her control over their homeland. Ligurians, highlanders from the coastal Italian Appennines, were light-armed warriors of rather loose discipline. The western Mediterranean thus regularly furnished manpower for the republic's armies till the year 201.

Greek mercenaries, the most highly valued in the east, were not recruited by Carthage until the mid-4th Century, unless perhaps in small numbers earlier. They are first mentioned in the Carthaginian forces facing the liberator Timoleon of Corinth when he arrived in Sicily in 344. Greek cities' allied troops were a separate matter: as early as 480 Selinus in south-west Sicily offered cavalry to Hamilcar's army, and 'Greek allies' – unspecified – earn a mention in his grandson's army in 409. Valued though they were, Greek professionals played a part in Carthage's armies only on and off, and for only about a century. Their loyalties may have been slightly suspect to generals in wars against Greeks. One story tells how in 344 excessive friendliness between Timoleon's and the Carthaginian Mago's Greek mercenaries alarmed Mago into evacuating Sicily altogether. Nor are Greeks mentioned in the next army sent over against Timoleon, or in the war against Agathocles in Libya near the end of the century.

Fighting the Romans was a different matter, as the timely role of Xanthippus of Sparta in 255 illustrates, but Greek mercenary numbers then seem to have run down again as the long war dragged on and the republic's finances deteriorated. When the great revolt of the mercenaries broke out in North Africa in 241, the only Greeks in the rebel forces were what Polybius calls *Mixellenes*, 'mixed Greeks' or possibly 'half-Greeks' – most of them slaves and deserters, he adds disdainfully – who are not afterwards reported in events. They may have been a composite of Greeks and others from south Italy, rather than mercenaries from the east. The armies of the Barcid generals over the next four decades, Hannibal's in Italy included, had no Greek mercenaries at all: we do not know why.

How contingents of a Carthaginian army were organised is not known in detail, but each contingent would consist at least of a number of sub-units like infantry companies and cavalry squadrons. In large formations there may have been other subdivisions, just as a Roman legion of Agathocles' time was made up of *manipuli* subdivided into *centuriae*. The Carthaginian republic paid their mercenaries' and conscripts' wages – though sometimes with lengthy gaps between payments – and presumably paid citizen troops too when these were in service, though the fancy armour and other accoutrements of bodies like the Sacred Battalion must have been at a warrior's own expense (cf. *Illustrations 25, 26*).

In every period the highest officers in an army were, it seems, all Carthaginians, though below them the various contingents, both conscript and mercenary, commonly had commanders and officers of their own. Some senior Carthaginian officers are known, most of them from the era of the wars with Rome. We do meet a 'Synalos' (probably Eshmunhalos) in 357, military governor of Carthaginian-controlled Heraclea Minoa in Sicily, who gave much-needed help to his Syracusan friend Dion in the quest to free that city from tyranny.

Illustration 25 Heavy-armed infantry on the march: jasper scarab from Kerkouane, 4th Century BC

In the following century, a Hanno was the garrison commander at Messana in 264 whose ineptitude contributed (at least in his compatriots' eyes) to bringing about the First Punic War; at the war's end one Gisco was the subordinate left in charge in Sicily by the departing Hamilcar Barca. Hannibal's cavalry commander Maharbal gave his famously fruitless advice to march directly on Rome, supposedly after Cannae in 216; another trusted subordinate was Hannibal's best friend Mago, nicknamed 'the Samnite' (we do not know why),

159

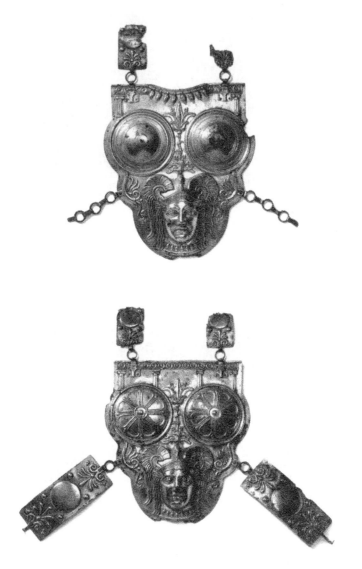

Illustration 26 Front and back parade armour (4th–3rd Centuries BC) found at Ksour Essaf, near Sousse

who served with him for twenty years; and Hannibal's own nephew Hanno was still another, and one of the best, of his lieutenants in Italy.

African and foreign officers are sometimes heard of, again chiefly during the Punic Wars. It was a Spartan mercenary, Xanthippus, who against all tradition at Carthage was granted practical – though not official – command in 255 and destroyed the Roman invaders under Regulus. Just a few years later, the fortress seaport of Lilybaeum was saved for the Carthaginians by Alexon of Achaea, who thwarted a treacherous scheme by other mercenary officers to hand it over to its Roman besiegers. In the great rebellion of 241 in North Africa, one of the most bloodthirsty rebel leaders was the Gaul Autaritus, leader of the Gallic mercenaries in Hamilcar Barca's old army. On the other side, Hamilcar gained the loyal support of a Numidian prince, Naravas, whose cavalry played a vital part in his campaigns and who may afterwards have married one of Hamilcar's daughters. Hippocrates and Epicydes, two officers in Hannibal's army in Italy, were brothers of part-Syracusan ancestry (their grandfather had lived in exile at Carthage): sent to Syracuse in 213 to manoeuvre that city into alliance with Carthage, they succeeded brilliantly, at least in the short term. Then, after the Roman sack of Syracuse, Hannibal sent a vigorous Libyphoenician cavalry officer, Mottones (Mattan) of Hippacra, to rally Carthaginian forces in the island.

Non-Carthaginians' services were not always fully appreciated by the republic, in later times anyway. Xanthippus found it discreet to exit North Africa after the victory that saved the city; a few years later, some unpaid and mutinous mercenaries were dumped on a small island (Ustica north of Sicily, perhaps, or Linosa between Malta and Byzacium) by their general. The Gallic chief Autaritus shared and sharpened his men's widespread discontent at their employers' shabby efforts to haggle over their overdue pay. The Numidian Masinissa, perhaps Naravas' nephew, served Carthage well in Spain in Hannibal's time but was then dropped in favour of his rival Syphax (a slight for which the republic was to pay dearly). Mottones' prowess so annoyed Hanno, the general in Sicily, that in the end the disgusted Hippacritan went over to the Romans – who in appreciation made him a Roman citizen, Marcus Valerius Mottones, as he shows in his and his sons' votive inscription at Delphi, set up twenty years later.

Carthaginian armies, like those of many other Mediterranean states, included a wide range of combatants. Heavily-armed infantry and agile, often Numidian cavalry formed their core, while among other important arms were lightly-armed infantry and distinctive contingents like the Gauls – ferocious though loosely-disciplined warriors, wielding fearsome broadswords – and the small but valued companies of Balearic slingers. A 4th-Century jasper scarab-ornament from Kerkouane depicts a group of heavy infantrymen on the march (*Illustration 25*): their armament of plumed helmets, shin-greaves and spears is fully Greek, and their purposeful stride implies a high level of discipline (the plumes perhaps suggest officers). The sort of parade armour available at least to generals and their immediate subordinates is illustrated by the magnificently wrought bronze armour, for breast and back, found at Ksour Essaf near the coast about 30 kilometres south of Sousse (*Illustration 26*). It is apparently a south Italian product and 4th- or 3rd-Century in date. Its owner could have served against Agathocles (or indeed with him) or in one of the great wars of the following century, and then took this item of personal treasure with him to the grave.

War chariots figured in some important 4th-Century campaigns, for instance against Agathocles, while one or two surviving *stelae* attest chariot-makers such as the Mago son of Himilco mentioned earlier. All the same the weapon, a survival from old Near Eastern warfare, was about as ineffective in the republic's conflicts as Persian chariots were against Greek enemies like Alexander. After 300 or so they were given up in favour of elephants.

Elephants are of course the popular symbol of Carthaginian warfare. In reality, like Greek mercenaries they were used for a much more limited period than often thought. The great powers of the eastern Mediterranean had started to use them in the wars after Alexander the Great's death. They first appear in 262 in Sicily – though possibly some had been used there in 278–276 against Pyrrhus, who had elephants of his own – and are mentioned for the last time at Zama in 202. Most of their service, then, was against the Romans in the first two Punic Wars. Carthage's elephants were acquired from the forests of the Atlas mountains; smaller than those from India which the eastern kingdoms used, they could carry only their riders but could inflict serious damage when skilfully used, especially against troops and horses unaccustomed to them. At the same time they needed large amounts of food, were difficult to trans-port across water, and could be neutralised – or even turned against their own side – by a resourceful enemy, as Scipio did at Ilipa in Spain in 206 and four years later at Zama.

Elephants were a mixed success for Carthage. In their first major battle against the Romans, at Acragas in 262, they made little impact and nearly all were captured. By contrast, Xanthippus' use of them seven years later against Regulus contributed to his victory. Hamilcar Barca similarly made good use of elephants in fighting the rebel mercenaries and Libyans from 240 to 237, and thereafter in his campaigns in Spain where the Barcid generals built up a powerful elephant corps supposedly, though maybe exaggeratedly, 200 strong (*Illustration 24i*). Hannibal's feat in 218, shepherding 37 from Spain across the Alps and into Italy, both helped him to his first big victory at the river Trebia and immortalised him in the memory of future ages – but then all save one died in the bitter winter that followed. When next he had a large body of elephants (80 at Zama) they inflicted a more devastating impact on his own army than on Scipio's.

CARTHAGINIANS AND GREEKS IN THE 5TH CENTURY

Carthage's dominance over the western parts of Sicily, established under the first Magonids, led to recurrently strained dealings with other peoples in the island, above all the Greek city-states. These had been founded between the later 8th and early 6th Centuries, Syracuse for example in 734 and Acragas in 580. Many quickly grew in size and wealth, often competing and sometimes co-operating with one another. The Sicilian Greeks, as warlike as their kinsmen in Greece, developed a populous and powerful civilisation (their repetitive conflicts notwithstanding) even more impressive than their colonial brethren's in southern Italy. Competition, though, could be lethal. Syracuse destroyed its own recalcitrant colony Camarina not once but twice (in 533 and then 484) as well as another, Megara Hyblaea, in 483. Naxos, on the east coast near Mt Etna, was depopulated first by Gela in the 490s and then by Dionysius ninety years later.

As noted earlier, Greeks from further east sought more than once, too, to plant themselves in districts under Carthaginian influence: Pentathlus in the west of Sicily around 580, then Dorieus towards the end of the same century – first near Lepcis in the Emporia region and then in western Sicily again. Carthage treated them, like Corsica's Phocaean settler-pirates, as threats. When, in the 480s, Syracuse under Gelon and Acragas under his kinsman Theron seemed intent on imposing a shared hegemony over the rest of Greek Sicily, the republic reacted anew. A conflict around 485 was indecisive and probably was small-scale: we know of it only because in 480 Gelon complained to envoys from Greece that Athens and Sparta had earlier refused to help him against the Carthaginians' 'barbarian army', while Justin vaguely alleges 'constant wrongdoings' inflicted by the Carthaginians on the hapless Sicilians. Disconcertingly, Justin also makes these summon the Spartan prince Leonidas to lead them (in fact he was to die that year at Thermopylae) – no doubt a blurred confusion with the Spartan Dorieus a generation earlier.[80]

The great clash came when Hamilcar the Magonid and his army landed in 480, reportedly after three years of preparation. The enterprise was not a clash simply of Carthaginians versus Greeks. Hamilcar himself was responding to an appeal from friendly Greeks: Terillus the ex-ruler of Himera on the north coast – recently deposed by Theron – and his powerful father-in-law Anaxilas, tyrant of Rhegium on the straits opposite Messana which was under Anaxilas' control too. Terillus was a guest-friend of Hamilcar, himself of course half-Greek on his Syracusan mother's side, while Anaxilas was so keen for intervention that he gave Hamilcar his own children as hostages. Selinus on the south-west coast also aligned itself with Carthage, even promising a contingent of cavalry (Anaxilas in the end supplied no troops). Theron and Gelon's power bloc, of quite novel size in the island, plainly alarmed not just Magonid Carthage but other western Greek states, while the links between all the leading individuals remind us that – whatever propaganda might claim – the Carthaginians were far from genuine outsiders or mysterious aliens in the Greek world.

To them the new bloc posed a far worse threat to their Sicilian *epikrateia* than Dorieus ever could. Given this sound reason for confronting the expansionist tyrants, it is not essential to believe the story in Diodorus – not in Herodotus – that Hamilcar's enterprise was concerted to match Xerxes' mighty expedition against Greece. Possibly enough Carthage kept in touch with Persia, via Tyre, about their two expeditions, but anything beyond that looks like imaginative Greek embroidery. Hamilcar landed at Panormus with his impressive armament, but while he was besieging Himera for his friend and protégé he was attacked by Gelon and Theron, his army was crushed after a long battle, and he himself was killed or – according to Herodotus' Carthaginian informants – threw himself into the great fire in which he had been offering sacrifice after sacrifice for victory (the tale sometimes viewed as supporting claims of Carthaginian human sacrifice: Chapter VII). Herodotus was also told that memorials to him had been set up at Carthage and other cities, with Hamilcar himself receiving cult offerings. As with Elissa, all the same, this claimed divinisation has no trace in surviving Carthaginian evidence.

The wars of the 480s opened a long and fruitless cycle of Carthaginian-Greek struggles in Sicily, which was to last two centuries even though Gelon's and Theron's own bloc did not last beyond another decade or two. Each war followed a predictable path: either a Carthaginian thrust against hostile Greek cities – usually but not always including Syracuse – which after some successes was beaten back, or a Syracusan thrust into the *epikrateia* which, often after some successes again, failed to maintain itself. A peace that restored more or less the pre-war status quo then ensued until the next clash. Not only in 480 but in several later wars, Carthage had Sicilian Greek allies who preferred associating with her, an overseas and (relatively) distant overlord, to falling under the control of a powerful and dangerous Greek neighbour which, more often than not, was Syracuse.

The war of 480 was the shortest of them all, a few months at most. Its effects were limited. The victors did not follow up their success by moving against Carthage's *epikrateia*, Selinus was not victimised for supporting her, Anaxilas made his peace with Gelon, and the prospect of Syracusan-Acragantine hegemony over Sicily disappeared after Gelon and Theron died in the 470s. The cost in men, materials and money to Carthage must have been severe even if the entire expedition was not annihilated (as our sources claim), but she maintained her grip over western Sicily while turning her attentions to imposing control over Libya. The Magonids continued in power even though Hamilcar's son Gisco was scapegoated for the disaster, to die in exile at Selinus.

Trade and relations with the Greek world went on. Although the shame of the defeat was not forgotten, the Carthaginians for the next seventy years left the rest of Sicily politically and militarily to itself. They were not tempted to intervene when a powerful native Sicilian leader, Ducetius the Sicel, united most of the remaining independent native peoples in a league that proved a temporary match for Syracuse and Acragas in the 460s and 450s; nor when Syracuse and Acragas, having defeated the Sicels, fell out. Carthaginian restraint is all the more striking in face of Syracuse's expanding strength and adventurousness. Its naval victory of 474 over the Etruscans in waters near Naples, and sea raids in the 450s against the Etruscan coasts and even Corsica, failed to upset the Magonids. Nor did they react against Syracuse's broadening hegemony over other Sicilian states, both Greek and Sicel. When Rhegium, Syracuse's neighbour Leontini, Camarina and Segesta wanted support against

Syracusan expansionism in the 430s, they made alliances with Athens – without much benefit until years later.

The Magonids' hands-off attitude to Greek Sicily for most of the 5th Century contrasts remarkably with their warlike policies down to 480 and, still more so, from 409 on. The benefits that accrued from this restraint, combined with the vigorous development of Carthaginian power in Africa, much impressed Greeks. Thucydides reports the Syracusan Hermocrates in 415 extolling Carthage's wealth in gold and silver; around the same time Athenian general Nicias (at least according to Diodorus) was insisting that her military strength far outdid his own city's. Hermocrates claimed, too, that she was as worried as Syracuse about Athens' ambitions for conquest. But throughout the great Athenian expedition against Syracuse, from 415 to 413, Carthage stayed aloof. The destruction of the invaders was achieved by the Syracusans with some help from Sparta – while the Magonids' attitude to Athens, at any rate after the catastrophe, may be gauged from a treaty of friendship made between Carthage and the Greek city in 406, marble fragments of which survive in Athens.

CARTHAGE VS DIONYSIUS I

Had Carthage maintained her hands-off policy towards Greek Sicily, simply staying on guard against any incursions that might be made into her territories, much wasteful bloodshed could have been avoided over the next century and a half. The changeover to vigorous and even vengeful aggression from 409 on is therefore surprising. As noted earlier, the claim that Carthage's leading citizen Hannibal, the now elderly grandson of Hamilcar the Magonid, was eager to avenge his forebear's disaster hardly seems reason enough – especially as the war began with the total obliteration of Selinus, Carthage's ally in 480 and his own father Gisco's home in exile later. At odds with nearby Segesta, Selinus had turned to Syracuse for help, prompting Segesta to call on Carthage. It looks as though the republic now decided deliberately on a reversal of dealings with Greek Sicily, for which she enlisted native Sicilian allies as well: now it was to be projection of power well beyond the *epikrateia*. Apart from the current Magonids' likely keenness for military distinction, the impulses for change must have been Carthage's success in developing an effective empire in North Africa and her concern at Syracuse's expanding dominance in Sicily. Diodorus in fact mentions this concern, which Hannibal played on to persuade his fellow citizens to act. Greece and the Aegean world, moreover, were now absorbed in the last stages of the Peloponnesian war, with Athens so uninterested in the fortunes of Greek Sicily as to become a formal ally of Carthage.

The ferocious energy of the offensives that began in 409 stunned the Sicilians. Selinus was besieged, sacked and depopulated, then Himera. Two years later Carthaginian and other North African colonists founded a new city, Thermae Himeraeae, at hot springs not far west of Himera. Then a new campaign began in 406, led by Hannibal and Himilco, which led to the sack of Acragas after most of its inhabitants had fled. There followed in 405 the same treatment for Gela and Camarina. Tens of thousands of refugees were left to wander across the island.

The remorseless Carthaginian advance in those years was only briefly halted by a plague that killed Hannibal among others (it was to appease Baal Hammon that Himilco then sacrificed a boy victim), and by Syracusan forces led by the ambitious and devious Dionysius, soon to make himself tyrant of his city. With most of central and eastern Sicily occupied but his forces beset by sickness, Himilco made peace on very favourable terms: the *epikrateia* in western Sicily recognised, the southern Greek cities from Acragas to Camarina made tribute-payers to Carthage, and others in Sicily's centre and north-east guaranteed their independence.

The peace of 405 looked like a triumph for Carthage and her Magonid leadership. In reality it was fragile, as every informed Carthaginian must have realised. Himilco brought back not only victory but plague. Dionysius soon moved to take over many eastern and central Sicilian cities, like Leontini, Catana and the Sicel strong-hold Enna, despite their promised independence. After an ostentatious military and naval build-up over the next few years, including his newly-invented warship the quinquereme, he opened a new war in 397 using huge military forces – reportedly eighty thousand infantry, three thousand cavalry and two hundred warships. He matched the sack of Selinus, Himera and Acragas by besieging the island city of Motya with massive siege machines, building a causeway to the walls from the mainland. Motya's last hours saw fighting in a tableau which one day would be strangely recalled in the sack of Carthage herself, as the attackers fought on wooden plank-bridges from one tall house across to the next on the crowded island:

The Sicilian Greeks found themselves in a very difficult position. For, fighting as they were from the suspended wooden bridges, they suffered grievously both because of the narrow quarters and because of the desperate resistance of their opponents, who had abandoned hope of life. As a result, some perished in hand-to-hand encounters as they gave and received wounds, and others, pressed back by the Motyans and tumbling from the wooden bridges, fell to their death on the ground. (Diodorus 14.51.5–52.4 (Loeb tr.))

What had been one of Phoenician Sicily's most flourishing centres was reduced to a deserted wreck. Himilco retook it the following year but it was never fully restored. Instead the Carthaginians founded a new port named Lilybaeum on the mainland, a short way south, which proved to be impregnable against all attackers, even the Romans.[81]

Himilco struck back in 396, but his and his deputy Mago's new series of successes – Messana taken and razed, Dionysius' fleet defeated, Syracuse laid under siege – were ruined by a fresh onslaught of plague. This was the occasion when the Carthaginians sought to appease Demeter and Kore, whose shrine outside Syracuse had been destroyed along with many others, by inducting their cult into the city. Himilco himself bribed Dionysius to let him and the surviving citizen troops sail home, abandoning everyone else. This disgrace drove him to his suicide. More calamitously for the Carthaginians, it led to the great Libyan and slave rebellion which for a time threatened the city's own existence.

The rather wearisome sequence of wars went on. The new general in Sicily was Himilco's deputy Mago – not, it seems, a member of the Magonid family, which now disappears from record – who put down the Libyan rebellion, warred with large forces against Syracuse in 393 and 392, but then negotiated a new peace. It kept the gains of 405, but conceded the Sicel communities in the central regions to Dionysius' unsympathetic rule. This step backwards may reflect difficulties at home resulting from the recent revolt and the long-lasting plague. Dionysius, left alone for the next nine years, used ruthless methods to create an impressive Syracusan dominion in eastern Sicily and even southern Italy, along with naval interventions in the southern Adriatic and a spectacular raid on Pyrgi on Italy's Etruscan coast. The Carthaginians probably foresaw a new war with so dynamic a power, so when Dionysius (predictably) began to seek alliances with cities in the island's west – ignoring Carthaginian remonstrations – they sent Mago against him in 383.

A disaster followed, with Mago defeated and killed in battle; but when Dionysius countered a peace offer with ill-advised demands that Carthage abandon Sicily altogether and pay him a large indemnity, she put Mago's son in command of fresh forces which shattered the Syracusans at Cronium (a place apparently near Panormus) probably in 382 or 381. Carthage still wanted peace, as Dionysius too now did, but not surprisingly her terms were sharp: he had to pay a thousand talents and accept a demarcation line at the river Halycus, today's Platani just west of Acragas, and in the north at the territory of Thermae Himeraeae (the city founded by Hannibal and Himilco in 407 to replace Himera).

The name of Mago's son and the date of the new peace are not certain. An anecdote in Polyaenus of a military stratagem might refer to him (a general called Himilco deceiving Dionysius' men outside Cronium), but in the same paragraph another Himilco story is about the earlier general who later committed suicide. On Diodorus' evidence, the peace soon followed the victory at Cronium. But Carthage in 379 or 378 re-established the town of Hipponium in southern Italy, destroyed earlier by Dionysius – an action which, if part of the same war, would put the peace during the 370s. This is not a strongly convincing argument, all the same, for peace before then would not ban Carthage from intervening at the edge of the tyrant's area of south Italian dominance.

In the later 370s fresh troubles at home afflicted the republic. The plague came back to kill large numbers in the city. This in turn encouraged both Libyans and Sardinians to rebel once more, rebellions successful so long as the epidemic continued to rage. The Libyans made no attack on the city, unlike in 396; perhaps they simply renounced Carthaginian authority, refusing to pay tribute and resisting efforts to bring them back into obedience. The Sardinians 'attacked the Carthaginians', which must mean the settler population, but seem not to have taken any cities like Tharros, Sulcis, Carales or Olbia. As soon as Carthage recovered her strength she put down this revolt fairly quickly, which suggests that the Sardinians had made only limited gains. Control was reimposed in Libya perhaps rather earlier, for only with her African territories secure could the republic feel free to act decisively beyond.

By this time Hanno 'the Great' was directing affairs: he was the general who achieved the submission of Libya (Chapter VIII) and he then had to face the latest challenge from Dionysius. Encouraged by Carthage's troubles, according to Diodorus, and further heartened by news of the disastrous fire in Carthage's dockyards, the ageing tyrant mobilised for yet another war in 368 but (not for the first time) his plans went awry. Despite the dockyard blaze, no fewer than 200 Carthaginian warships annihilated his fleet anchored near Drepana and Mt Eryx; little happened after that, with Dionysius dying in 367 and his son and namesake leaving the war in limbo until a formal peace years later. The two sides' regions of dominance seem to have stayed much as before.

Carthage had not wanted the war any more than the previous one. Hanno had other concerns, like keeping the Libyans subject and dealing with his enemy 'Suniatus'. The supposed ban in 368 against studying or speaking Greek – whatever its real content – would fit a resentful attitude towards Greek Sicily. The results of the four decades of conflicts were mostly bad, particularly for Sicily with their countless sieges and sackings, enslavements and at times slaughtering of cities and their populations. Carthage did replace Motya with Lilybaeum and Himera with Thermae Himeraeae, both destined to prosper, and settled war refugees at Tauromenium near the destroyed town of Naxos on the east coast (it would soon be the birthplace of the historian Timaeus). Dionysius founded the city of Tyndaris in 396, on the north-east coast, with war refugees from Greece. These creations hardly compensated, though, for the damage inflicted in southern Italy as well as Sicily.

CARTHAGE AND TIMOLEON

The general peace in Sicily after 367 was overthrown from 357 on, although the Carthaginians still stayed carefully aloof. The younger Dionysius, cultivated and feckless, was deposed by his high-minded but unbending brother-in-law Dion (helped initially by his friend 'Synalos' or Eshmunhalos, the commandant at Heraclea Minoa). The cost was anarchy at Syracuse and across Greek Sicily, with Dion murdered in 353, petty tyrants seizing power in other cities, and the ousted Dionysius II trying twice between 356 and 344 to retake Syracuse by force. That city from 345 on was held by one Hicetas, who like so many Sicilian Greeks had good relations with Carthage and who, faced with the ex-tyrant's return, called on her for help.

Hanno 'the Great' was gone, and with him the hands-off policy towards Greek Sicily. Whatever faction or competing factions had taken over, they needed military as well as political successes, for Hanno's group remained active even though his son Gisco was exiled. The republic had recovered prosperity, as her powerful and lavish armaments of the next four years imply; the convulsions in eastern Sicily offered the real chance of repeating, even outdoing the achievements of 409–405. Hicetas was sent help: 50,000 infantry (including many Greek mercenaries), up to 10,000 cavalry and 300 chariots under a Mago, whose colleague Hanno had 150 triremes. There were, Diodorus states, 'weapons and missiles of all kinds, a profusion of siege engines, and a great quantity of food and other supplies'. Mago was able to place some troops actually in the sector of Syracuse held by Hicetas against Dionysius II – the first and last time that Carthaginian forces ever set foot there.

Yet again a promising start ended badly. Hicetas had earlier sought help from Syracuse's mother city Corinth. An elderly Corinthian leader, Timoleon, now arrived with a few hundred Greek mercenaries, to make an immediate impact on events. Dionysius II agreed to go and live in Corinth. Next, reportedly after Mago's and Timoleon's mercenaries began fraternising, the Carthaginians abandoned their mission entirely to march back to the west (it was now 343). This aroused such anger at home that Mago killed himself, though his unforgiving fellow citizens insisted on crucifying his body; his deputy is not heard of again. Two new generals, named Hamilcar and Hasdrubal, took the field in 341 with still larger forces, as described earlier.

The lengthy preparations, though, had given Timoleon time to strengthen his position in Sicily. He met the Carthaginians at the river Crimisus (probably today's Belice) north of Selinus, in late May or early June, where his army – badly outnumbered, but aided by a gigantic thunderstorm – shattered the Carthaginians. The Sacred Battalion of 2500 eminent citizens, and with it over 7000 other citizen troops, were destroyed, thousands more soldiers were captured, and the booty was colossal. The Carthaginian army virtually ceased to exist as a fighting force. Although Timoleon was content to return in security and glory to Syracuse, at Carthage there were panic-stricken fears of a Greek invasion. The city's next move was to recall Gisco, son of Hanno the Great, and appoint him general, or possibly general and sufete together for full control. Gisco opted for caution and the status quo, making a peace which returned the island to the dividing-line of 367 at the Halycus.

Carthage's expeditions of 343 and 341 failed not through inadequate resources but because of poor generalship. None of the generals performed well, while the Greek side found a totally unexpected rescuer in the charismatic Timoleon – not only a phenomenally successful commander, but a remarkable political and social leader. He had much to do: grass was growing in the *agora* of a wrecked and depopulated Syracuse; other cities were in a similar plight; and tens of thousands of new migrants from Greece were needed to rebuild the devastated and depopulated island. Yet in a few years his measures began to revive Greek Sicily, which of course promised to make any Carthaginian attempt to overpower it still more problematic. Gisco preferred to take the republic back to his father's non-interventionist attitude; so did his successors until around 320.

THE AGE OF AGATHOCLES:
CARTHAGE AT BAY

The Carthaginians had other overseas developments to watch. Alexander the Great's conquest of the Persian empire – including Tyre and then Egypt – threatened to re-order Carthage's priorities, especially given the king's unsubtle threats that he had military ambitions for the west too. We saw earlier that Hamilcar, the secret agent at his court, was later put to death by his unappreciative countrymen: perhaps it was because he had failed to wean Alexander off this idea. The breakup of the empire after Alexander died in 323, and Egypt's new ruler Ptolemy's indifference to westward ventures, finally eased that worry.

Timoleon's pacification measures began to unravel in the 320s. The oligarchs he put in change at Syracuse sought to imitate the elder Dionysius' interventions in southern Italy, while their rule was challenged by a new popular leader, Agathocles – born, it so happened, at Thermae Himeraeae around 360 to a father exiled from Rhegium. Rather than see another tyrant take over Syracuse, the Carthaginians supported the oligarchs, even helping them in 319 with troops led by the Hamilcar whose obscure link with Gisco's family has been mentioned before. Then, paradoxically, Hamilcar and Agathocles came to a hands-off agreement that allowed the Syracusan to become, in practice, tyrant after all. In a style that became one of his trademarks, Agathocles cemented his rule in 316 by massacring his oligarchic opponents with their families.

Why Hamilcar switched his support is hard to tell, yet he was not punished. Perhaps he and his friends at home reasoned that the oligarchs had no long-term future, making a good relationship with their rival the only prospect for stability. If so it was mistaken optimism. The next decade and a half became a saga of evenly-matched and dramatic conflict never before seen in Carthage's or Sicily's history.

Agathocles soon began to reimpose Syracuse's old dominance over the rest of Greek Sicily. This naturally drew anxious attention from Carthage. In 315 her envoys put a stop to him attacking Messana; then in 314 Hamilcar brokered a peace of sorts between Syracuse and its growing number of opponents, though this failed to last and tension now grew between Syracuse and Carthage too. When a Carthaginian fleet stopped Agathocles in 312 from taking Acragas after at last seizing Messana, he invaded the *epikrateia* to bring a number of places (unnamed) under his power. So began the next great Sicilian war, defeating Carthage's long efforts at averting it.

Hamilcar died before he could be recalled in disgrace, to be replaced by his kinsman or friend Hamilcar son of Gisco. The new general, combining his own troops with anti-Agathocles Greeks, defeated the tyrant near Gela in 311, won over most of eastern Sicily with a (slightly paradoxical) message of liberation, and laid siege to Syracuse by land and sea. Agathocles responded with astonishing bravado, which at the time surely seemed mad. On 14 August 310 (the day before a solar eclipse), he slipped out of Syracuse with a small army of 13,500 on 60 ships, evaded pursuit, and landed near Cape Bon. Burning the ships, he marched on Carthage.

This epic expedition lasted three years, causing upheavals even worse than those of the Libyan rebellions earlier in the century, partly because yet again the Libyans launched their own revolt. The Carthaginians were taken utterly by surprise. Their first resistance measures, drawing on the city's own resources because the invaders had largely cut it off from the *chora* and Libya, were disastrous. Of the two generals, Hanno was killed along with most of the new Sacred Battalion, while his political rival Bomilcar retreated to focus on the city's own security. This led to the notorious mass sacrifice of hundreds of children from aristocratic families which Diodorus describes. Agathocles could not assault Carthage but established his headquarters at Tunes, then marched through the countryside plundering it. He brought the east coast under his power, from Neapolis and Hadrumetum to Thapsus, and in 309 defeated another Carthaginian army.

The war was also going badly for Carthage in Sicily. Hamilcar failed in two attempts to capture Syracuse – and the second, in 309, ended with his army totally routed and Hamilcar himself captured by the Syracusans. They tortured him brutally to death in the streets, sending his head over to Agathocles. Disgusted at these defeats,

Carthage's Sicilian Greek allies including Acragas broke away to act for themselves, convulsing much of the island with fresh fighting, sieges and sackings. Carthaginian fortunes seemed bleak enough to encourage Bomilcar to make his coup attempt late in 308, just at the time when Agathocles was reinforced from Cyrene by a fresh army under an ambitious commander named Ophellas. Ophellas' notion of a North African kingdom for himself was promptly snuffed out by his murderous ally, but Agathocles kept his soldiers and went on to capture both Hippacra and Utica, just to Carthage's north.

Then, as so often in previous wars, the situation reversed itself. Syracuse's own fortunes in Sicily worsened, causing the tyrant (by now calling himself 'king' like Alexander's successor generals) to leave the expeditionary forces under his son Archagathus' command while he returned home. Stalemated at Tunes, the invaders turned to raiding inland. An officer named Eumachus made a profitable sweep through western Libya, taking Thugga and later Hippo Regius on the coast. His next foray took his division into Numidia, though we have seen that the places in Diodorus' narrative – Miltine and three 'cities of the apes' – cannot be identified. Eumachus' booty-haul was again great, but the pressure on Carthage had eased. Three new armies, small but efficiently led by the new generals Hanno, Himilco and Adherbal, fell on the equally divided invasion forces. What was left of these retreated to Tunes where they were themselves blockaded.

Agathocles hurried back from Sicily, only to be defeated in his turn. The Carthaginians did give him some unintended respite, accidentally setting their own makeshift camp ablaze with much loss of life (allegedly they were sacrificing their choicest prisoners by fire, but this is a dubious Greek claim: Chapter VII). Nevertheless Agathocles realised that the game in Africa was lost. With the same rational ruthlessness as always, the self-styled king slipped away by sea late in October 307, abandoning even his two sons whom the furious soldiers at once murdered.

The Carthaginians ended the war quickly in both theatres. Most of the deserted army took service with them; the rest were enslaved and put suitably to work restoring the ravaged countryside. We happen to know that Archagathus' killer Arcesilaus, an officer and former friend of the king, settled at Carthage as an exile: he would have interesting grandsons (Chapter XI). Rebel Libyans were brought back under control, no doubt with heavy penalties. Agathocles, still facing bitter enemies in Sicily, was ready to make peace, and the Carthaginians were prepared to make it bearable for him.

The division of the island at the Halycus was confirmed; he earned (ironically enough) a large Carthaginian subsidy too; and he remained free to subdue his Greek enemies, bringing virtually all Greek Sicily under his rule. Some years later he copied Dionysius I by intervening in southern Italy and across the Ionian sea.

On the evidence we have, this war, one of the longest – and surely the costliest – that Carthage had ever waged, had not been sought or planned by her. She had made repeated efforts to keep Sicily stable, against continual prodding and provocation from Syracuse. Nor was it well waged. The attempt to fight it on traditional lines was met by Agathocles' untraditional, desperation-born response; her generals in both theatres showed little ingenuity and élan, in contrast to Agathocles in Libya and some of his lieutenants in Sicily.

What did distinguish Carthage was her solid resolution not to give in. At no stage were the invaders offered terms. The war in Libya showed that she could maintain access to munitions and manpower although most of the hinterland was cut off. The defeat of one army was followed by the raising of another, just as was done in Sicily after Hamilcar's first siege of Syracuse failed. Even with the city short of food, in early 307, the authorities could still assemble, equip and send out the armies that turned the tables. The war illustrated, too, the mixture of fragility and strength in her dominion in North Africa. Subjects and even allies could turn readily against her when an inviting opportunity came, yet were soon brought back under control. Another striking feature was the secondary role played by her navy. Besides transporting armies and supplies, it was used mainly in blockading Syracuse by sea – not always successfully.

A further feature of Agathocles' war was the unquenchably, often viciously competitive energy of Greek Sicilians. They waged wars more often among themselves than against Carthage; repeatedly inflicted and suffered slaughter and devastation; then regouped, recovered and, after a generation, fought bitterly again over territory, plunder and hegemonies.

The only real gainer from the century of wars from 409 to 306 (at horrendous cost) was Syracuse. Under Dionysius I and then Agathocles it achieved a level of hegemonial power in Sicily and southern Italy that made it almost the equal of the great powers of the eastern Mediterranean, reducing one-time rivals like Acragas and Gela to local autonomy at best. In the west, Carthage had for long been the only great power, though never powerful enough to impose dominance on the many Greek and Italian states with which she did business. The imperial greatness of Syracuse would not last; but, halfway up the Italian peninsula, another concentration of power and hegemony was growing, which would one day sweep up all the rest.

The Carthaginians gained few lasting benefits from the wars. The gains that did come their way were short-term, like the wider Sicilian hegemony won in 405. Peace based on the limited status quo of the Halycus or, arguably, even the narrower status quo of 480–410 would have avoided the social, economic and physical damage of the wars on Carthage while (arguably) doing far more for her prosperity. The growing impact of Greek culture would quite likely have been still greater, and Carthage's own contribution to western Mediterranean life likewise.

CARTHAGE AND PYRRHUS

The peace of 306 lasted until Agathocles died in 289. Carthage had to be watchful, for the king's dominions kept growing: southern Italy as far north as Croton, and for a few years the island of Corcyra, modern Corfu, once he had amassed a 200-strong navy. His daughter married Pyrrhus, the ambitious warrior-king of Epirus. Still dissatisfied, according to Diodorus, he was planning a new war against Carthage when he sickened and died.

This was no doubt a relief to the republic, but the outcome was to renew her involvement in the rowdy affairs of Greek Sicily. Quite soon her general in the *epikrateia* intervened to settle political strife at Syracuse; but before long a new tyrant named Hicetas (maybe a descendant of the tyrant of the 340s) took power there, while inter-city enmities blossomed anew. Agathocles' Campanian mercenaries, forced to leave Syracuse, seized Messana – slaughtering or expelling the male citizens – then under the warlike name of 'Mamertines' (Mamers was the Campanian war-god) became a plundering terror to the entire island for decades. Tyrants again arose in cities everywhere, Diodorus dolefully remarks. Acragas' tyrant, Phintias, asserted his city's ambitions in typical ways: he emptied Gela of its population to make them found a new city nearby named Phintias (Licata today), and warred against Syracuse.

Hicetas defeated Phintias, then chose to invade Carthaginian Sicily, perhaps hoping for quick booty and more prestige. Instead he was so badly defeated that a rival overthrew him in 280. Phintias' successor also intervened at Syracuse. Now roused to action, the Carthaginians sent troops and ships to lay the city and the warring leaders under siege, rather as they had done in 344–343 against Dionysius II and the earlier Hicetas. The reprise was completed when another Greek outsider joined the action: Pyrrhus of Epirus, who was waging war against the Romans in southern Italy as Tarentum's ally and rescuer. Pyrrhus' own ambitions were grander than just saving the Tarentines – a western empire appealed to him – but his victories over the Romans, like Agathocles' over the Carthaginians, merely produced a stalemate. At this point an invitation from Syracuse to be its rescuer arrived. Of course he agreed.

While he was negotiating (fruitlessly) with the Romans about peace, the Carthaginians made a pact with them – backed up with a large subsidy delivered by an admiral, Mago – requiring that, if either state made an alliance with the king, this should still allow each to aid the other if it was attacked (obviously by Pyrrhus). It also set the rules under which that help might be rendered. As matters turned out, the Romans did not make peace with Pyrrhus, who then warred on Carthage and later against Rome again.[82]

Pyrrhus crossed to Sicily in 278, eluding a patrolling Carthaginian fleet to lead an alliance of Sicilian Greeks in a new drive against the 'barbarians'. But much the same happened as with his Italian war: success followed by frustration. First he swept right across the *epikrateia*, capturing one place after another – even the mountain fortress of Eryx above Drepana, and Panormus – until the Carthaginians held only the heavily-fortified port of Lilybaeum. It was a blitzkrieg unparalleled in their two and a half centuries in western Sicily. They offered him terms, including an indemnity and ships for transport (back to Italy, apparently) – terms which ignored Rome despite the recent pact. Pyrrhus rejected the offer. But his Sicilian allies were aghast at his proposal to invade Libya; they began to suspect his ambitions and were affronted at his high-handed behaviour towards them. As defections spread, the king left the island in disgust in 276 to rescue Tarentum all over again – only to be defeated by the Romans the following year and abandon Italy too. Tarentum capitulated in 272 to become Rome's newest subject ally.

At Syracuse a new and intelligent general, Hiero, came to power in 275 or 274, more concerned to curb the lawless Mamertines than to prolong hostilities with Carthage. The old status quo along the Halycus was restored, with the modest improvement that Acragas remained free from, and suspicious of, Syracuse and therefore had friendly relations with Carthage. The Carthaginians continued to watch Syracuse's doings carefully, but now they kept an eye on events in Italy too, where by 270 Rome exerted total control.

X

THE FIRST WAR WITH
ROME, AND AFTER

THE SECOND AND THIRD TREATIES
WITH ROME

Carthage's relations with Rome went back many centuries, as shown earlier. They were mainly commercial and were regulated from 509 on by the first treaty between the two, which laid down how merchants from Rome should and should not do business in Carthaginian territories, and made stipulations about attacks on cities in each other's neighbourhoods. These stipulations, so far as is known, never had to be acted upon.

Livy and Diodorus report another treaty in 348, without details, while Polybius gives the text in Greek – this time with no comment on its archaic Latin. It declared friendship between the Romans and their allies on one side, and 'the Carthaginians, Tyrians and Uticans' and their allies on the other. Some provisos resembled the old treaty. Should Carthaginians take any 'city in Latium' not subject to Rome, they could keep the booty and prisoners but must hand the city over to the Romans; a Roman could do business freely at Carthage and in Sicily 'which the Carthaginians govern', and a Carthaginian ditto at Rome; but Romans were not to sail past the Fair Cape (either Cape Farina or perhaps Cape Bon); and if a Roman or Carthaginian had to stop over in the other state's territory for provisions, he should not harm the locals and must leave within five days.

On the other hand, the new treaty put some fresh bans on Romans. No sailing, either, past Mastia Tarseion – apparently the Iberian town in south-eastern Spain which Carthage later refounded as New Carthage – and no raiding, commerce or city-founding in Libya or Sardinia (the old treaty had allowed trade in both). For the Carthaginians, if they captured any persons who had 'a written peace', meaning formal treaty links, with Rome and brought them into a Roman port, a Roman could free them; this applied vice versa to Romans.[83]

Much in this new agreement surprises. Rome was far more powerful and prosperous in 348 than around 509, so banning Roman traders from Libya and Sardinia must have been very disagreeable to them. Perhaps, after the rebellions around 370, the Carthaginians aimed to recoup the economic and financial damage by monopolising Libyan and Sardinian commerce. Banning Romans from sailing past a given site in south Spain looks superfluous if they could not sail westwards past Cape Farina in any case; perhaps it was just fussy drafting. Again, to ban Roman city-foundings in Libya and Sardinia is peculiar, for such settlements were being planted only in the regions around Rome itself, such as southern Etruria and Latium. Diodorus does have the Romans send a small colony 'to Sardinia' (*Sardonia* – not the usual *Sardo* or *Sardous*) in the 380s: but this may well be an error for the one they placed at Satricum in Latium in 385.

Peculiarly too, the Carthaginians were not banned from planting a city anywhere they might like in Italy or indeed Latium. Nor was Rome banned from founding one in Sicily – in or outside the *epikrateia* – though it was surely out of the question, from Carthage's viewpoint, to let that happen. The Campanians already in the island, like the mercenaries who had taken over Entella in the west in 404 and those settled by Carthage herself near Mt Etna later, gave enough trouble.

Aristotle's description a few years later of treaties made 'to prevent unjust acts by anyone' and 'for mutual commerce and dealings' – noting those between Carthaginians and Etruscans as examples – fits this one well. All the same, it put more prohibitions on the Romans than on the Carthaginians. Strikingly, it offered no fuller recognition of Roman hegemony in Latium than the first one did, and it only implicitly acknowledged Rome's diplomatic ties beyond Latium (in the 'written peace' clause, which did not specify Latin persons alone). The treaty seems something of a selective potpourri: modifying some existing rules, adding new ones which included superfluous or very hypothetical provisos, and leaving out other matters that were arguably just as or more relevant. Conceivably it may have been based on a standard template that Carthage used for territorial and commercial agreements. We might even wonder whether the text that Polybius saw was in Greek and was used by both signatories.

Polybius, who found the first two treaties, the anti-Pyrrhus pact of 279, and the later Roman–Carthaginian treaties in an archive at Rome, found too that neither Romans nor Carthaginians in his time knew of them. Later writers were just as uninterested, apart from registering treaty dates (real or supposed): thus Livy reports a 'third' renewal in 306 and a 'fourth' in 279. An exception was the pro-Carthaginian Philinus of Acragas, who reported that Rome and Carthage had a treaty banning the former from Sicily and the latter from Italy. This allowed him to put the Romans in the wrong over the outbreak of war in 264, when Roman legions crossed to Messana. Polybius, the only source for his claim, dismisses it because Philinus knew none of the other treaties and his supposed text was not in the archive. By contrast, many moderns dismiss Polybius instead.[84]

The chief argument for the 'Philinus' treaty is that it fitted international conditions in 306 better than a renewed 348 treaty, for by 306 Rome directly controlled not only all Latium but much of Italy, notably Campania and Etruria. By 279 in turn, Roman hegemony covered the entire peninsula except its Greek south. This could seem to make nonsense of Polybius' report that the pact against Pyrrhus 'confirmed the existing agreements', if that meant confirming the seventy-year-old treaty. Later ancient historians, Livy included, certainly tried hard to find some Carthaginian act before 264 which could count as an incursion against Italy: obviously they were seeking to turn Philinus' claim to Rome's benefit.

Yet in 306 Carthage was in no position to think about warring in Italy, and the Romans were still fighting the Samnites and Etruscans. Neither had military or political grounds for making an agreement like Philinus' – even apart from the obvious fact that neither had control over 'all Sicily' or 'all Italy' in 306. Later writers' anxiety to put the Carthaginians in the wrong before 264 proves only that they had read and believed Philinus. The one item in the 348 treaty making no sense in 306 or 279 was the 'cities in Latium' clause: but, without the words 'in Latium', even this could still apply as late as 279, though Polybius might well ignore (or overlook) the omission.

Philinus very probably knew of the 279 pact, for he not only recorded the First Punic War but began with an introductory book leading up to it. As outlined above, the terms added in 279 bound each state, if it were to ally with Pyrrhus, to retain the right to help the other militarily. Carthage would supply naval transport for troops of either state, and would send warships too to help the Romans 'if need be'. As it proved, neither Rome nor Carthage did ally with Pyrrhus, or ask the other for help – not even when the Carthaginians were confined to Lilybaeum by the king's blitzkrieg. The only fruit of the pact was that before he crossed to Sicily, a small Carthaginian force went over to Italy via Roman-held Rhegium, to do minor damage to a Greek ally of his. Philinus might draw the seemingly clear deduction that military intervention in Italy or Sicily was normally disallowed. He did not know the real treaties of 509 and 348, which envisaged and regulated just such acts.

THE OUTBREAK OF THE WAR

Pyrrhus supposedly remarked on sailing from Sicily: 'What a fine wrestling-ground we are leaving for the Romans and Carthaginians!' This may be *ben trovato* rather than true, for at the time those states were trading partners and allies (of a sort) against him, the Tarentines' war was not yet lost, and the remark left out of account the other great power in the island. All the same the wrestling began just a few years later, in strange circumstances.[85]

In 264, facing destruction from Hiero of Syracuse, the trapped Mamertines at Messana appealed both to nearby Carthaginians – a fleet at Lipara under one Hannibal – and to the more distant Romans. As in 315 against Agathocles, once again Carthage saved Messana, putting some troops into the city to deter the Syracusans. The Mamertines accepted the troops until they learned that Rome would also help: then they sent the Carthaginians away. Their appeal to Rome had made much of their Campanian background, but at Rome a good deal of debate had taken place over whether to agree to an alliance with such thuggish freebooters. According to our sources, Polybius included, the interventionists – among them the consuls, Rome's equivalent of sufetes – argued that Italy was menaced by Carthaginian expansionism, and also that there would be plenty of plunder. Finally one consul, Appius Claudius, was sent with a consular army of two legions to cross the straits at Rhegium to aid the new allies.

In reality aid was not needed, as Hiero (now King Hiero by acclamation) had taken his forces home. But when word reached Carthage that her force at Messana had been dismissed, her reaction was both fast and thoroughly unexpected. The force's commander was crucified (for stupidity), troops were set in motion, alliances were made both with Acragas and – unprecedentedly – with Syracuse, and together the new allies Carthage and Syracuse put Messana under siege by land and sea. Facing this remarkable turn of events, the consul at Rhegium belied his earlier warlike stance by sending an offer to negotiate. It was rejected by both the Carthaginian general (another Hanno) and Hiero, an act they may soon have regretted.

Eluding Carthaginian warships, Appius ferried his legions across to Messana; then defeated first the Syracusan and next the Carthaginian army, which retreated to their own territories. In this way hostilities began.

The reasons for the outbreak of war have been debated from that time to this. One standard explanation basically accepts the ancient one: the Romans feared Carthage's expansionism and acted to avert it militarily. Another reverses it: the Romans were aggressive, expansionist, and greedy for the wealth of both Sicily and Africa, and therefore launched the war – while of course seeking to cover this up by blaming their opponents. A blended view (going back to the later Roman historian Cassius Dio) sees both powers as greedy, aggressive, suspicious of each other, and keen to annex each other's territories. The events themselves suggest a different and less easily defined set of causes. The Mamertines had sought Rome's help against Hiero; Appius offered talks when he found himself facing not just Syracusan forces but also Carthaginian. Having driven them off, he and then his campaigning successors the consuls of 263 focused their offensives on Syracuse until Hiero in summer 263 asked for peace. The Carthaginians sent Syracuse no help until too late (a fleet sailed up just after Hiero made peace; then sailed away). Once Hiero was out of the war, on easy terms, one consul returned home with half the Roman forces.

In sum, these events indicate that in 264 the Romans had expected to fight alongside their new Mamertine allies against Syracuse. Eastern Sicily was renowned for its wealth (even if this had not recovered fully from past wars) while Hiero's city, though far below its Agathoclean power, was rebuilding its strength and reach. The Romans, having replaced Agathocles' and Dionysius' mastery over southern Italian Greeks with their own, could feel entitled to worry. Carthage had been concerned about Syracuse, too, as the rescue of Messana showed, yet was prepared to hold her nose and ally with her old enemy against the town she had just rescued: the reasonable inference is that she feared letting the Romans into Sicily, whatever Appius' peaceful protestations. They had been her trading partners and nominal allies for two hundred and fifty years; but to have them permanently in the same island as the *epikrateia* was plainly seen at Carthage as a threat – rightly or wrongly. The astonishing speed with which Rome thrust Syracuse out of the war, and thus effectively achieved dominant power over eastern Sicily, made the threat still more critical.

If so, hostilities resulted from a series of fears and miscalculations, starting with the Roman decision to accept the Mamertines as allies and Carthage's double volte-face in reaction, attacking Messana and allying with Syracuse. It was another mistake to refuse to talk with Appius at Rhegium – not to mention the failure after that to block him from crossing with some 16,000 troops – and yet a third error was to leave Hiero to carry on the war alone. Syracuse's capacity to fight wars for years, and its physical impregnability, had so impressed the Carthaginians for more than a century that they no doubt expected the same again, only to find that they had miscalculated.

PHASES OF WAR: 264 TO 257

The First Punic War turned into something entirely new in Carthaginian experience. It lasted almost a quarter of a century, nearly as long as all of Carthage's 4th-Century Sicilian wars put together. It demanded large and lasting forces both on land and at sea, with operations that ranged over all her territories. Her fleets played a much more crucial role than ever before, without enjoying more than a few successes. At no time in twenty-three years did she use her naval strength to send military forces into Italy, not even after the Romans' invasion of Africa in 256–255. Of course, doing so might have had no better luck than that adventure. On the other hand, the impact could have been crucial to her fortunes.

Instead the Carthaginians showed themselves more conservative than their enemies in waging war. They had always warred in Sicily, Africa or Sardinia: this one brought no change of practice. By contrast the Romans moved their war effort outside Italy for the first time (Polybius notes the historical significance of this); and then after a time took a still more momentous initiative – becoming a naval as well as a land power. It may have been only because they waged the war with remarkable clumsiness that Carthage was able to keep fighting until 241.

Another novel feature was that most of the war in Sicily was fought in the island's west, especially the *epikrateia*. Already in late 263 Segesta there declared for the Romans. A planned Carthaginian counter-offensive in 262 was derailed by the new consuls (Roman commanders changed yearly). Four legions besieged Acragas, defended by the Mamertines' rescuer Hannibal, and routed a relief army under Hiero's old collaborator Hanno, whose 60 elephants were badly mauled – incidentally, the first Carthaginian elephant corps we hear of. When the Carthaginians left Acragas to its fate in early 261, Greek Sicily's second city was sacked yet again, with up to

50,000 people made slaves. More significantly still for Carthage, it was now (as Polybius tells it) that the Romans decided to drive her altogether out of Sicily. To put it another way, three years into the war Rome finally resolved to impose its own hegemony over the entire island.

The fateful resolve to create a Roman navy followed, once Carthaginian warships started raiding Italy's western coasts from Sardinia. A Carthaginian quinquereme captured by Appius Claudius three years before gave the Romans their model; their Italian coastal allies, Greeks included, supplied most of the crews; and an unknown designer hit on a device to combat the Carthaginians' greater battle-skills – fitting a long wooden bridge attached, through a slot at one end, to a pole on each ship's foredeck and with an iron spike at its other end. It could be swung with ropes to fall immovably onto an enemy deck as the two ships closed for action, allowing the 300 or so waiting Roman troops to charge across and overwhelm the enemy. This was the famous 'raven' (*corvus*), another Roman initiative. In 260 the grand fleet (built in sixty days, says Polybius) of about 120 ships under the consul Duillius met and thrashed Hannibal's 130 off Mylae. The *corvus* took the Carthaginians by surprise, accounting for heavy losses in ships and men. As was noted earlier, even for Carthaginian crews the quinquereme was probably still a fairly recent acquisition, and they lacked much combat practice. The tactic of head-to-head ramming could be outmatched, they discovered, if a Roman ship swerved aside a little and then dropped its boarding-bridge, for Roman and Italian allied heavy infantry were too much for the Carthaginians' shipboard troops.

A later copy of Duillius' understandably pleased triumphal inscription survives, rather damaged, to tell both of his exploits on land (he rescued Segesta from siege) and of his naval victory over the Carthaginian 'dictator' Hannibal with copious booty and prisoners. Yet even with naval equality established, the Romans for some years merely raided Sardinia and Corsica. Another victory, off Sulcis in 258, so shamed the defeated Carthaginian crews – many if not most of them citizen sailors – that they themselves crucified their admiral Hannibal (probably the same man as before). This lesson failed to prevent a third setback off Tyndaris in 257. It is another example of their conservative approach to war that the Carthaginians never copied the *corvus* or devised some means of countering it.

AFRICA INVADED AND SAVED:
256–255

On land the war briefly moved eastward in 259 with a Carthaginian victory near Thermae Himeraeae and the capture of both Enna and Camarina, but the Carthaginian forces were pushed back to Panormus the following year. Then the entire struggle stalled. This led the Romans to try a fresh initiative: invading Africa. A hugely increased fleet – Polybius' perhaps exaggerated figure is 330 warships – led by both consuls of 256 used the *corvus* to demolish a comparable Carthaginian fleet off Cape Economus west of Heraclea Minoa, and disembarked four legions of Romans and Italian allies on the Cape Bon peninsula. These then took the little town of Clupea (Aspis to Greeks) and marched south. A few old Carthaginians surely had vivid memories of Agathocles landing near there half a century before.

In spite of a surprising, and hard to explain, order from the senate at Rome now recalling one consul, the fleet and part of the army, the invasion force of some 15,000 Romans and Italian allies under Marcus Atilius Regulus rolled forward much as Agathocles' had. The same wealthy countryside was plundered, some twenty thousand people were seized for enslavement, and numbers of enslaved prisoners from Italy were freed. The Carthaginian army that confronted Regulus at 'Adys', probably Uthina near the river Catadas 40 kilometres south of Tunes, was totally defeated on a hilltop (where its elephants proved useless). It had probably not been helped by having no fewer than three generals in command: Hasdrubal and Bostar appointed at Carthage, and Hamilcar summoned over with troops from Sicily. Things grew worse, with refugees flooding into Carthage and, again as in Agathocles' time, revolts starting to erupt in the countryside. Though Polybius calls the rebels 'Numidians', he all but certainly is writing about the Libyan subjects of Carthage. Over the winter of 256–255 the Carthaginians did what they had refused to do with Agathocles: they sent envoys to Regulus to ask for his terms.

We know of his demands not from Polybius but from Dio, whose list gives some which look plausible: Carthage to abandon Sicily, free all her prisoners of war and ransom her own prisoners from Rome, and indemnify the Romans for their war costs. Others in his list, tacked on like an addendum, are invented exaggerations of later peace terms (no fleet, no war or peace without Rome's permission), but even the plausible demands were more than the Carthaginians would accept. Instead they succeeded in turning the tables by accepting the guidance of a newly-arrived Spartan mercenary officer named Xanthippus (not that it made him popular with his employers, as mentioned earlier). The Romans were brought to battle in spring 255, on level ground, by a roughly equal army 16,000 strong, with no fewer than 100 elephants across its front. These broke up and trampled the Roman infantry while on the wings the Carthaginian cavalry drove off the enemy's: then it was virtually inevitable that the victorious horsemen would strike the legions in flank and rear, causing a catastrophe. Regulus and a few hundred others fell into Carthaginian hands; 2000 survivors got away to Clupea, where a fresh Roman fleet eventually arrived to rescue them after first smashing an opposing fleet off Cape Bon. A further and still grimmer Roman disaster followed, for a summer storm caught the returning Romans off Sicily's unfriendly south-eastern coast, sinking all but 80 of their several hundred ships and drowning the nearly unbelievable total of some 100,000 seamen and soldiers.

The Roman invasion had lasted only about a year, in contrast to Agathocles's three. Its failure no doubt delighted the Carthaginians, but offered them some sobering though perhaps unappreciated lessons too. The Romans might have done better had they not reduced their invasion force and had Regulus made some effort to collaborate with the Libyan, or 'Numidian', rebels. The Carthaginians might well have done better had they put one general, such as the experienced Hamilcar from Sicily, in command from the start. They owed the final victory to a foreigner – something they resented, it seems, for Xanthippus soon left their service for that of the king of Egypt. (That the ungrateful Carthaginians had him murdered is a myth, like the famous tale of them later torturing Regulus to death when he would not urge the Romans to make peace.)

VICTORIES, DEFEATS, STALEMATE: 254 TO 242

The war, already almost a decade old, shifted focus back to Sicily where in 254 it began to go wrong again for Carthage. An unusually sophisticated amphibious Roman assault on Panormus in 254 cost her the richest city in the shrinking *epikrateia*, where the Romans extracted ransom in the usual way from the residents who could pay (some fourteen thousand altogether) while the rest, about thirteen thousand souls, were sold into slavery. Other places, such as Solous and the isolated allied town Tyndaris, were lost too. When a Carthaginian general, Carthalo, retook shattered Acragas, he could not hold it and therefore razed it. By 253 the *epikrateia* was merely a stretch of the west coast from Drepana in the north (now a strongly fortified port) round to Heraclea Minoa in the south. Thermae and the Lipara islands were still in Carthaginian hands, but went the way of Panormus and Tyndaris a year later. On the other hand, the rebels in Africa were subdued by Hamilcar, and a large new Roman fleet which raided Libya's east coast in 253 was devastated by another storm on the open sea between Sicily and Sardinia, with thousands more men drowned. On one theory the *corvus* was given up after these tragedies, because its weight could overbalance ships in heavy weather. At any rate, it never reappears in the historical record.

Both sides were by now under severe strain. Carthage had suffered much lower losses of life overall, but around 250 approached Ptolemy II of Egypt to lend her 2000 talents (12,000,000 Greek drachmas, a very large sum), a request which he diplomatically turned down. The war, again limited to western Sicily, continued more or less at a standstill until a sudden pounce at Panormus, at harvest-time in 250, by the then Carthaginian general Hasdrubal. He had no fewer than 140 elephants and hoped to retake the city, held by two legions under Lucius Caecilius Metellus, but once more the animals brought trouble on his army – running amok under a hail of spears and javelins from the walls to trample the Carthaginian infantry – with the catastrophe then completed by a bold Roman sortie. Not only were the Carthaginians bloodily beaten but scores of elephants (if not the entire herd) were captured by Metellus, who sent them off to Rome for display. Hasdrubal suffered the regular fate of disgraced generals at Carthage.

By now she had lost all of her old territories in Sicily except the two fortress ports Drepana and Lilybaeum. The rest of the war focused on these two closely-besieged places; save for Hiero's moderately-sized kingdom, the rest of the island was controlled by Rome.

Carthage's first victories since the defeat of Regulus, and her last in the war, were won in 249. When one consul tried to take out the Carthaginian fleet anchored in Drepana's harbour, Adherbal the general there brilliantly outmanoeuvred him to sink or capture 93 of his 120 ships and thousands of prisoners. Next his colleague Carthalo, arriving from Africa with naval reinforcements, first mauled the surviving Roman warships anchored near the army besieging Lilybaeum, then sailed round against a second enemy fleet escorting a large supply convoy along the south coast. Without a battle he forced them to beach on the unfriendly shores between Camarina and Phintias, where he left them to the even unfriendlier mercies of yet another giant storm. The 800-strong supply convoy was wrecked, as were all but two of the other consul's 120 warships. In perhaps a couple of weeks, in a sequence of remarkable fleet actions, two enterprising Carthaginian commanders thus wiped the existing Roman navy off the sea.

Yet the victories were not effectively followed up, partly because the Carthaginians were now financing the war on a shoestring, despite squeezing massive taxes out of their Libyan subjects. Adherbal's and Carthalo's victories did not break the twin sieges; by 247 both were replaced, never to reappear. The agile fleets and crews of 249 were reduced to convoying and raiding. The Romans, too, made no new naval push but maintained the relentless pressure on the western ports, while also encouraging private citizens' ships to harass Carthaginian merchant craft. In 247 the new general in Sicily, an officer named Hamilcar, tried to shift the focus of action by seizing a broad mountaintop in the hinterland of Panormus – various locales have been suggested – to launch attacks on enemy forces in Sicily and renew seaborne raids on Italy's coasts. The Romans responded by putting him, too, under blockade on the mountaintop, though he still broke out from time to time. After three years he made a lightning move over to Mt Eryx above Drepana, obviously hoping to have greater impact on the besiegers there. But this time, able to occupy only a ridge under the enemy-held summit and above their siege camp outside Drepana, he was still more restricted.

Hamilcar's raiding style, or his skill at fighting on in these hard positions year after year, earned him the nickname 'Barca' – *Baraq* in Punic, meaning either 'lightning' or (rather likelier) 'blessed' – and quite unstinting admiration from Polybius, who judges him the war's most outstanding general. His achievements were very limited in fact, mainly because the forces he had were small and funds hard to find. By war's end the mercenary and Libyan troops in Sicily, including the garrisons of the ports, numbered only about 20,000, a far cry from the imposing armies of previous decades, and they had not been paid in a long while.

One brighter spot for Carthage was that in these years her Libyan territories expanded. This was achieved by another newcomer on the scene, the second Hanno to be called 'the Great' in Greek and Roman authors. While Hamilcar operated in Sicily, Hanno campaigned in the hinterland, around 247 taking – and treating humanely – the town of Theveste in the fertile plateau-country some

250 kilometres south-west of Carthage. He may well have annexed Sicca too, again in a fertile countryside north of Theveste and about 175 kilometres west of Carthage, for this town was under the city's control by 241. Their regions, and those nearby around Mactar and Zama, meant fresh taxpaying sources at a time when the republic's finances were under worse pressure than ever. Even though Hanno the Great later became Hamilcar Barca's irreconcilable opponent, they probably began as political collaborators around 248–247: Hamilcar as general in Sicily, Hanno as an equal-ranking general in Libya. Hanno in these years certainly enjoyed military success, and therefore prestige, denied to Hamilcar. He seems to have been Carthage's leading figure politically, with Hamilcar relying (partly anyway) on his support to keep his own command across the water.

PEACE AND REVOLT

The seemingly endless war was at last decided on the sea. The Romans raised a citizens' loan in 242 to launch a brand-new fleet, again modelled on an up-to-date Carthaginian quinquereme (this one recently captured outside Lilybaeum). Somehow taken by surprise when the fleet arrived in west Sicilian waters unseasonally early in 241, the Carthaginians had a desperate scramble to resupply the blockaded ports with munitions and troops. In the first week of March a different Hanno sailed out with ill-prepared ships, poorly-trained crews, and laden transports. On the 10th, in rough seas, the consul Gaius Lutatius Catulus and his deputy, the praetor Marcus Valerius Falto, met the Carthaginians off the Aegates Islands just west of Drepana. Fifty of Hanno's warships were sunk, 70 taken, and 10,000 prisoners captured. On his return to Carthage the authorities put him on a cross (ironically, the fate of the first Hanno at Messana twenty-three years earlier), while authorising Hamilcar at Eryx to negotiate peace.

Unsurprisingly, the terms agreed on were painful. Carthage withdrew from western Sicily, three hundred years after the first campaigns by Mazeus. She paid Rome 1000 talents (6,000,000 Greek drachmas) at once, with another 2200 payable over ten years. Hiero was guaranteed against attack: that ancient rivalry, too, was done. Yet there was no ban on trade with Roman-dominated Sicily or Hiero, or any control over what the Carthaginians could do elsewhere. The implications for Rome of acquiring, in effect, the first province of a future empire took time to be realised: the subject

Sicilians were lightly controlled until the 220s or even later, while Syracuse held on to a modest level of independence. The Romans were soon ready for business with Carthage once again, even ready to help their ex-foes when they fell into dire straits.

Carthage had suffered rather fewer losses than Rome in ships and lives, but was financially desperate, especially after paying the 1000 talents. The war cost her a strategic and revenue-rich buffer in Sicily. It inflicted a severe blow to both her prestige and – more severely perhaps – her sense of security. The fleets had not in practice justified her reputation for unequalled naval skills, nor had most Carthaginian generals been any better than their Roman opposite numbers. Under the current Hanno the Great's exacting supervision as general in Libya, countryside and towns had to pay the harsh taxes and levies described earlier: yet all that their rulers could show in return were losses and tragedies. It was not the first time that setbacks abroad caused a backlash in Africa, but this proved to be the worst.

The republic misguidedly tried to bargain down the arrears of pay owed to Hamilcar Barca's returned army. Hamilcar himself, no longer general, stayed in the background. The men – 20,000 foreign mercenaries and Libyan conscripts – were sent out with their families from Carthage to Sicca, nearly 200 kilometres inland, where Hanno tried but failed to negotiate reductions. The angry troops marched back to Tunes to force fresh talks. Then, just after the Carthaginians finally conceded their demands, a violent coup at Tunes late in 241 installed new and radical leaders who murdered the old commanders and instigated a revolt.

The new generals were a Libyan, Mathos, a Campanian Roman deserter called Spendius, and Autaritus the leader of the Gallic mercenaries. What caused the revolt is not clear in Polybius' narrative, the only detailed source. It may be that the radicals exploited Carthage's current military weakness (she now had only Hanno's small army in the countryside) and fears by the Libyan troops for their own fate once the foreign mercenaries were paid off and departed. Since most or all the Libyan communities promptly joined the revolt, the rebels no doubt hoped for a swift victory with plunder and the end of Carthage's hegemony. The foreign mercenaries may well have looked forward to settling in Libya, on the lines of the Campanians at Entella and Messana in Sicily.

The 'Truceless War', as Polybius calls it, lasted over three years with abrupt changes of fortune and a grim level of brutality by both sides. It again brought out the dogged and resourceful side of the Carthaginians when faced with possible disaster. With Hanno achieving little, Hamilcar was reappointed general during 240. He organised a small army of citizens and others, sortied from Carthage in spite of the rebels' blockade, and put fresh vigour into the fight-back by defeating Spendius beside the Bagradas and then marching inland to begin reimposing control. His resources were limited and his strategy risky. At one point he was surrounded by Spendius' and Autaritus' troops and by a force of Numidian cavalry, actuated perhaps by sympathy for their Libyan kinfolk as well as hopes of booty – but persuaded Naravas the Numidians' leader to change sides and help him defeat the rebels. Naravas looks like a son of the Massylian king Zilalsan mentioned earlier (Chapter VIII), for an inscription set up by a Numidian lord at Mactar in 128 names an ancestor as *Nrwt* son of Zilalsan (*Zllsan*). Hamilcar promised the young prince one of his daughters in marriage, a promise he seems to have kept.

Hamilcar's strategy focused on the Libyan heartland and largely ignored the coastlands. There Carthage was blockaded from Tunes, Hippacra and Utica besieged, and Hanno (it seems) able only to keep the rebels from doing worse. Other misfortunes occurred: the mercenaries in Sardinia seized the island, slaughtered all the Carthag-inians they could, and won over a force sent to confront them. Probably during 239 Hippacra and Utica both changed sides. The war's savagery intensified – the rebels mutilating and killing their prisoners, Hamilcar retaliating (he had his elephants trample captives, a method imitated from Alexander's successor generals). He then had to call on Hanno to combine forces with him, but their disagreements paralysed their military efforts. The authorities at Carthage directed the soldiers themselves – no doubt the citizen troops and officers – to decide between them: Hamilcar was chosen by the men, resuming operations with Hanno's more compliant replacement and with Naravas' sterling cavalry. Nevertheless Carthage's troubles encouraged Mathos at Tunes to tighten the blockade into a closer siege for several months, roughly from late summer 239 until early 238.

The Libyans, or at any rate their military leaders, were empha-sising the solidarity of their movement by striking coins (in some cases, overstriking Carthaginian coins) with the Greek word *Libyon*, 'of the Libyans' (*Illustration 24h*). This and the coins' find-spots in Sicily, not North Africa, suggest that they were used to pay traders from the island who dealt in arms and other supplies. Roman and Italian traders took part in this commerce too at first, leading to hundreds being intercepted by Carthaginian warships. After a

Roman protest they were freed: a sensible step, since the Romans then banned such trading and rendered Carthage valuable other help, like repatriating thousands of war-prisoners ransom-free. Hiero of Syracuse, aware of the peril of losing Carthage as a counter-balance to Rome, was another generous helper.

Even so the tide was very slow to turn. Hamilcar cut off Mathos and his men from the interior so effectively that they gave up besieging Carthage to fall back on Tunes. Still too weak, it seems, to attack them directly, Hamilcar returned inland to continue reasserting Carthaginian control, shadowed by another large rebel army under Spendius and Autaritus. The climax of a lengthy campaign of manoeuvres, marches and clashes came when this army was trapped at a place that Polybius calls 'the Saw' (*Prion*), seemingly a mountain ridge somewhere in Libya. After holding out to the point of canni-balising their captives and slaves, the rebels tried to capitulate, only for Hamilcar to turn on them and wipe them out save for the two generals and their lieutenants. These he took with him back to Tunes to crucify on a hilltop (perhaps in today's Parc du Belvédère) in full view of Mathos' troops. Mathos revenged Spendius and the others by defeating Hamilcar's colleague there – Hamilcar's division was on the far side of Tunes – and crucifying him and other eminent prisoners on the same crosses.

Politics and common sense intervened at Carthage to impose a temporary reconciliation on Hamilcar and Hanno, who from then on cooperated intelligently to force Mathos from Tunes out to Byzacium, where they were conclusively crushed. All Libya capitulated, as did Hippacra and Utica by early 237. The last scene of all, Polybius records, was the young men of Carthage leading Mathos in triumph through the streets while torturing him to death – much like the fate in 309 of the Hamilcar captured by the Syracusans. The punishments inflicted on the rebel communities are not reported. This time the Carthaginians may have acted with restraint: Utica at least did not lose its special relationship with Carthage and was stubbornly loyal under Scipio's siege thirty-five years later, nor did Libyan communi-ties defect to him during his marches through their lands. The resources to rebuild the shattered state would be found in Spain.

XI

THE NEW EMPIRE AND
HANNIBAL

THE SARDINIA CRISIS

Hamilcar Barca had effectively saved Carthage, if with invaluable help from Naravas the Numidian and Hanno the Great. It was Hamilcar and his supporters who reaped the benefit: over the next thirty-five years their 'Barcid' group dominated the republic's affairs. First Hamilcar, then his politically skilful son-in-law Hasdrubal, and finally his eldest son Hannibal were in turn elected generals and, in effect, the commanders-in-chief of Carthaginian armed forces, able to have their own choices appointed as subordinates. At Carthage their kinsmen and political supporters had similarly effective control of offices, though probably never a monopoly. Barcid generals commanded in all the important theatres of war (and some less important ones) from 237 to 201, while at Carthage the *adirim* and sufetes – whenever a glimpse of them occurs – are found seconding Barcid wishes and voting down rival arguments. Hanno the Great and his group were completely ineffectual (as they complained repeatedly), at least until the end of the Second Punic War.[86]

Ironically, the Barcids' dominance at Carthage was a fact that both they and their opponents wanted to deny by the end of the war. Their opponents, and Roman friends of these like the contemporary historian Fabius Pictor, argued that the Barcid generals in Spain had launched the war in the teeth of universal opposition at home. The Barcid side, Hannibal included, claimed that he lost because the home authorities had refused to support him properly. Both claims are still widely believed, though neither is convincing. The reality is that in the Barcids, as in the Magonids and the family of the first Hanno the Great, Carthage found a new ruling house, its success resting on military prowess and adept political skills until these assets collapsed.

Hamilcar's planned expedition to southern Spain in 237 made sound sense from Carthage's point of view. The old Phoenician cities there, notably Gades, were suitable bridgeheads. Hamilcar had a veteran army that he could count on for success. The land was well developed, its towns and peoples long in close contact with Phoenician and Carthaginian civilisation, and its regions rich in mineral resources: silver above all. Spain was also on the opposite side of the western Mediterranean from Rome.

Besides this expedition, another was readied to recover Sardinia where the rebel mercenaries had been thrown out by the native Sardinians and appealed to Rome for help. The Romans now made a sudden, this time unwelcome, return to Carthage's affairs. Claiming that Italy and not Sardinia was the real target, they refused to negotiate but instead declared formal war on Carthage to get their way. In no condition to resist, she had to give up Sardinia and pay out no less than 1200 talents more. These extraordinary actions Polybius himself condemns as unjust, without trying to explain them. The Romans, however, surely knew that their renowned recent adversary Hamilcar was now effectively in power. With Sicily lost, Sardinia's position and wealth would be invaluable in efforts to rebuild Carthage economically and militarily. The immediate payment exacted – larger than in 241 – strengthens the impression that the Romans sought to check a rapid Carthaginian recovery.

Hamilcar felt the humiliation keenly. His son in later life told the famous story of how his father agreed to take him, aged nine, to Spain once Hannibal swore on the altar of 'Zeus' – Baal Hammon or Baal Shamim – 'never to be friendly towards the Romans' (often misrepresented as always to be the enemy of Rome, a very different attitude). Polybius and others, rightly or wrongly, judged the seizure of Sardinia to be the first of the causes of the next war.

THE NEW EMPIRE IN SPAIN

From 237 until his death in 229 Hamilcar extended Carthaginian domination over most of southern Spain, especially the lower and middle valley of the river Baetis (modern Guadalquivir). The Carthaginians, based at Gades, conquered some communities by force while winning over others as allies, though the excerpts and passing comments in Polybius, Diodorus and others give minimal details. As in the war in Libya, Hamilcar could use brutal methods when it suited him – for instance mutilating and crucifying Indortes, a defeated Iberian chieftain – but this seems to have been rare. By 228 the province extended across southern Spain, with military forces over 50,000 strong and a corps of 100 elephants from Africa. Hamilcar's control of affairs over there is well illustrated by his despatch of his son-in-law Hasdrubal at one stage to put down a rising by a Numidian people, called by Diodorus the 'Micatani' (they may have been foes of Naravas' Massyli).

Hamilcar made Carthage more of a land power than ever before. While the Spanish territories expanded, the navy contracted. While in the first war with Rome Carthaginian fleets numbered between 120 and 350 ships, on the outbreak of the second the quinqueremes and triremes at Carthage and in Spain totalled just over 100 – with nearly 20 of them unfit to fight. His successes had the desired impact at home. According to Cornelius Nepos' brief biography, 'with horses, weapons, men and money he enriched all Africa'. The horses and men (probably war-prisoners) may have been sent over to work in towns and the countryside like the enslaved men from Agathocles' army after 307, while the weapons would include highly-regarded swords and javelins, all of iron. The money of course came from booty, tribute, and increasingly from mines – old ones like the workings in the Río Tinto region by the Atlantic, newer ones in the mountains north of the Baetis and around Mastia, the later New Carthage.

How the new province was governed is obscure. The Phoenician cities such as Gades, Malaca and Abdera must have been formal allies, tribute-free but perhaps required to provide ships and crews for transport, even maybe a few warships. The Iberian and Celtic communities allied with Carthage would provide stated contingents of infantry and cavalry, while those subdued by force probably had to supply both soldiers and tribute. Some, if not all, of the mines were state-owned, though in practice leased to contractors, as was done in Greece and by the Romans. Pliny the Elder's report of 300 pounds of silver mined daily in Hannibal's time at a place (unknown) called Baebelo may really be a misunderstanding of the yield – equivalent to some 9,000,000 drachmas or 1440 talents a year – from all the mines in Barcid Spain by then. The silver coins, shekels and other denominations, struck by the Barcid authorities in strongly Greek styles, were products of this wealth (*Illustration 24i*).

Hamilcar's constructive activities included founding a new city which Diodorus calls Akra Leuke – White Cape or White Fort. It may be the Lucentum of Roman times, today's Alacant (Alicante) on the south coast, though other identifications are possible. Akra Leuke, if it was Lucentum, was both a good port linking Barcid

Spain with North Africa and also advertised the growing grandeur of Hamilcar himself as leader of his state. The Carthaginians had not been noted city-founders like the Phoenicians, with Lilybaeum and Thermae Himeraeae their only creations in centuries. Hellenistic rulers on the other hand were enthusiastic about it, starting with Alexander whose Egyptian Alexandria was only his most famous foundation.

In winter 229–228, campaigning somewhere in mountainous country above Mastia, Hamilcar lost his life, attacked by a supposedly allied king from further north. He saved his sons Hannibal and Hasdrubal, but perished on horseback in a torrential river. His son-in-law Hasdrubal was acclaimed general in his place by the troops and confirmed by the citizens at Carthage. A winning though not always mild personality, the new leader consolidated the province as well as extending its borders up to the river Tagus. Perhaps by now a widower (or perhaps not), he married the daughter of a Spanish king, encouraged his brother-in-law Hannibal to take a Spanish wife too, and convened a gathering of Spanish leaders, no doubt carefully chosen, to declare him their supreme general: *strategos autokrator*, according to Diodorus, though what term the Spaniards used is not known.

In 227 or 226, Hasdrubal in his turn founded a city, transforming or entirely replacing the old Iberian town Mastia with a grandly conceived creation which he named *Qart-hadasht*, New City: a 'Carthage' for Spain. Sited between a safe harbour along its south side and a salt-water lagoon along the other, on its many hills stood the temples mentioned earlier of Baal Hammon, Eshmun, perhaps Kusor and the perhaps Iberian deity Aletes (Chapter VII), while the splendid palace of the generalissimo himself crowned another. That Hasdrubal thus declared his independence from his native land is an idea going back to his contemporary Fabius Pictor, who passed on accusations from Carthaginian anti-Barcids. This ignores the other Carthages in the Mediterranean such as the even older one in Cyprus (Chapter I); a possible one in Sardinia; Neapolis, as the Greeks called the *Qart-hadasht* on the gulf of Hammamet; and Carthage's own outer suburb the 'New City'. Rather, Spanish Carthage – with its striking hilltop – announced the renewed strength of the Carthaginian state to the Mediterranean at large and also to the Spanish peoples whose loyalty Hasdrubal was working to win.

He was not simply the peace-builder as later ages liked to paint him. He increased the regular army in Spain to 60,000 foot and 8000 horse, putting his brother-in-law Hannibal in 224 in charge of his cavalry forces where, we are told, the young man saw plenty of action. Other army officers would become famous, such as Hannibal's brothers Hasdrubal and Mago, and the cavalry commander Maharbal. The territories under Barcid rule now covered roughly half the Iberian peninsula. The Romans were among those who noticed.

They had paid Carthage limited attention, if any, after the Sardinia affair. A supposed fact-finding embassy to Hamilcar in 231 (mentioned only by the later historian Dio) is probably fiction and, even if genuine, nothing came of it. The Romans were more active both in continental Italy, where the dominant peoples were Gauls who had given them repeated trouble since around 390, and from 229 in Illyria and Dalmatia across the Adriatic, where they fought a serious war to impose a loose control. Then in 226–225 they faced the threat of a huge Gallic invasion from the north, causing them not only to mass powerful forces against it but also to send envoys to Spain. They persuaded Hasdrubal to promise that the Carthaginians would not campaign beyond the river Iber (Ebro) in north-eastern Spain.

This agreement, not formally a treaty since it was signed off by him alone, came to play a role in arguments ancient and modern over why the Second Punic War broke out, with Roman writers claiming that it also protected Saguntum, a small but rich city on Spain's east coast trading with Rome. This was a fiction, caused by the agreement's plain implication that Rome had no objection to the Carthaginians campaigning – and of course subduing everything – up to the Ebro. This was a necessary fiction because Hannibal's later capture of Saguntum was the shaky basis for Rome declaring war in 218. The Ebro-line may have seemed apt to the Romans because it would keep Carthaginian expansion well south of the Pyrenees, beyond which lay Gaul with its restless and excitable warrior peoples. Hasdrubal surely agreed to the line because it tacitly promised him freedom, in turn, from Roman interference to its south. The agreement once made, the Romans destroyed the invading Gauls and conquered their lands, then in 219 fought a second Illyrian war to confirm their trans-Adriatic hegemony. From 225 to late 220 they paid Spain and Carthage no further attention.

THE COMING OF THE
SECOND PUNIC WAR

Hasdrubal's assassination in 221 by an aggrieved Spanish warrior passed the generalship to his brother-in-law Hannibal, again by vote of both the army in Spain and the people at home. This was the third, and so far as we know the last, time that citizen troops had a say in who should command them. At twenty-six the new general had spent most of his life in the new province, had as a wife the daughter of a Spanish king – making the Barcid family kin to two sets of royal families, in Spain and Numidia – and was already a charismatic leader at the head of well-tested troops. Events moved swiftly from now on.

Hannibal at once showed himself a pugnacious commander: campaigning in late 221 and then in 220 across central and north-western Spain as far as the river Duero, storming towns, and defeating a regional Spanish army along the Tagus, near Toletum, by letting them start to ford the river and then striking with elephants and cavalry followed by a general attack. Other communities, overawed, sent offers of submission, so that by autumn 220 he could claim to rule Spain as far as the Ebro (except Saguntum). In twelve months he had added nearly as much territory to the province as his predecessors had done in sixteen years, though his conquests were not so populous or developed.

This drew Rome's attention for the first time in half a decade. Two envoys arrived late in 220 to urge him not to cross the Ebro and, additionally, not to molest Saguntum. With Cisalpine Gaul (as north Italy was now called) in their hands, the Romans were clearly interested in stalling any further Carthaginian expansion north-wards. It seems to have suited them, too, to demand that friendly but non-allied Saguntum should be left alone, perhaps to be a Spanish listening-post for them or – since it had been acting as one for years and been consistently ignored – more likely to symbolise to Hannibal and Carthage that the victor of the previous war was never going to acknowledge them as its full equal.

In either case the move backfired, for Hannibal treated it as a threat. As Polybius implies in his account, he will have remembered how the Romans had used the mercenaries from Sardinia as the pretext for seizing it. He may also have had in mind their interven-tion over Messana. In spring 219 he put Saguntum under siege as a deliberate challenge to them. After a difficult siege of over seven months – Saguntum was a very different target from his previous captures – he took and sacked the city.

The Romans had done nothing to help it. Why, remains a much-debated question. Essentially it seems that, just as in 264, they were at odds over whether or not to act until Hannibal's success finally pushed them into acting. In March 218 envoys, this time travelling directly to Carthage, declared war when the *adirim* predictably refused to hand their general over.

HANNIBAL INVADES ITALY

The new war was as unnecessary as the previous one, for neither Carthage nor Rome needed conflict. Hannibal still had much of Spain to be busy in, not to mention vast areas of western North Africa. The Romans, on existing evidence, were more interested in the eastern Mediterranean. Trade and hospitable contacts between both states were as busy as ever. Yet – as in Europe in 1914 – these features were overbalanced by mutual suspicions, insecurities and ambitions.

Carthage, with her new resources and territorial dominions, was once again at least as powerful as Rome. The Romans with their Italian allies could call on about three-quarters of a million men of military age, in a total population of three to four million. Carthage with her *chora*, allies and subjects from Lepcis Magna to Gades will have had a population roughly similar. In 218, according to Hannibal's own figures (so they seem from Polybius' account), she put into service some 122,000 troops, while Rome's field armies totalled 71,000. Nor was any Roman general of the day – or the first decade of war – any match for Hannibal. Two drawbacks did exist: the fleets in both Spanish and African waters were puny compared with Rome's 220 fully-equipped warships; and none of the other Carthaginian commanders in the entire war, even Hannibal's brothers, proved better than the enemy's.

Hannibal had expected war before the Romans declared it. He readied a large army to invade Italy: for the alternative, to wait for them to attack him in Spain – and invade Libya too – was out of the question. The first years of his Italian expedition are by far the best known, marked by his crossing of the Alps and three great victories over one Roman army after another: at the river Trebia in December 218, Lake Trasimene in June the year after, and Cannae in Apulia in August 216 which put most of central and southern Italy at his mercy. The brilliance of these victories has made his reputation immortal – the only Carthaginian, indeed, with a name still instantly recognisable. Much of southern Italy changed sides to ally with him after 216, so that Carthage by 212 had Rome hemmed in on almost every side.

Besides these new supporters, she had as allies the Numidian kings, the Gauls in northern Italy, Syracuse in Sicily, and the kingdom of Macedon across the Adriatic. She also controlled most of Spain. From late 216 to the middle of 207, Carthage was the greatest power in the western Mediterranean, facing a shrunken and tormented Rome.

This supremacy was not easily won or free of severe flaws. When Hannibal crossed the Pyrenees in mid-218, leaving his brother Hasdrubal in charge of Spain, he had 59,000 troops – but, after he arrived in northern Italy, only 26,000. The usual explanations for this staggering loss are attacks by the Gauls along the route and Alpine snow and ice; but in reality the Gauls' off-and-on attacks, all told, amounted to just seven days' fighting, while snow and ice were met only in the final week, on the pass and the way down to Italy. Supplies en route were plentiful, even in the autumnal Alpine valleys. Nor did he leave garrisons in Gaul. The likeliest explanation is that numbers of the Libyan, Numidian and Spanish troops simply deserted – both in southern Gaul, and later in north Italy before his roll-call. Luckily, the Gauls in north Italy had risen against their Roman conquerors and brought him valuable extra forces.

The Romans' response from 218 to 216 was to confront the invaders head-on, in the normal way of Mediterranean warfare. It was Hannibal's way, too. Alexander the Great had shown how a series of devastating victories could bring down even the most imposing enemy; after his three, Hannibal looked to the shattered Romans to talk. Their response, unconventional by Mediterranean great-power standards but entirely in line with their own responses to Pyrrhus and to their First Punic War disasters, was to refuse talks of any kind. Meanwhile they changed their military strategy.

Hannibal did have at least two opportunities to put crushing pressure on them, but avoided it. After Trasimene, the Romans and his own side expected him to march direct on Rome, only four days away for an army and fewer for cavalry. A fleet from Carthage sailed to the Etruscan coast to link up with him, only to find that he had swung east to the Adriatic. After Cannae a year later, with almost no Roman forces left in the field, he again chose not to advance on the city. Livy's famous tale has his bold cavalry general Maharbal comment sourly that 'you know how to win, Hannibal; you don't know what to do with victory'. It was certainly impossible to take Rome by siege. Cutting it off from outside, though, was feasible especially when there were no organised Roman forces in the countryside to cause trouble, and could have been done as early as the aftermath of Trasimene. Like Mathos' and Spendius' mutiny at Tunes in 241, this could also – and perhaps decisively – have been the signal to all of Rome's restive fellow-Italians to come over to the clearly dominant invader.

HANNIBAL, MASTER OF
SOUTHERN ITALY

Hannibal preferred to operate in central and southern Italy and seek to win over their cities and cantons. He sent home non-Roman prisoners without ransom to spread word that he had come to free Rome's oppressed allies. Nothing came of it until his crushing victory at Cannae: then a series of Italians, beginning with the Campanians of Capua – despite their shared citizenship with Rome – began to defect. Between late 216 and summer 212 the Capuans were joined by most of the Samnites, Lucanians and Bruttians, several Apulian cities, and many of the southern Italian Greeks – especially Tarentum, won over by a bloodless coup in 212. Cannae also encouraged the king of Macedon, Philip V, to make an alliance in 215 with the conquering Carthaginian, for he too had resentments against Rome. A year later the ring around Rome tightened further when Syracuse – no longer ruled by old Hiero – joined Hannibal's coalition largely through the efforts of a resourceful pair of brothers, Hippocrates and Epicydes, officers in Hannibal's army and grandsons of Arcesilaus, the Syracusan exile at Carthage who had killed Agathocles' elder son in 307.

Carthaginian aims in the war must be inferred from events. No statement of aims survives apart from Livy reporting that Hannibal assured Roman prisoners after Cannae that 'for him it was not war to the death: his fight was about honour and power'. Whatever later ages thought, physically destroying Rome was not a goal, nor even reducing it to a political nullity. The alliance with Macedon guaranteed that each state would help the other should another war occur with the Romans – taking for granted that there would still be a Rome capable of making war. In fact Hannibal had already sent one of his senior lieutenants, Carthalo, to sound out the Romans about talks (Carthalo had a family guest-friendship with the Roman leader Quintus Fabius Maximus, famous for his 'delaying' tactics against the invaders), though the senate at Rome refused him access.[87]

Even if Rome continued as a state, common sense required Hannibal and Carthage to make sure that it would be as shackled as possible. The treaty with Philip V promised Macedon the districts in and around Illyria which the Romans controlled, while Carthage's alliance with Syracuse in 214 notionally divided Sicily between the two signatories at the old Halycus line. In Italy Hannibal had to be tactful. Treaties with Capua and other Italian states guaranteed their freedom and self-government, and compulsory military support was not required from all (not from Capua, for instance). The Capuans, and maybe others, expected him to go home after the war – in the Capuans' opinion, it was their turn to dominate Italy. But this was hardly an outcome that Hannibal could envisage, even if he had to pretend he did. Only a strong postwar Carthaginian presence, no doubt with him or another Barcid leader in charge, could prevent Italian chaos from erupting, enabling the surviving Roman state to regain its dominance or Philip V to be tempted to intervene.

LIMITATIONS AND SETBACKS

The unyielding determination of the Romans brought Carthage's hopes down. Instead of seeking terms after their defeats as other states commonly did (Carthage included), they returned to Fabius' tactics of avoiding battle, shadowing Hannibal's movements, and attacking the rebel Italians. By 212 there were 25 legions in the various theatres of war from Italy to Spain, as well as powerful fleets at sea. Up to a third of Roman and loyal Italian manpower was under arms. Despite his victories and new allies, Hannibal was put essentially on the strategic defensive, with the Romans as early as 214 beginning to subdue places that had defected. This solid fight-back was an important reason why he sought allies beyond Italy, to stretch Roman resources as widely as possible.

Carthage's own war-effort was comparable to Rome's. Hannibal built up his forces with Samnite, Lucanian and Bruttian recruits to numbers big enough to enable him, for a couple of years, to detach a secondary army under his nephew Hanno for operations further south while he fought in Campania. Overseas, large armies operated against the Romans in Spain and Sicily, and the navy was revived with fleets in African and Spanish waters. It may well have been in these years, too, that the Barcid authorities governing Carthage constructed the famous artificial ports to accommodate her expanding fleet (Chapter VI). With the Roman navy regularly raiding her coasts, protected harbours for both naval and merchant shipping would be vital.

The years from 212 to 210 began a slow turn in the fortunes of the war. Macedon and Syracuse proved useless as allies, with Macedon soon pushed out of Illyria and Syracuse captured in 212 by the redoubtable general Marcellus. Carthaginian relief forces failed both before the capture, when an army with its general perished (not for the first time) in Syracuse's malarial marshlands, and after, when, as mentioned earlier, a new general's arrogance towards his best officer Mottones caused the latter to join Marcellus and contribute to defeating his ex-friends. In Spain, Hannibal's brothers and a colleague named Hasdrubal son of Gisco succeeded in shattering the Roman invaders in 211 (with able help from Numidian cavalry led by Naravas' young kinsman Masinissa), yet did nothing to exploit their victory. Hasdrubal made no effort to lead forces to Italy, either, where he had been awaited since 215. Hannibal himself could neither prevent nor break the Roman siege of Capua which began in 212 – not even by launching his famous march on Rome in 211, for he could not pull the besiegers to pursue him and the city was firmly garrisoned. After Capua surrendered, he spent the next eight years in southern Italy: trying to defend his shrinking parcel of allies as one after another fell back into Roman hands, still winning or drawing occasional battles, but being constantly harassed – especially by Marcellus until the latter's death in action in 208.

The loss of Capua was followed by a thunderbolt in 209. Publius Cornelius Scipio, the twenty-five-year-old new Roman commander in Spain, captured New Carthage in a surprise attack by sea and land while all three Carthaginian generals were over-confidently quartered elsewhere. In 208 and 206 Scipio defeated them in two great battles, at Baecula and Ilipa, which ended Carthage's thirty-year rule in the peninsula. Scipio returned to Rome to become consul in 205 and prepare to invade Africa.

METAURUS, ZAMA AND PEACE

Hannibal's brother Hasdrubal did leave Spain to reach northern Italy in 207, but brought no help to his increasingly beleaguered elder brother in the south. Hannibal was so circumscribed by Roman armies that the consul Gaius Claudius Nero could lead an élite force northwards to join his colleague Marcus Livius Salinator facing Hasdrubal. They destroyed the new invasion at the river Metaurus, just inland from the Adriatic. Nero took Hasdrubal's head back to deliver to his brother: Carthaginians might remember how in 309 the Syracusans had sent the head of Hamilcar son of Gisco over to Agathocles.

Hannibal hung on in the very south of Italy for four more years. Now he probably hoped that, as long as he stayed, he would keep Africa safe from invasion; indeed old Fabius Maximus opposed Scipio's project for this very reason. Moreover in 205 Italy was yet again invaded by a Barcid, Hannibal's surviving brother Mago. Yet by landing in Liguria Mago gave himself no better chance than Hasdrubal of reaching their brother; eventually his invasion was crushed and he himself mortally wounded. By then Scipio was conquering Libya, and Hannibal was finally called home.

The defence of North Africa was first led by the Barcids' ally Hasdrubal son of Gisco and Syphax, king of Numidia. Originally king of the western Numidian Masaesyli, Syphax had united the country by driving out the would-be king of the Massyli – Masinissa – and had married Hasdrubal's daughter, the cultured and beautiful Saponibaal (in Latin, Sophoniba, often misrendered 'Sophonisba'). They failed to repel Scipio, who landed near Utica in 204 to be joined by Masinissa. After a lengthy period of insincere negotiations, he destroyed their camps and armies in a night attack early in 203, then defeated their new armies inland on the Great Plains near Bulla in the upper Bagradas valley. With Syphax captured, Masinissa was recognised by Scipio as king of all Numidia – though the new king was forced to renounce his new wife Sophoniba, whom he married after falling in love at first sight (or so the tale was told). At his command, she took poison, completing the romantically tragic story.

The last two years of the war limited it to North Africa. After the Great Plains, the Carthaginians sought and accepted Scipio's peace terms, which removed Carthage's military and naval capabilities, annexed Spain, and exacted a large indemnity, but left her home territories intact. Peace was then confirmed at Rome, but meanwhile the Carthaginians had sent Hannibal and Mago a recall – and when Hannibal landed at Hadrumetum with his veterans, to be joined by the survivors of his brother's army, he continued to act as though the peace did not apply to him. Nor, it seems, did his countrymen object, causing Scipio in turn to renew operations inland.

It took Hannibal most of 202 to build up and train a new army, so that only in October did he set out to find Scipio. Before the last battle, the two leaders held a famous personal meeting near Naraggara, 40 kilometres west of Sicca, which resolved nothing but let each get to know the other. Next day, probably 19 October, Scipio defeated his opponent in the so-called battle of 'Zama' – a misnomer perpetrated by Nepos – by routing his elephant corps and cavalry, then beating down each of Hannibal's three rather disconnected battle lines in turn. The battle was still in the balance, with Hannibal's third line of mainly Bruttian veterans fighting Scipio's legionaries (most of them survivors of Cannae), when the Roman and Numidian cavalry returned to strike the veterans in the rear, a reversal of Hannibal's coup at Cannae. Hannibal got away with a few horsemen and told his countrymen to seek peace.

Scipio's new terms were rather harsher: no Carthaginian navy except ten ships, no overseas wars at all and none in Africa without Rome's permission, an indemnity of 10,000 talents over fifty years (60,000,000 Greek drachmas or Roman *denarii*), and – a clause which would bring future trouble – Masinissa was entitled to the lands held by his ancestors. But Carthage remained intact, independent and in control of Libya: in fact Scipio surveyed and confirmed her existing borders. Hannibal was left untouched.

In 201, as his last act in Africa Scipio anchored the navy of Carthage, large ships and small, in sight of the city and burned them: the symbolic end of Carthage as a great power. From then on she had to make her way in a changed world.

HANNIBAL'S WAR: AN ASSESSMENT

Could Carthage have won the Second Punic War? Rome's military strength is often pointed to as the critical factor for victory – as a contest of Goliath versus David in which Goliath won. Another argument, less popular today though going back to Polybius, is that a nation of comfortable merchants who paid others to do their fighting had no chance against a tough farming people who each year went out to inflict massive damage on their foes. In reality, as mentioned above, Carthage's military strength from the start was at least equal to Rome's. Even in 207, when some 130,000 troops were still serving in Roman armies from Italy to Spain, Carthage's armies as reported by Polybius and Livy totalled as much as 150,000. Moreover her revived navy grew to well over 100 quinqueremes. The unwarlike-merchants picture is just as flawed: the ruling élite was as much, or more, a landowning class accustomed to military as well as naval leadership. Roman society, in turn, was already commercially developed by 264 and still more so by 218, while the Roman authorities were alert to the importance of trade: so the fuss with Carthage in 240 over the arrested Italian traders showed, and then the war with the Illyrians in 229 over Illyrian piracy.

The war might, arguably, have been won had Hannibal marched directly on Rome after his crushing victory at Lake Trasimene in 217, or after Cannae the year after. He might have retrieved the situation as late as 207, if he had made a better effort at leaving Apulia to join forces with his brother (as Hasdrubal was expecting).

A less noticeable point, but just as important, is that large reinforcements sent to Italy by sea – not to Spain or Sicily, as they were –
could have made the difference even as late as 212; Hannibal's only
reinforcements were 4000 men and 40 elephants in 215. Indeed, had
Mago in 205 brought his 25,000 troops and elephant corps to
Bruttium, the Romans might not have authorised Scipio to go to
Africa, although by then the best that Carthage could hope for
would be a compromise peace.

As for the Romans, they may have thrown away their best chance
for an early victory, saving tens of thousands of lives, by electing to
abort the planned invasion of Africa in 218 while continuing the
expedition into Spain. An African invasion would have met no
Carthaginian general of Hannibal's abilities (nor were Greek mercenaries in service by now), while there was as yet no navy able to
prevent a Roman blockade of the city by sea as well as land. The
Carthaginians' greatest weakness – or inhibition – was over an
invasion of their home territories, as both Agathocles and Regulus
had shown and as Scipio proved. It took Scipio only two victories in
one year to bring them to terms, even if Hannibal's return then
required a third before peace finally came.

XII

REVIVAL AND
DESTRUCTION

POLITICS AND REFORMS

The loss of Spain's mines and taxes, the seaborne raids during the war, and the ravaging of parts of Libya by Scipio all left Carthage in a poor state. An instalment of the indemnity, 200 talents in silver coin, paid to Rome in 199 was found to be one-fourth base metal, while a late Roman writer tells of Hannibal putting his 'legions' to work in Africa planting olive trees. All the same, a year after the peace, Carthage thought it best to send as a gift 200,000 bushels of grain to Rome and the same amount to the Roman troops operating in Greece once more against Philip V – gifts, incidentally, matched by Masinissa of Numidia. Politically the Barcids' dominance was over. Carthage was governed by an anti-Barcid faction which Livy calls 'the order of judges', apparently a resurgent court of One Hundred and Four. For even if many of these judges were Barcid allies or at least appointees, most surely switched sides after 201, some even earlier as the Barcids' prospects soured. Hanno the Great, their longest-lasting opponent and still active in 202, may soon have died as he is not heard of again, but his supporters – one of them is known, Hasdrubal 'the Kid' – probably belonged to, or were, the dominant element among the 'judges'.

The new faction was close-knit and intolerant, with the added advantage of judicial power, but the drawback of incompetence. By 197 or 196 it had landed the republic in strife with Masinissa and was proposing a new tax on citizens to fund the next war-indemnity instalment. This led to Hannibal being elected sufete, no doubt on a programme of reforming abuses and with an unknown but compliant colleague. Whether he openly promised to reform the One Hundred and Four, too, is less clear – but as soon as he was defied by the 'quaestor' allied with them – probably the *rb mḥšbm*, 'head of the treasurers' – the new sufete proposed successfully to the citizen assembly that judges be elected annually but not in two consecutive years. He next carried out a thorough investigation of public accounts and peculations, which enabled him to stabilise the public expenses, recover substantial embezzled funds, and cancel the personal tax measure. There may even have been enough funds recouped to pay for the urban building project of the 'Hannibal quarter' on Byrsa's southern slope, which dates to just about this time (Chapter VI). He could not settle the dispute with Masinissa, though.[88]

How the reforms were applied in detail is not recorded, for Livy (our sole source) prefers to focus on how Hannibal was driven into exile. Even earlier his enemies had used their contacts with leading Romans to accuse him of intriguing with Rome's latest opponent, Antiochus III the Seleucid 'great king' of the east. When the Romans – against Scipio's urging – sent over envoys in 195, supposedly to settle the quarrel with Masinissa, Hannibal avoided arrest by taking ship to join the king, never to return. With his going, the revived Barcid faction lost its last taste of power.

PEACE AND PLENTY

The reforms seem to have endured, all the same. The Barcid group continued to be influential for some years: Hannibal sent a Tyrian friend, Aristo, to consult them in 193 in hopes – which proved unsuccessful – of securing his return. The 'judges' faction seems never to have regained its monopoly, though very likely its members pursued politics under other colours, as perhaps did pro-Barcid Carthaginians.

Nothing is recorded of who held office or influence over the next forty years but, whoever they were at any given time, they always showed submissive respect towards Rome as that state advanced to dominate the entire Mediterranean. Not only were the indemnity instalments now paid without trouble but in 191, when Rome was at war with Antiochus, the Carthaginian authorities sent an offer to repay – at once – the remaining forty years' worth, meaning 8000 talents or 24,000,000 *denarii*, equal perhaps to nearly two years of Rome's average revenues in the early 2nd Century. In practice it might have been a strain to fulfil the offer, had the Romans accepted it. But coming from a state that, just half a decade earlier, had been in dire straits over paying a single instalment, it indicates the impressive fiscal progress that Carthage had made. The Romans preferred to keep the symbolic dependence of year-by-year payments, and they also paid for – rather than accept as a gift – large quantities of grain (perhaps 800,000 bushels) and barley (500,000) at the same time. These suggest Carthage's and Libya's agricultural recovery too. Other offers of foodstuffs are reported in later decades, while Polybius' glowing eyewitness description has already been quoted on how prosperous the countryside was in his time (Chapter V).

Trade seems to have been busy, too. Besides Plautus' comically versatile merchant Hanno the 'Poenulus' in the 190s, pottery vessels and figurines identified as Carthaginian-made occur at plentiful sites along western Mediterranean shores as late as the mid-2nd Century. At Carthage in turn, Campanian-made pottery products (bowls and dishes, for instance) were imported at a steadily growing rate from the early years of the century until 149. Second-Century Carthag-inian and Numidian coins have been discovered in the Balkans; while a late-era Carthaginian coin found in the Azores may suggest that a Carthaginian – or Gaditane? – trader sailed even that far (of course this is no proof of regular trade).

As noted earlier, archaeological work on Carthage's circular port has turned up very few items datable before the mid-2nd Century; but rather than showing that she was now rebuilding a navy and so breaking the peace terms, this suggests that the port had substantial work done on it then. The likeliest reason for the overhaul would be that merchant shipping had outgrown the capacity of the outer commercial port. The reported claim by Roman envoys to Carthage in 153, that they had seen quantities of wood stored for building a war fleet, may misrepresent this project; similarly Masinissa's son Gulussa's allegation to the Roman senate in 151 that the Carthagin-ians were evilly scheming a fleet – a claim he had already wrongly made over twenty years earlier. The senate, it is worth noting, treated all these assertions with remarkable sang-froid, probably aware that there were no such plans.

One dissident aspect of the picture is the monetary quality of Carthaginian coinage, which had not been very high for a long time but grew worse after 201 (*Illustration 24j*). This needs a cautious appraisal. By itself it might seem to show economic decline, but it is not a compulsory explanation. Carthage's coins had been struck primarily to pay mercenary troops or subsidise allies in war. After 201 neither existed. At Carthage and in Libya the other, traditional means of exchange – weighed pieces of precious metal, barter, and even foreign coins – should have continued. Masinissa struck coins, too, but his kingdom's economy did not use or need them as a necessary engine for development.

It was in this last period that the city's population, according to Strabo, numbered 700,000. So great a throng could never have lived within the walls, while Megara was mostly a garden suburb, but Strabo may have mistaken a credible figure representing both city and *chora* as applying to just the city (or expressed himself badly). Where he found the number he does not say, but it would seem most likely to be from a census of citizens and resident Libyphoenicians, for Libyphoenician cities shared some political rights with Carthage (Chapter IV). If so, the physical city's inhabitants, excluding slaves but counting in resident Libyphoenicians and Libyans, may be estimated at around 200,000 or a little more – for they had to fit into two or at most three hundred hectares, the built-up 'New City' area of Megara included. Adult male Carthaginians, who alone could vote, hold office, or serve in war, would probably not number above 180,000 in city and *chora* together. The Libyphoenician cities and the Libyan peoples must have had a much larger population all told – up to two or three million – but not even an ancient guess survives.

Carthage continued to be a cosmopolitan centre, open to comers from around the Mediterranean. Numidia was a close social and cultural neighbour. Masinissa had been educated there before 218, while a niece of Hannibal's, probably during the war, had married an elderly uncle of his (and so briefly became queen of the Massyli). One of Masinissa's daughters in turn married a Carthaginian sometime in the 190s or 180s, no doubt an eminent citizen: they had a son Hasdrubal who was to be elected a general in 149. By the 150s he was a member of the faction that vigorously supported good relations with the king at whatever cost. Other Numidians too had Carthaginian connections. For instance, two high-ranking Numidian officers chose to desert to Carthage in the war between the two states in 150 (Appian names them Hagasis and Subas). Still later, in 148 during the Roman siege when the city's prospects were already dimming, so did another lord named Bithyas (was this the Phoenician name Bitias or *Pdy* ?).

In 149 there were Italians residing in the city, no doubt mostly merchants. Leading Carthaginians continued to have social contacts with their Roman opposite numbers, too. They used these to whip up suspicions at Rome against Hannibal in the 190s, as we have seen. Four decades on, one of the best commanders in the Third Punic War was a dashing cavalryman named Himilco, always

called by his nickname Phameas (a Greek version of Pumay?) who
– like Hannibal's officer Carthalo the ancestral guest-friend of
Fabius' family – had a family friendship first formed with Scipio
Africanus' father nearly a century before. In the end Phameas too
went over to the besieging Romans, whose most vigorous officer
was Africanus' grandson Scipio Aemilianus. Among Romans of the
time, one Decimus Iunius Silanus had so complete a grasp of the
Punic language that he was put in charge of translating Mago's
agricultural encyclopaedia after 146; he too surely had close
Carthaginian contacts.

Dealings with the Greek world remained strong. In Hannibal's
lifetime (he died in Bithynia in 183) there appeared the histories of
Philinus on the First Punic War, and Silenus' and Sosylus' on the
Second. Hannibal's own war memoir, inscribed in Punic and Greek
in the temple of Hera at Cape Lacinium in Italy, has been mentioned
too, and his pamphlet twenty years later about improper Roman
activities in Asia Minor. Again as noted earlier, by the middle years
of the century there was enough interest in Greek philosophy at
Carthage to enable a young thinker named Hasdrubal to give
Platonist lecture courses in his own language.

CARTHAGE AND NUMIDIA

Carthage's gifts and offers to Rome, as well as her instant decree of
exile against Hannibal after he sailed away and the Roman envoys
denounced him, showed how well the authorities realised that the
world had changed. Between 200 when the Romans went to war
again with Philip V and humbled him, and 188 when they imposed
peace on the beaten Great King in the east, meanwhile strengthening
their hold over southern and eastern Spain, Carthage could only
watch as her former foes imposed an entirely unprecedented
hegemony across the Mediterranean's countless states and peoples.
The eastern kingdoms, once-fractious successors to Alexander's
empire, now performed all their circumscribed actions under a
thoughtful, if sometimes uninterested, Roman gaze. The middling
and minor eastern states – such as Athens, Sparta, the Aetolian and
Achaean leagues, Pergamum, Rhodes, and Hannibal's last refuge
Bithynia – treated Rome frankly as their new hegemonial lord.
Nearer home, Carthage's ancient rival and sometime equal Syracuse
was a tribute-paying component of the Roman province of Sicily.
Worst of all from the Carthaginians' point of view, Numidia was

now a single kingdom under the ambitious, wily and ostentatiously Rome-friendly Masinissa.

Masinissa was determined to make his kingdom a state to be reckoned with. He encouraged economic life, with great benefit to his revenues, made his capital Cirta an impressive and populous city, and gave his royal court (if nowhere else) a solid veneer of Greek as well as Carthaginian culture. One son, Mastanabal, is commemorated in an inscription at Athens as taking part in sacred chariot races, another – the king's eventual successor Micipsa – as a student of philosophy. Maybe he attended some of Hasdrubal Cleitomachus' early lectures. Masinissa predictably eyed Carthage's prosperous Libyan hinterland with interest. He could argue that because the peace of 201 allowed him to recover ancestral lands, he was entitled to parts of Libya, for the region or much of it must have belonged to his (very distant) ancestors. His dispute with Carthage in the 190s was over territory, though our information is confused and contradictory. Livy offers implausible details: a Numidian rebel named Aphther fleeing through Emporia, Masinissa later attacking the same region. Polybius more convincingly dates these to the 160s. Whatever the dispute was, it fizzled out after Scipio led an embassy in 193 to mediate. Appian, not always a reliable authority, has the quarrel ended by a treaty which – he writes – ceded territories to the king but also established unbroken peace for fifty years, all of which looks exaggerated if not made up.

In 182 Livy reports a new dispute, over unnamed territory, suppos-edly leading to a fierce military clash; but in reality Carthage was forbidden to make war unless Rome permitted, and the senate's reportedly tepid reaction to the affair gives this episode too the suspicious look of later invention or (at best) gross exaggeration. Then Livy reports a third occurring in 174–172 and supposedly costing Carthage seventy towns and forts: so he has their envoys complain at Rome. If Masinissa did carry out such a land grab, he may have been forced by the Romans to hand it back, for Appian has him seize the Thusca region with its 'fifty towns' – a description which sounds similar – only in 153 or 152, a period for which Appian's chief source seems to have been Polybius. It is rather likelier that the earlier episode is again an overblown exaggeration, involving details borrowed from the events of 153–152.

But during the 160s Carthage lost the entire Emporia region in a royal grab which the Roman senate condoned. It looks as though the ageing king, now in his seventies, at last decided on a frankly expan-sionist programme. Maybe the barely-known rebellion (and escape to Cyrene) of Aphther a few years before had seriously hurt his resources and prestige. Some years before 162 he invaded and took over Emporia's open country but could not capture the towns (Lepcis Magna and its sisters). When the dispute went before the Roman senate, however, he was awarded them as well – even though it is hard to see how he could have a genuine ancestral claim – with the Carthaginian envoys' counter-arguments failing utterly. Carthage had to hand over not only Emporia but also 500 talents – supposedly the revenue which the king should have received from the towns since his original invasion.

His incursions nine or ten years later took away a huge slice of her western lands, if Appian's report is accurate. Both the *pagus* of Thusca and the Great Plains region further north, around Bulla and the upper Bagradas, were seized probably in 152. The Theveste region, too, must have gone now if not earlier. Geographically and ethnically these regions perhaps better fitted a claim that they had once been Massylian, or at any rate Numidian. These thefts pushed Carthage's Libyan territories back to where they had been three hundred years before, and perhaps halved her agricultural and tax resources. Her reaction was drastic, and fatal.

POLITICS AT HOME AND WAR WITH MASINISSA

The course of events in the 150s is not at all clear, for the chief accounts are in an epitome of Livy's lost books and the idiosyncratic history by Appian. Appian writes of three political factions at Carthage: a pro-Roman one led by 'Hanno the Great'; a pro-Masinissa faction led by one Hannibal nicknamed 'Starling'; the third a 'democratic' one, with Hamilcar 'the Samnite' and Carthalo at its head. These factions, plausible at first sight, look less so when scrutinised. How a pro-Roman faction would differ from the Masinissa-friendly one in practice is not clear, for by the 150s Rome's attitude had become fairly pro-Masinissa. If the Masinissa faction simply urged complying with his demands, it cannot have been too popular, for the demands seemed endless. Nor is it obvious why a 'democratic' faction should be at odds with either of the others; the issue of popular rule was internal, not one of attitudes to foreign states.[89]

The true basis of the mid-century factions was probably much the same as in the past: allegiances to powerful individuals through kinship or other ties. It is true that Hannibal Starling's group were seen as favouring Masinissa, for after the king's new success forty of them were exiled by the 'democrats', who had used the crisis to win the political upper hand – and the exiles fled to Cirta. Meanwhile Hamilcar the Samnite's and Carthalo's supposed people's-rule platform may be simply a Greek view of the popular support which they earned by urging resistance to Numidia. As for the 'Roman' faction and this latest 'Hanno the Great', they played no recorded part in events and quite possibly are a mistaken hangover in Appian.

Neither Carthage's appeals to Rome about previous encroachments, nor a series of Roman embassies during the 150s, reversed Masinissa's various hauls. She did not appeal again after losing her western territories, but Masinissa's son Gulussa told the Romans that she was preparing both military and naval forces: a fairly obvious effort at arousing Roman hostility. The senate was not that interested (though the Carthaginians were indeed readying troops), since it took no action except perhaps to authorise yet another embassy. Livy's epitome has the senate vote for war unless the Carthaginians undid the alleged preparations: an unconvincing claim, for no fleet existed nor did war follow when Carthage went on to use the new army.

Early in 150 Masinissa besieged another Carthaginian town, 'Horoscopa' (perhaps Thubursicu near Thugga). The Carthaginians sent out the new army under one of the 'democrat' faction, Hasdrubal, but after a chequered campaign his force was trapped by the ninety-year-old warrior king, forced to surrender, and then mostly massacred – events which recall Hamilcar Barca's dealings with the rebels at 'the Saw' in 238. Scipio Africanus' grandson, Scipio Aemilianus, had been visiting the king and had offered to broker a compromise peace, but Hasdrubal had unwisely refused its terms. Whether a newly-arrived Roman embassy now arranged a truce is not known, but hostilities seem to have ended. Hasdrubal, still active, was condemned to death by the Carthaginians along with Carthalo and perhaps others in their faction like Hamilcar – though in fact the general lived to fight another day. The Carthaginians, however, found themselves in deadly danger. The Roman envoys went home to report that the peace of 201 had been broken, with the Carthaginians at war without Rome's permission and against Rome's ally.

THE OUTBREAK OF THE
THIRD PUNIC WAR

Polybius, in a surviving excerpt, and Appian assert that Rome had decided on war long before declaring it in 149. Livy's epitome is more nuanced: it reports Cato the Censor constantly demanding a pre-emptive war from 152 on because he had observed Carthage's revival, the equally eminent Scipio Nasica (a cousin of Aemilianus) equally constantly urging restraint, and the Romans coming to no decision as a result. Whether or not to engage in a third Punic war was as debated at Rome as the previous two had been.

The pace of events is not fully clear. Carthage now sent two embassies to Rome, one after the other, essentially to ask forgiveness and avert war. The first was told enigmatically that it would depend on 'if the Carthaginians give satisfaction to the Romans'. The ensuing embassy received the still more delphic reply that 'the Carthaginians knew very well' what this meant. Was this a cat-and-mouse game to keep them from readying their defences? But the defences were already in excellent shape, with impressive stocks of military equipment available, as the recent Roman envoys could have reported. The opaque responses may hint that the debate over how to deal with the situation in North Africa had still not ended.

All the same, Cato and his supporters were close to success. Now unexpectedly Utica, Carthage's oldest sister colony, her loyal ally during Hannibal's war, declared itself in Rome's power. Utica not only had a safe harbour within a day's sail of Carthage but, more important, was a signal that Carthage might lose the support of the other Libyphoenicians. With Masinissa already close to the city, the prospects of Rome forcing her immediate capitulation – and then unimpededly plundering her accumulated wealth – surely looked excellent, provided that impressive forces were sent. In winter 150–149 the Romans formally declared war.

Why they wanted war, not just a capitulation, was debated at the time and has been ever since. Polybius in another surviving excerpt sets out different views that he found in Greece: some approved the war because of the violated treaty of 201, or because Carthage was Rome's inveterate enemy; others ascribed it to Roman duplicity, arrogance and greed. Modern judgements are still more divided. That the Romans feared Carthage is no longer very widely believed, for after nearly half a century of being consistently submissive to Rome, as well as disarmed, she was utterly beaten by a Numidian army. Moreover the Romans expected a fairly easy victory or even a prompt surrender. Another once-influential view saw Rome acting to prevent Masinissa from mastering all North Africa as well as Carthage's maritime potential. Masinissa himself certainly seems to have been disappointed at their intervention. This explanation looks unlikely, all the same – the obvious way to keep Carthage out of the king's hands would have been to ally with her against him, not to attack her (and expect him to help).

Other suggested reasons are greed both for Carthage's commercial advantages and more immediately for the huge plunder from a sack; and direct aggressiveness, since military successes supposedly were vital to a leading Roman's success in politics. An economic motive is hard to judge; yet, if Carthage's excellent site and hinterland were such objects of desire, it is strange that the Romans left the city a deserted wreck for a hundred years and gave privileges (notably tax-free status) to the towns like Utica and Hadrumetum which had defected to them during the war. A wish for military glory perhaps did lend impetus – but the strongest advocate for war was the eighty-four-year-old Cato, whose military career was long over; while its strongest opponent Scipio Nasica, if in no need of glory himself, had a son and a nephew who would surely have welcomed it (and did serve in the expedition). Again, the consuls who commanded the invasion of Africa in 149, Manilius and Marcius Censorinus, were neither of them particularly distinguished – surprising choices when many other Romans of grander status should have been fighting for the opportunity to crush the homeland of Hannibal.

The Romans' motives were no doubt varied. The attractions of easy Carthaginian booty (which did draw in plenty of ordinary recruits), a push by perhaps some participants to earn war -renown, and a vengeful bitterness among those like Cato who remembered Hannibal's invasion may all have influenced Romans for war. Just conceivably some leaders may have worried, too, that the nonagenarian Masinissa would leave behind a fragile kingdom which Carthage would dominate, thereby becoming a real danger to Rome's Mediterranean dominance. On the surviving information, all the same, the full reasons for the war will always remain elusive.

THE THIRD PUNIC WAR

The consuls of 149 had no problem in assembling large forces because, unlike the wars then being waged in Spain, this one was expected to be short, easy and profitable. The armament that crossed to Sicily in the spring is reported as having 80,000 foot and 4000 horse, with 50 quinqueremes and 100 smaller warships. Another desperate embassy from Carthage, arriving meanwhile at Rome with full powers to negotiate, could only match Utica by offering unconditional surrender. The Roman concept (*deditio in fidem*) was much like the one applied to Germany and Japan in 1945. The surrendering side put itself absolutely into the other's power and must submit to whatever the victors imposed. The Carthaginians certainly knew this standard Roman practice, nor had their own habits been very different in their Greek Sicilian wars.

Now the Romans did start a cat-and-mouse game. The consuls in Sicily first required three hundred children of the city's leading families to be handed over to them as hostages. They then sailed over to Utica in full strength, where the Carthaginians at their demand delivered all their military stores – no fewer than 200,000 sets of armour, 2000 pieces of artillery, and other weapons. Then came a last demand: the citizens must leave their city and settle 80 *stadia*, about 16 kilometres, inland. The figure was not realistic, for it would have placed a quarter of a million Carthaginians along the difficult range of heights stretching from Tunes to the Bagradas. It really meant any distance that the Romans would judge convenient, leaving the city to be plundered and demolished.

Carthage exploded with anger and outrage, vividly recorded by Appian. The unfortunate envoys who came back to report the ultimatum were lynched by furious crowds, as were senators who had urged appeasement. Resident Italians were manhandled or killed. On the same day, the *adirim* declared war, freed the slaves in the city, and sent an appeal for aid to the recently-condemned Hasdrubal – now commanding 30,000 troops in the countryside and probably shadowing Masinissa. The other Hasdrubal, Masinissa's grandson, was elected general too and took command in the city. Temples and squares became *ad hoc* weapons workshops; women cut off their hair to make cords for catapults. The Romans meanwhile marched down from Utica to open the siege. Masinissa, it seems, retired to Cirta to watch.

The siege of Carthage lasted three years. Her 23 Roman miles (34 kilometres) of walls – including the triple line across the flat isthmus outside Megara – defeated repeated assaults from the isthmus, the sea and the lakeshore. The citizens within the walls were not completely alone. The forgiven Hasdrubal operated in the countryside with his army, while Hippacra, Nepheris and Clupea-Aspis near Cape Bon held out too. According to Appian, the Romans were supported locally only by Utica and (on the east coast) Hadrumetum, Leptis, Thapsus and Acholla. Hasdrubal was able to send supplies in to the besieged, and until the summer of 147 foreign merchants could still reach the city despite the Roman blockade. Parts of Megara itself were probably cultivated for food.

In 149 and 148 the Carthaginians kept the besiegers at bay. Attacks on the walls were met by counter-attacks; early on, much of the Roman fleet was set ablaze by fire-ships, and Censorinus' troops on the lakeshore were hit by an epidemic in the hot summer. Hasdrubal moved to Nepheris near the coast and could not be dislodged. Even after Himilco Phameas changed sides following a conversation with his friend Scipio Aemilianus, now an officer with the army, Carthage's situation largely held firm. Piso, the consul in command in 148, spent that summer failing to capture Hippacra, while on Masinissa's death the Numidian lord Bithyas with his 800 horsemen joined Hasdrubal's army. Carthaginian spokesmen moved around Libya encouraging resistance. By now discipline in the besieging army was badly deteriorating due to setbacks and poor leadership. What had promised to be a straightforward and profit-able expedition was now a war as strenuous, expensive and long-lasting as those in Spain.

The situation began, nevertheless, to worsen for the Carthagin-ians. The army at Nepheris could not seriously harass Carthage's besiegers. Sometime in 148 its general Hasdrubal, now in the city and suspicious or merely jealous of his namesake the grandson of Masinissa, convinced the Carthaginians that this general – despite his vigorous leadership – was a traitor. Masinissa's grandson was bludgeoned to death by his fellow citizens. More ominously still, Scipio's exploits during the siege gained him election as consul for 147 and the command in Africa. With him, incidentally, he brought his friend Polybius the historian.

Scipio reinvigorated the army and the siege. New fortified camps on the isthmus cut all land communications. He frightened Hasdrubal into abandoning Megara, built a mole out into the sea below the southern city wall to block off the Cothon – the artificial ports – and seized the 'Falbe quadrilateral'. A small Carthaginian fleet, built by the citizens from leftover materials in the circular port and launched through a channel secretly dug through to the sea alongside, was poorly led and suffered defeat. In the city Hasdrubal became virtual tyrant, murderously intolerant of criticism and reportedly living in luxury with his troops while the citizens starved. Deaths and deser-tions mounted dramatically. During the winter, Scipio attacked and destroyed the army at Nepheris under its Greek (or Greek-named) commander Diogenes and captured Nepheris itself, with up to 70,000 enemy troops and civilians reportedly killed and 10,000 taken. All of Libya now capitulated, including the Libyphoenician loyalists such as Hippacra.

No hope remained for Carthage. In spring 146 the Romans launched the final assault.

Attacking first through the naval port, then over the lakeshore wall, they moved past the '*tophet*' and Cothon to reach the *agora* with its surrounding public buildings, like the senate house and the golden – and instantly looted – temple of 'Apollo' (Reshef). Byrsa's citadel, the last refuge of thousands of surviving citizens, was connected to the *agora* by three streets lined with six-storey apartment houses where many people were still trapped. Each had to be taken against bitter hand-to-hand resistance on every level: assault troops reaching the upper floors used planks to fight their way across to another while more fighting raged on the ground far below – a struggle recalling the horrors of Dionysius' capture of Motya. Once his men reached the walls of Byrsa, Scipio had all the houses along these streets destroyed to clear access.

Next day, the seventh since the assault began, Byrsa capitulated. The last Carthaginians, fifty thousand men, women and children, came out to be enslaved. Hasdrubal and 900 Roman deserters held out in the temple of Eshmun until the general emerged, alone, to surrender to Scipio. In a Dantesque scene the deserters set the temple on fire and hurled curses on him before perishing in the flames. So did his own wife, who then slew their two small sons and threw both them and herself into the inferno.

Scipio put the city to the torch and pronounced a solemn curse on any who might seek to dwell there. Polybius saw him weeping as he watched Carthage's funeral pyre: the general explained that he was thinking that one day this could happen to Rome.[90]

XIII

CARTHAGE IN HISTORY

The Romans annexed Carthage's remaining territory as the province 'Africa', granting tax freedom and other privileges to Utica and the other towns which had deserted her, while the rest paid taxes and were subject to the Roman governor. Not all Carthaginians perished or became slaves: many had fled to Numidia during the war, some had deserted to the Romans, and the three hundred child hostages (we may hope) lived out their lives. They may have been among the survivors for whom Hasdrubal-Cleitomachus in Athens wrote his work of consolation. The site of Carthage itself remained desolate – apart from a failed effort to create a Roman colony alongside it twenty-five years later – until Rome's new despots Caesar and then Augustus ignored Scipio's curse to found a city which, like the rest of North Africa, would flourish far into the future. (They did not, incidentally, need to scrape away any salt: it was not Scipio in 146 BC but a historian in 1928 who scattered that over the ruins.) Masinissa's expanded kingdom continued to thrive too, even after being annexed by Caesar in 46 BC.

Carthage's language, civilisation and religion did not disappear. We have seen St Augustine five and a half centuries later reporting that the country folk around Hippo Regius still spoke Punic at home; and when asked who they were, they replied 'Chanani' – *Kn'nm*. The cities and towns of Libya and Numidia for centuries used Punic on the hundreds or thousands of inscriptions in their temples and tombs, public buildings, and artworks. Baal Hammon was Latinised as Saturn, Tanit as Juno Caelestis; and with agriculture growing ever more productive, the cult of Demeter – Ceres in Latin – and Kore flourished as 'the two *Cereres*'. Local grandees, even in Africa *provincia*, kept their Carthaginian names until Augustus' day, as shown in the patronage inscription of 12 BC linking the governor of the province (the emperor Nero's grandfather) with

220

pagus Gurzensis near Hadrumetum through the *pagus*' magistrates Hamilcar, Bomilcar and Muttunbal.

Carthage made lasting impact on the ancient Mediterranean, practical, cultural and political. The practical included Mago's farming encyclopaedia and a range of everyday items and techniques: the mosaic decoration of patterned terracotta pieces called *pavimentum Punicum*, the *plostellum Punicum* threshing-cart, pomegranates which the Romans called *mala Punica* ('Punic apples'), and the fish-sauce called *garum* which had helped Carthage grow rich and became an obsession for the Romans. Culturally her influence spread not only through Libya and Numidia but to Sardinia, Sicily and southern Spain, promoting urban life in towns both old and newly-founded.

Her political impact included creating a system of hegemony over several different lands, few under direct rule from the city (only perhaps her *chora* was) but still producing the benefits of rule: taxes, regulated or monopolistic trade, centres where citizens could settle, foodstuffs, and military and naval supplies and personnel. Moreover, the Carthaginians evolved a republican political system which in subtlety and openness matched any Greek state, not to mention Rome. They showed that such systems were not a monopoly of those peoples. Their own could attract tempered praise from a serious analyst like Aristotle – as well as a backhanded compliment in Polybius' suggestion that it had been better (because not so democratic) before Hannibal's war.

After 146 BC Romans and Greeks had harsh things to say about the Carthaginians. Plutarch's is the classic example, anachronistically writing of them two and a half centuries later in the present tense:

> the character of the Carthaginian people ... is bitter, sullen, subservient to their magistrates, harsh to their subjects, most abject when afraid, most savage when enraged, stubborn in adhering to its decisions, disagreeable and hard in its attitude towards playfulness and urbanity.

He contrasts them with the tolerant and lighthearted Athenians of old, naturally ignoring Athenian actions like the savagery at Melos, their judicial murder of Socrates, and their fawning over successive Hellenistic monarchs. Diodorus, Livy and later writers delight in telling of Carthaginian cruelty, treachery and irreligion, even though their own narratives contradict the claims. Livy insists on

Hannibal's viciousness and atheism, just after reporting his boyhood oath on the altar of 'Jupiter' and not long before describing how he worshipped at Gades' temple of Melqart and later dreamt of being divinely guided to Italy. Of course, as Carthage receded into memory while Rome's devious and harsh behaviour towards her from 150 to 146 caused discomfort to later generations, exaggerations and plain fictions could flourish.

Such moralising accusations are much less in evidence before 146, when Greeks and Romans from Herodotus to Plautus and Polybius actually knew the Carthaginians. Complaints then were political and military: their endemic bribery for office (noted by Aristotle), reliance on mercenaries (as by Polybius, ignoring the roles of Libyan recruits and often of citizen soldiers), or the supposed menace of Carthage, along with the Campanians, to the Sicilian Greek way of life (thus the author of a 4th-Century essay once ascribed to Plato). Criticisms by one society of how another ran its affairs were common, then as now. In the same centuries Greeks saw great faults in the Persians, not to mention in other Greeks, while the increasingly Greek-influenced Romans grew more and more contemptuous of the Greeks they actually dealt with. Cato the Censor was notorious for this, and at the same time it is worth noting that he ranked Hamilcar Barca alongside three historic Greeks – Themistocles, Pericles, Epaminondas – and the Roman general Manius Curius Dentatus as leaders superior to any king.[91]

Carthage was a vigorous cultural crossroads. Beginning as a Phoenician settlement, she soon formed close links with her Libyan neighbours and kept them after making the Libyans her subjects. From the start, too, Carthaginians traded and intermarried with Greeks, perhaps also with Egyptians and other Mediterranean peoples. They added and adapted Libyan, Egyptian and Greek art forms and religious practices to their own, developing a lively civilisation which they then carried to other western lands. The accusation, still sometimes made, that Carthaginian civilisation was a commercially tainted dead-end is essentially an offshoot of the embarrassed, and maybe guilt-ridden, criticisms by Greeks and Romans after 146. By the time they were destroyed as a state and people, the Carthaginians had a growing literature, strong if eclectic artistic and architectural traditions, advanced economic skills, and were kin to almost every other Mediterranean people. Had they and not the Romans become masters of the Mediterranean world, taking in the vast energies of Italy, the far western lands and the Hellenistic world, the civilisation that resulted would have spoken Punic and Greek rather than Latin and Greek, but would certainly have made an equally momentous contribution to history.

NOTES

ABBREVIATIONS

Appian, *Lib.*	Appian, *Libyca*
Aristotle, *Pol.*	Aristotle, *Politics*
CIS	*Corpus Inscriptionum Semiticarum*
DCPP	*Dictionnaire de la civilisation phénicienne et punique*
FGrH	*Die Fragmente der Griechischen Historiker* (F. Jacoby *et al.*, eds.)
HAAN	*Histoire ancienne de l'Afrique du Nord* (Gsell)
HaP	*Hannibal ad Portas* (Peters)
ILS	*Inscriptiones Latinae Selectae*
KAI	*Kanäanische und Aramäische Inschriften* (Donner and Röllig)
Kl P	*Der Kleine Pauly*
Pliny, *NH*	Pliny the Elder, *Natural History*
Pol.	Polybius, *Histories*

1. Canaans (*Kn'nm*): St Augustine, *Letter to the Romans* 13. Ponim (alternatively *Ponnim*): Krahmalkov (2000), 11.
2. Sidon and Tyre: Herodotus 2.45; Strabo 16.2.22–4; Justin 18.3.5; Aubet (2001), 20–1, 29; Markoe (2000), 33. Sidon's area: Markoe (op. cit.), 68, 199. Tyrian 'skyscrapers': Strabo 16.2.23, C757. Old Testament denunciations: Aubet (op. cit.), 119–26, and her Appendix II. Cassiterides: Note 35.
3. Ithobaal I: Josephus, *Jewish Antiquities* 8.317, 9.138; Aubet (2001), 46; *DCPP* 233 s.v. Ittobal 2. Governor or vice-regent (*soken*) of the 'New City' of Citium: Manfredi (2003), 341–2. Tyrian annals, Menander of Ephesus: Josephus, *Against Apion* 1.116–27. Nora and its *stele*: Pausanias 10.17.5; Aubet (2001), 207; Lipiński (2004), 234–47.
4. Philistus on Carthage's foundation: *FGrH* 566 F47; cf. Euripides, *Trojan Women* 220–1. Appian on 'Zorus' and 'Carchedon': *Lib.* 1.1.

Foundation-date for Utica: Pliny, *NH* 16.216; Pseudo-Aristotle, *De Mirabilium Auscultationibus* (*Observations of Marvels*) 134; Velleius Paterculus, 1.2.1 and 3, gives 1103 BC for Gades. Timaeus' date for Carthage and Rome: Dionysius, *Roman Antiquities* 1.74.1. Archaeological evidence: e.g. F. Rakob in Lepelley and Lancel (1990), 31–43; Aubet (2001), 212–26; Docter (2002–3).

5. Trogus' foundation story: Justin 18.4.3–6.10. Zakarbaal high priest of 'Jupiter': Justin 18.5.2; Virgil *Aeneid* 1.446 makes him priest of 'Juno', which some moderns prefer – e.g. Alvar and Wagner (1985). Earliest houses and animal bones: Docter *et al.* in Bartolini and Delpino (2005); opposed by M. Botto, ibid., 579–627. 'Byrsa': different interpretations by E. Lipiński in Lepelley and Lancel (1990), 126–9; in *Itineraria Phoenicia*, 481–4; Aubet (2001), 216. Elissa 'Theiosso': Timaeus, *FGrH* 566 F82. Phoenician *'lt*: Krahmalkov (2000), 56–7.

6. Yadomilk's pendant: Krahmalkov (1981), in *DCPP*, 394 s.v. *Pgmlyn*, and in Kaltner and McKenzie (2002), 213–14; illustr. in *HaP*, 269 no. 4. Bitias: Livy in Servius' commentary on *Aen.* 1.738; Krahmalkov (op. cit.), 190–1.

7. Site and size of early Carthage: Lancel (1995) 41–5; F. Rakob in Vegas (1998), 15–46; Aubet (2001), 218–19; Docter (2002–3), with remarks too on Carthaginian iron-smelting. Water supply: Fantar (1993), 1.138–41.

8. Carthaginians sent out to Libyan countryside: Aristotle, *Pol.* 2.1273b; 6.1320b. Libyphoenicians: Diodorus 17.113.3, 20.55.4; Livy 21.22.3; H. Ben Younès in Krings (1995), 820; Manfredi (2003), 397–404.

9. Bodmilqart son of Istanis: M. H. Fantar in Amadasi Guzzo *et al.* (2002), 230.

10. Thucydides 6.2 on Phoenicians and Greeks in Sicily. El-Haouaria quarries: *DCPP* 149; Lipiński (2004), 372. No obvious Carthaginian presence in hinterland before 400: Lund (1988), 50–4; cf. Greene and Kehoe (1995),.

11. Full citizens and lesser ones: thus Fantar (1993) 1.177–83. Safot (and others) as freedmen 'thanks to' former master: so Huss (1985), 497–8; see below, Note 48. Hannobaal and Esmunhalos: Krahmalkov (2000), 200. *Kyrious Karchedonious*: Pol. 7.9.5; Huss (1985), 467. Citizens and artisans at New Carthage: Pol. 10.17.6–9; 10.17.15; Gsell, *HAAN*, 2.227–9.

12. Associations, communal meals: Aristotle, *Pol.* 2.1272b; Ameling (1993) 164–8, 180–1. *Mzrḥ*: Krahmalkov (2000), 274 (translating *mzrḥ*-reference). Marseilles Tariff: text in *KAI* no. 69; illustration in *HaP*, 320–1.

13. Isocrates' praise, *Nicocles* 24; at Carthage 'tyranny' had given place to aristocracy, Aristotle, *Pol.* 3.1316a.

14. Sufetes: Aristotle, *Pol.* 2.1272b–73a ('kings'); Plato, *Laws* 674a–b; Nepos, *Hannibal* 7.4; Livy 30.7.5, 34.61.15 (*sufetes* judging cases in

193), cf. 28.37.2 (at Gades, 206); Festus, *De Verborum Significatu*,
404 s.v. 'sufes'; Huss (1985), 458–61. Four sufetes: Cato, *Fragmenta
incerta* 32 (ed. Jordan: from Festus, 154); cf. W. Huss, *Le Muséon* 90
(1977), 427–33.

15. 'The 120th year': Krahmalkov (2000), 478. Manfredi (2003), 379,
interprets the inscription as 'the twentieth year' – as does Krahmalkov
too in Kaltner and McKenzie (2002), 214. W. Huss sees no date at all:
(1986), 437–42).

16. Hamilcar 'king' in 480: Herodotus 7.165–7. Hannibal, Himilco and
Mago in 409–383: Diodorus 13.43.5, 14.49.1 and 54.5, 15.15.2;
below, Chapter VIII.

17. Abdmilqart and *Abd'rš*, and two generals: Krahmalkov (2000), 440
s.v. *rb VI*. Baalay, ibid. Arishat: *HaP*, 95 no. 4. *Pn* 'of the nation of
Carthage': Krahmalkov (2000), 434. 'Iomilkos' (Himilco) at Delos:
Masson (1979).

18. Carthage's senate: Aristotle, *Pol.* 2.1273a; Carthage 'democratically
ruled': *Pol.* 3.1316b. More democratic by Second Punic War: Pol.
6.51.3–8, disapprovingly.

19. Pentarchies: Aristotle, *Pol.* 2.1273a (Loeb tr.), 1275b. Board of ten for
sacred places and of thirty for taxes: Krahmalkov (2000), 400 s.v. *ps* ('the
thirty men who are in charge of the payments'); 404 s.v. *p'm* 3; 477 s.v. *špṭ
II*. 'Accountants', *mḥšbm*: Huss (1985), 465; Krahmalkov (2000), 277–8.

20. The *rab* (*rb*): Huss (1985), 464–5; Krahmalkov (2000), 439 s.v. *rb IV*
(cf. 440, *rb VI*). Bribery, money-making, corruption in public life:
Aristotle, *Pol.* 2.1273a–b; 3.1316b; Pol. 6.56.4. More than one office
held simultaneously: Aristotle, *Pol.* 2.1273b.

21. Generals: *Politics* 2.1273a. 'Second' general: Krahmalkov (2000), 441;
also 473 (interpreting *hšn'* as 'second general').

22. Court of 104: *Pol.* 2.1272b–73a; Justin 19.2.5–6 (100 senators).

23. Citizen assembly: *Pol.* 2.1273a, and cf. Note 19. Thugga's voting
'gates', *ILS* 6797; Sznycer (1978), 583–4; Huss (1985), 551.

24. Lepcis Magna: E. Acquaro (1998), 415. 'Altars of the Philaeni': Pol.
3.39.2; Sallust, *Jugurtha* 79; Strabo, 3.5.5 C171; 17.3.20 C836; Lancel
(1995), 93–4.

25. Ebusus: Diodorus 5.16.2–3; C. Gómez Bellard in Krings (1995),
762–75. 'All belongs to the Carthaginians': Pseudo-Scylax, *Periplus*
111; Lipiński (2004), ch. IX. Tribute of Lepcis *c.* 193: Livy 34.62.3.

26. Xenophon on Carthage and Libyans: *Memorabilia* 2.1.10. Gems from
African interior: Strabo 17.3.11 C830, 17.3.19 C835; Pliny, *NH*
37.92, 95–6, 104; Biffi (1999), 394–5. Mago the waterless traveller:
Athenaeus, *Deipnosophistae* 2.44E; Geus (1994), 177–8. Pharusii:
Strabo 17.3.7 C828.

27. Pithecusan and Euboean pottery dating 775–750 at Carthage: Aubet (2001), 218. 'A *puinel* from Carthage' – *mi puinel Karthazie ( )elps ... na*: F. W. von Hase in *HaP*, 72.

28. Phocaeans, Herodotus 1.165–6; Colaeus, 4.152. Pyrgi tablets: Lancel (1995), 84–6; Schmitz (1995); D. W. R. Ridgway in *Oxford Classical Dictionary*, 1282. Close Carthaginian–Etruscan trade links: Aristotle, *Pol.* 3.1280a (Loeb tr.).

29. First treaty with Rome: Pol. 3.22.4–-13; Scardigli (1991), 23–46; Huss (1985), 86–92; Ameling (1993), 130--3, 141--54; Bringmann (2001), dating it to 348/7.

30. Carthage in Sardinia: C. Tronchetti in Krings (1995), 712–42; P. Bernardini in *HaP*, 142–83. Battle of Alalia: Herodotus 1.166; Krings (1998), 93–160. Mago and his sons: Justin 19.1.1–2.1.

31. Carthaginian 'conquest' of Sicily: G. Falsone in Krings (1995), 674–97; A. Spanò Giammellaro in *HaP*, 184–92. Pentathlus: Diodorus 5.9; Pausanias 10.11.3–4; Krings (1995), 1–32. Dorieus in Sicily: Herodotus 5.43–48, 7.158; Diodorus 4.23.3; Pausanias 3.16.4--5; Justin 19.1.9 (preposterously replacing Dorieus with Leonidas of Sparta).

32. Very early pottery from Spain: F. Rakob in Ennabli (1992), 31–33. Carthage's supposed aid and treachery to Gades: Justin 44.5.2–3.

33. Carthaginians' silent trading on Africa's Atlantic coasts: Herodotus 4.196; cf. Picard (1961), 233.

34. Hanno's *Periplus*: Pliny, *NH* 2.169; 5.8; 6.199–200; Demerliac and Meirat (1983); Geus (1994), 98–104; Lipiński (2004), 435–76. 'Gorillas': Lipiński in Geus and Zimmermann (2001), 79–85; K. Brodersen, ibid., 87–98.

35. Himilco's voyage: Pliny, *NH* 2.169; Avienus, *Ora Maritima* 117–29, 380–9, 402–15. Cassiterides: Herodotus 3.115; Strabo 3.2.9 C147, 3.5.11 C175–6 (quoted), 3.5.11 C175–6 (ship-captain story); Pliny, *NH* 4.119, 7.197.

36. Carthage's wealth and power: Thucydides 6.34.2; Diodorus 12.83.6; Pol. 18.35.9; Cicero, *Republic* 2.7.

37. Penteconters: O. Höckmann in *HaP*, 101–2. Carthaginian merchant ships: P. Bartoloni in Krings (1995), 282–8; Lancel (1995), 121–5; Höckmann (op. cit.), 96–9. Large-scale imports from Greece, especially Athens: J.-P. Morel in Lepelley and Lancel (1990), 67–99; Lancel in Hackens and Moucharte (1992), 269–81. Olive oil from Acragas: Diodorus 13.81.4–5. Wide-mouthed *amphorae*: Lancel (1995), 275–6. Tagomago and Marsala wrecks: M. E. Aubet Semmler in *HaP*, 325–6.

38. Hanno in Plautus' *Poenulus*: lines 930–49 and various interjections between 994 and 1027; S. Faller (2004). Carthaginian cargoes at Rome: Palmer (1997), 31–52.

39. Greeks at Carthage in 396: Diodorus 14.77.5. Italians there in 149: Appian, *Lib.* 92.433–4; Zonaras 9.26. Cirta's *Hanno* the *gugga* (*ḥn' ḥgg'*): Krahmalkov (2000), 135. Nobas son of Axioubos: Rhodes and Osborne (2007) 216–18, no. 43. Aris' and Mago's *amphorae*: Lancel (1995), 275.

40. Carthage's *chora*: Pol. 1.71.1. Citizen population in late 3rd Century: Hoyos (2003), 225. Diodorus quotation: 20.8.3–4 (Loeb tr.); cf. Picard and Picard (1968), 129. Roman loot from *chora* in 256: Pol. 1.29.7. Wealth of countryside around 150: Appian, *Lib.* 69.312; Pol. 12.3.1–5 (tr. E. S. Shuckburgh); Strabo 17.3.15 C833; cf. Biffi (1999), 406.

41. Mago, Hamilcar and Cassius Dionysius: Varro, *de Re Rustica* 1.1.10, 1.38.1, 2.1.27; Cicero, *De Oratore* 1.249; Columella, *de Agricultura* 1.1.13 and 18, 12.4.2; Pliny, *NH* 17.63, 18.22–3 (Mago translated by order of Roman senate), 18.35, 21.110–12.

42. Some ordinary Carthaginians (from Krahmalkov (2000)): e.g. Abdmilqart, Ariso and Baalyaton, 325; Baalsamor and his son, 476 s.v. *š'r II*; Halosbaal, 341; Mago the butcher, 201 s.v. *ṭbḥ;* 'the craftsmen who made the female statues', 198–9; Abdeshmun the seal-keeper, 200. 'New Gate' inscription: Fantar (1993), 1.114–15; Lancel (1995), 142–4. Hannobaal and Safot: Note 11 above. Hannibal of Miqne: Krahmalkov (op. cit.), 34.

43. Safot's and Baalsillek's *stelae*: Krahmalkov (2000), 34. *Gry* the fuller: ibid., 223 s.v. *kbs.* On the sense of *bd* see Huss (1985), 497–8; Fantar (1993) 1.183–4; Krahmalkov (2000), 84–5, 98. Inscriptions with *š ṣdn* listed in Huss (1985), 498 n. 26.

44. Roman and Italian slaves of Carthaginians: Zonaras 8.12 (in 256); Appian, *Lib.* 15.61 (in 204). Hanno the traitor and slaves: Justin 21.4. Regulus' slave-haul: Pol. 1.29.7. Hasdrubal son of Gisco buys 5000 slaves for fleet: Appian, 9.35 (but not in Pol. or Livy). Great Libyan revolt 396 and slave recruits: Diodorus 14.77.

45. Artificial channel from lake of Tunis in 4th Century: L. Stager in Ennabli (1992), 72; Lancel, *Carthage* (1995), 182–9.

46. Alleged 5th-Century stagnation: Warmington (1964), 57–62; Picard (1968), 79–80, 111–15; Moscati (1968), 161–2. No stagnation: Morel in Lepelley and Lancel (1990), 78–84; Lancel in Hackens and Moucharte (1992), 269–81.

47. Megara: Appian, *Lib.* 117.559 (Loeb tr.), 135.639. Land surveys: Green and Kehoe (see Note 10), 111–12. Bomilcar's failed coup: Diodorus 20.43.1–44.6 (my tr.).

48. Temples: Lancel (1995), 212–15. Possible remnants of Eshmun's, Fantar in *HaP*, 226; of early 2nd-Century temple near *agora* (?): Rakob in Vegas (1998), 28–31. Flat-roofed temples: e.g. Lancel (1995),

313–14 (Thuburbo sculpture); Rakob (op. cit.), 30. Motya *stele*: Spanò Giammellaro in *HaP*, 186, with 195 no. 14.

49. Demeter and Kore *stele*: S.-M. Cecchini and M. G. Amadasi Guzzo in Lepelley and Lancel (1990), 101–11; G. Bergamini in *HaP*, 234 no. 10. Dougga mausoleum: G. Hiesel in *HaP*, 63, 66. Sabratha mausoleum: Lancel (1995), 309–11.

50. Henchir Jaouf mausoleum: Quinn (2003), 20, 23–4, 34. Mausoleum drawing, Clupea: Lancel (1995), 281. Jbel Mlezza paintings: ibid., 222–3. 'Tower' outside Megara in 147: Appian, *Lib.* 117.557.

51. Archaic Carthaginian houses: Rindelaub and Schmidt (1996); T. Schäfer in *HaP*, 216–20. The 'Hannibal quarter': Lancel and Morel in Ennabli (1992), 43–68; Lancel (1995), 152–72. Villa at Cape Gammarth: ibid., 280.

52. *Agora* in 308: Diodorus 20.44.3–5. In 146: Appian, *Lib.* 91.340 (with the senate-house), cf. Diodorus 32.6.4. Senate meetings in temple of 'Aesculapius': Livy 41.22.2, 42.24.3.

53. Carthage's outer walls: Appian, *Lib.* 95.449–51; Lancel (1995), 415–19. The ports: *Lib.* 96.452–5; 'Cothon', 127.605–8; cf. Strabo 17.3.14–15 C832–3; Picard and Picard (1961), 28–33, and (1983), 34–7; J. Debergh in Hackens and Moucharte (1992), 283–97; L. Stager in Ennabli (1992), 73–8; H. Hurst, ibid., 79–94; Lancel (1995), 172–88. Falbe's quadrilateral: Appian, *Lib.* 123.582–3 (*choma*); Fantar (1993), 1.126–7; Lancel (1995), 179–80.

54. Gods in Hannibal's treaty-oath: Polybius 7.9.2–3 (my tr.); Picard (1967), 26–35; Walbank (1957 ff.), 2.46–52; Barré (1983); W. Huss in Bonnet *et al.* (1986), 223–38; Lancel (1995), 208–9; Barceló (2004), 145–6.

55. Tanit at Carthage: Huss (1985), 513–16; Lancel (1995), 199–204; Lipiński in *DCPP* 438–9. Demeter and Kore: Diodorus 14.70.4, 76.4, 77.5. Hannabaal *khnt š krw'*: M. Le Glay, *DCPP* 128. Carthaginian deities with probable or possible Greek and Roman equivalents: Huss (1985), 521–5.

56. 'Awakener of the god', and 'scent of '*štrny*' or 'husband of '*štrny*': Krahmalkov (2000), 309; *DCPP* s.v. Astronoe. Hanno sufete and awakener, and Y'*zm* great-grandson of Masinissa: Krahmalkov, ibid. Rooster images: Lancel (1995), 223–5; G. Maass-Lindemann in *HaP*, 263.

57. Greeks and Romans on Carthaginian child-sacrifice: Cleitarchus, *FGrH* 137 F9; Diodorus 20.14.4–7 (in 310); Plutarch, *de Superstitione* 13; Curtius, *Alexander* 4.3.23; Tertullian, *Apologeticus* 9.2–4. Mazeus and his adult son: below, Note 65. Hamilcar's disappearance in 480: Herodotus 7.167, claiming Carthaginian informants. Boy sacrificed in

406, Diodorus 13.86.3; prisoners sacrificed in 307, 20.65.1–2. Silius Italicus' tale: *Punica* 4.763–829. Carthage's *'tophet'*: Lancel (1995), 227–56; Aubet (2001), 245–6; S. Ribichini in *HaP*, 247–56. *Stele* of priest with baby: *HaP*, 257. On child sacrifice: e.g. Gras *et al.* (1991); L. E. Stager in Ennabli (1992), 72–5; Schwartz (1993), 28–57, with forensic evidence; Fantar (1993), 2.300–3; Docter *et al.* (2001/2); Azize (2007); Shaw (2007), 12–18.

58. *mlk 'dm* a sacrifice of 'reddening' or 'rouging': thus Azize (2007), 199–201; cf. N. Wyatt, *Religious Texts from Ugarit*, 2nd ed. (London and New York, Continuum: 2002), 186 and n. 44 (red ochre). Nicivibus inscription about Concessa: Azize (2007) 191, 195–6, 202. On infant mortality in Roman times (one in three or four): e.g. Hopkins (1983), 70–3, 225.

59. 'The minor kings of Africa': Pliny, *NH* 18.22–3. Hiempsal's 'Punic books': Sallust, *Jugurtha* 17.7; Morstein-Marx (2001). St Augustine on 'Punic wisdom': *Letters* 17.2. Hidden sacred books: Plutarch, *Moralia* 942C. Hannibal's inscriptional memoir: Pol. 3.33.18, 3.56.4; Livy 28.46.16. Inscription on sack of Acragas: Krahmalkov (1974), and in *Beyond Babel: A Handbook for Biblical Hebrew and Related Languages*, ed. S. L. McKenzie and J. Kaltner (Leiden, Brill: 2002), 214; Schmitz (1994). Verse inscriptions at Mactar: Krahmalkov (1975). Julius Nasif: Krahmalkov (1994).

60. Milkpilles' biography: Krahmalkov (2000), 477 s.v. *špṭ*, 289 s.v. *Mlkpls*. The 'ancient Mactarian': *ILS* 7547. Silenus' and Sosylus' histories of Hannibal: Nepos, *Hannibal* 13.3; one papyrus fragment of Sosylus survives (*FGrH* 176 F1). Hasdrubal-Cleitomachus: Cicero, *Tusculan Disputations* 3.54; Geus (1994), 150–3.

61. Ivory of goat on sacred tree: *HaP*, 337 no. 6. 'Fez'-capped goddess with daughter: *HaP*, 236 no. 17. Wide-eyed dedicator: Picard and Picard (1968), plate 29. Enthroned Melqart (?) from 'Hannibal quarter': *HaP*, 237 no. 19. Amulet-case: ibid., 240 no. 33. Etruscan bronze figurine, ibid., 78; 'temple boy', 234 no. 9.

62. Phalaris' bull and other Sicilian booty: Cicero, *Second Verrines* 4.72–4; Diodorus 13.90.3–5. Ephebe of Motya: Lancel (1995), 323–5, denying implausibly that such art would have been favoured at Carthage. Boethus 'the Carthaginian': Pausanias 5.17.4; A. Rumpf, *Kl P* 1.916.

63. Kerkouane tambourine-player: Fantar (1995), 103. Ivory intaglios: *HaP*, 238 nos 24–5. Baalshillek's ossuary: *DCPP* 356, fig. 264. Priest's sarcophagus from Ste Monique: ibid., fig. 265. Isis-priestess: Lancel (1995), 326–7; M. Maass, *HaP*, 284–5 no. 61. Isis (?) statuette: *HaP*, 285 no. 63.

64. Carthaginian and associated coinage: Jenkins and Lewis (1963); *DCPP* s.v. Numismatique, 320–7; P. Visonà in Krings (1995), 166–81; H. R.

Baldus in *HaP*, 294–313 (pp. 302–13 show a large selection of coins). Half-destroyed coins from 146: ibid., 313 nos 88–9, with Baldus' notes.

65. 'Malchus': Justin 18.7.1–18; Ameling (1993), 73–9; Krings (1998), 33–92. Note *mzl* = 'good fortune': Krahmalkov (2000), 273.

66. Mago and his sons: Justin 18.7.19–19.1.17 (two generations before Himera, see 19.1.1–2.1). They decided everything, 19.2.5. Tribute still paid to Libyans until after 480: 19.1.3–4, 19.2.4.

67. Hamilcar Barca's victory parade in 237: Pol. 1.88.6; cf. Chapter X. Gisco's return in 338: Diodorus 16.81.4; Polyaenus, *Stratagems* 5.11; Picard and Picard (1968), 143, 160.

68. Hannibal's motives in 410–409: Diodorus 13.43.6. Himilco's defeat and suicide: Justin 19.2.7–3.12; Diodorus 14.70–76; Orosius 4.6.10–15 (dating it to Darius' reign!). Court of 104 in Justin: Note 22. Capture of Selinus, Acragas, Camarina and Gela in 410–406: Trogus, *Prologue* 19.

69. Revolt of Libyans and Sardinians in 370s: Diodorus 15.24.2–3, 73.1. 'The campaigns of Hanno the Great in Africa': Trogus, *Prologue* 20. Hanno and 'Suniatus': Justin 20.5.11–14. Tales of arrogant Hanno: Pliny, *NH* 8.55; Aelian, *Varia Historia* 14.30; Plutarch, *Moralia* 799E; Maximus of Tyre, *Dissertation* 32.3. Geus (1994), 106–8, 129, holds (unpersuasively) that three separate Hannos are involved – the 'Great', the traitor, and the lion-tamer. Hanno's fall: Aristotle, *Pol.* 5.1307a; Justin 21.4.1–8.

70. Carthage and Alexander: Arrian, *Alexander* 2.24.5, 7.15.4; Curtius, *Alexander* 4.2.10, 4.3.20, 4.4.18. Hamilcar the spy: Justin 21.6.5.

71. Accusations against and secret trial of Hamilcar in 312: Diodorus 19.72.2; Justin 22.3.3–5, 22.7.9–10. Bomilcar's attempted coup in 308: Diodorus 20.43.1–44.6 (his colleague Hanno a hereditary enemy, 20.10.1–2); Justin 22.7.7. Himilco, Adherbal and another Hanno appointed: Diodorus 20.60.3–4, 61.3.

72. Royal Numidian governor in 128 BC: Huss (1985), 260 n. 65; Lipiński in *DCPP*, 133 s.v. Djebel Massoudj. *Pagi* in Roman Africa: e.g. *ILS* 9482 (Muxsi); Picard *et al.* (1963) on Thusca and Gunzuzi; *ILS* 9399, 9404 (Thugga); *ILS* 6095 (*Gurzensis*); *ILS* 6118 (*Minervius*).

73. Taxes on Libya: Diodorus 20.3.3; Pol. 1.72.1–5.

74. *Glmt* and *Pḥls*: Manfredi (2003), 438. Zilalsan: *KAI* no. 101; Y. Thébert, *DCPP* 135 s.v. Dougga; Krahmalkov (2000), 306–7 s.v. *mqdš*. Sufetes in North Africa after 146: Manfredi (op. cit.), 376–80 (with list). *B'lm*: Manfredi (ibid.), 386–9, 404, 430, 436, 446.

75. Polybius on Carthaginian and Roman war-making: 6.52.1–6 (tr. E. S. Shuckburgh, slightly adapted); similarly Diodorus 5.38.2–3 (plainly thinking of the 3rd Century). Carthaginian warfare: e.g. Gsell, *HAAN*, 2.331–460; Connolly (1981), 147–52; Huss (1985), ch. 475–9;

Ameling (1993), 155–235, and in *HaP*, 88–93; Goldsworthy (2000), 30–6; Daly (2002).

76. Marsala wrecks: Frost (1991), and at www2.rgzm.de/Navis/Ships/Ship056/NaveMarsalaEnglish.htm (retrieved 20/02/2009); Höckmann in *HaP*, 96, 103–5. Dockyard fire in 368: Diodorus 15.73.3–4.

77. Quadrireme: Pliny, *NH* 7.207 (citing Aristotle); Diodorus 2.5.6; 14.41.3, 42.2, 44.7 (Dionysius I). Quinquereme: Diodorus 2.5.6; 14.41.3, 42.2–5 (but triremes still used in 307: 20.61.7). On all these warships see Steinby (2007), 23–7; on quinquereme battle-tactics, Murray (1999).

78. Carthaginians' armbands: Aristotle, *Pol.* 7.1324b. Citizen troops: e.g. Diodorus 13.44.5–6 (410–409); 13.80.3, 88.3, 110.6 (406); 15.15.2 (383); 16.80.4–5 and Plutarch, *Timoleon* 27.4–5, 28.10 (at Crimisus); Diodorus 20.10.5 (309); Pol. 1.75.2 (240).

79. Claimed army strengths: e.g. in 480, Herodotus 7.165, Diodorus 11.20.2; in 409, Diodorus 13.54.1, 54.5–6, Greek allied troops, 58.1. In 396 plague kills 150,000: 14.76.2; troops at the Crimisus, 16.77.4; Plutarch, *Timoleon* 25.1; in 262, Diodorus 23.8.1; at Cannae, Daly (2002), 29–32; at Ilipa, Pol. 11.20.2; Livy 28.12.13; Appian, *Iberica* 25.100. Mercenaries: e.g. Ameling (1993), 183–225; Daly (2002) ch. IV.

80. Gelon's complaint in 480: Herodotus 7.158; Krings (1998), 312–13. Carthaginians' 'constant wrongdoings': Justin 19.1.9.

81. Fall of Motya: Diodorus 14.51.5–52.4 (Loeb tr.). Carthage's dealings with Greek Sicily: e.g. Gsell, *HAAN*, 3, ch. I; Warmington (1964), chs. II–V; Meister (1984); Asheri, (1988); Franke (1989); Lewis (1994); Picard (1994); L.-M. Günther in *HaP*, 81–7; cf. Zambon (2008). Dionysius I: Caven (1990). Timoleon: Talbert (1974). Agathocles: Consolo Langher (2000).

82. Pact with Rome in 279: Polybius 3.25.1–5; Walbank *Commentary on Polybius*, 1.349–51; Huss (1985), 210–12; Scullard (1989), 532, 535–7; Scardigli (1991), 163–203; Hoyos (1998), 11–14.

83. Second treaty with Rome, 348: Polybius 3.24.1–16; Walbank, *Commentary* 1.345–9; Scullard, 526–30; Scardigli (1991), 89–127; Hoyos (1998), 7–9.

84. Treaties 'to prevent unjust acts by anyone' etc.: Aristotle, *Pol.* 3.1280a–b. Philinus' claimed treaty: Pol. 3.26.3–5; Huss (1985), 204–6; Scardigli (1991), 123–62; Lancel (1995), 380–3; Hoyos (1998), 9–11; Serrati (2006); Steinby (2007), 78-84.

85. The Punic Wars: e.g. Gsell, *HAAN*, 3, chs. 2–8; de Sanctis (1968), vols 3.1 and 3.2; Lazenby (1978, 1996); Caven (1980); Harris (1989), 142–63 on the Third Punic War; Lancel (1995), 361–427; Goldsworthy (2000); Le Bohec, *Guerres puniques* (2001); K. Zimmermann,

Rom und Karthago (Darmstadt, Wissenschaftliche Buchgesellschaft: 2005; 2nd edn., 2009).

86. Hannibal and the Barcids: Picard (1967); Seibert (1993); Lancel, *Hannibal*; Hoyos (2003); Barceló (2004); Hoyos (2008).
87. Hannibal to Roman prisoners after Cannae: Livy 22.58.2–4. Text of treaty with Philip V: Pol. 7.9; Livy (23.33.10–12) and later writers give a distorted Roman version. See Walbank, *Commentary*), 2.42–56; Seibert (1993), 240–6.
88. 'Order of judges', and Hannibal's sufeteship and exile: Livy 33.45.6–49.8.
89. Factions in the 150s: Appian, *Lib*. 68.304–5.
90. Scipio's tears at Carthage: Pol. 38.21–22; partly in Appian, *Lib*. 132.628–30.
91. Plutarch on the Carthaginians: *Moralia* 779D. Cato's admiration for Hamilcar Barca: Plutarch, *Cato Major* 8. Essay claiming to be a letter from Plato: [Plato], *Letters* 8.353e.

SELECT BIBLIOGRAPHY

Acquaro, E., 'Giustino XVIII, 4–7: riletture e considerazioni', in *Archäologische Studien in Kontaktzonen der antiken Welt*, ed. R. Rolle and K. Schmidt (Göttingen, Vandenhoeck and Rupprecht: 1998), 413–17.

Alvar, J and Wagner, C. G., 'Consideraciones históricas sobre la fundación de Carthago', *Gerión* 3 (1985), 79–95.

Amadasi Guzzo, M. G., Liverani, M. and Matthiae, P. (eds), *Da Pyrgi a Mozia: Studi sull' Archeologia del Mediterraneo in memoria di Antonia Ciasca* (2 vols.: Roma, U. di Roma 'La Sapienza': 2002).

Ameling, W., *Karthago: Studien zu Militär, Staat und Gesellschaft* (München, C. H. Beck: 1993).

Asheri, D., 'Carthaginians and Greeks', *Cambridge Ancient History* 4 (1988), ch. 16.

Aubet, M. E., *The Phoenicians and the West: Politics, Colonies, and Trade*. 2nd edn, tr. Mary Turton (Cambridge, Cambridge University Press: 2001) [originally published as *Tiro y las Colonias fenicias del Occidente*: Barcelona, Ediciones Bellaterra: 1987; 2nd edn., 1994].

Azize, J., 'Was there regular child sacrifice in Phoenicia and Carthage?', in Azize, J. and Weeks, N. (eds), *Gilgameš and the World of Assyria: Proceedings of the Conference held at Mandelbaum House, The University of Sydney, 21–23 July 2004* (Leuven-Paris-Dudley MA, Peeters Publishing: 2007), 185–206.

Barceló, P., *Hannibal: Stratege und Staatsmann* (Stuttgart, Klett-Cotta: 2004).

Barré, M. L., *The God-List in the Treaty between Hannibal and Philip V of Macedonia: a Study in Light of the Ancient Near Eastern Treaty Tradition* (Baltimore and London, Johns Hopkins University Press: 1983).

Bartoloni, G. and Delpino, F. (eds), *Oriente e Occidente: Metodi e Discipline a Confronto: Riflessioni sulla Cronologia dell'Età del Ferro in Italia. Atti dell'Incontro di Studi, Roma, 30–31 ottobre 2003* (Pisa-Roma, Istituti Editoriali e Poligrafici Internazionali: 2005).

Biffi, N., *L'Africa di Strabone: Libro XVII della* Geografia (Modugno, Edizioni del Sud: 1999).

Bonnet, C., Lipiński, E. and Marchetti, P., *Religio Phoenicia. Acta Colloquii Namurcensis ... anni 1984* (Studia Phoenicia 4: Namur, Peeters: 1986).

Bringmann, K., 'Überlegungen zur Datierung und zum historischen Hintergrund der beiden ersten römisch-karthagischen Verträge', in Geus and Zimmermann (2001), 111–20.

Cambridge Ancient History, 2nd edition (Cambridge: Cambridge University Press): vol. 4, ed. J. Boardman *et al.* (1988); vol. 6, ed. D. M. Lewis *et al.* (1994); vol. 7 Part 1, ed. F. W. Walbank *et al.* (1984); vol. 7 Part 2, ed. F. W. Walbank *et al.* (1989); vol. 8, ed. A. E. Astin *et al.* (1989).

Caven, B., *The Punic Wars* (London, Weidenfeld and Nicholson: 1980).

Caven, B., *Dionysius I: War-lord of Sicily* (New Haven and London, Yale University Press: 1990).

Connolly, P., *Greece and Rome at War* (London, Macdonald: 1981).

Cornell, T., Rankov, B. and Sabin, P. (eds), *The Second Punic War: a Reappraisal* (BICS Supplement 67: London, Institute of Classical Studies, University of London: 1998).

Consolo Langher, S. N., *Agatocle: da capoparte a monarca fondatore di un regno tra Cartagine e i Diadochi* (Messina, Dipartimento delle Scienze dell'Antichità dell'Università degli Studi di Messina: 2000).

Daly, G., *Cannae: the Experience of Battle in the Second Punic War* (London, Routledge: 2002).

Demerliac, J.-G. and Meirat, J., *Hannon et l'empire punique* (Paris, Les Belles Lettres: 1983).

Dictionnaire de la civilisation phénicienne et punique: see Lipiński, E. *et al.*

Docter, R. F., 'The topography of archaic Carthage: preliminary results of recent excavations and some prospects', *Talanta* 34–35 (2002–3), 113–33.

Docter, R. F. *et al.*, 'Research on urns from the Carthaginian tophet and their contents', *Palaeohistoria: Acta et Communicationes Instituti Archaeologici Universitatis Groninganae* 43/44 (2001/2002), 417–33.

Docter, R. F., *et al.*, 'Radiocarbon dates of animal bones in the earliest levels of Carthage': in Bartolini and Delpino (2005), 557–75.

Donner, H. and Röllig, W., *Kanäanische und Aramäische Inschriften*, 2 vols (Wiesbaden, Harrassowitz Verlag: 1962–1964; 5th edn, 2002).

Ennabli, A. (ed.), *Pour Sauver Carthage: Exploration et conservation de la cité punique, romaine et byzantine* (Paris, UNESCO/INAA: 1992).

Faller, S., 'Hanno und das punische Personal im *Poenulus*'. in T. Baier (ed.), *Studien zu Plautus' Poenulus* (Tübingen, Gunter Narr Verlag: 2004), 163–202.

Fantar, M. H., *Carthage: Approche d'une civilisation*, 2 vols (Tunis, Alif: 1993).

Fantar, M. H., *Carthage: la cité punique* (Tunis and Paris, Alif/CNRS: 1995).

Franke, P. R., 'Pyrrhus', *Cambridge Ancient History* vol. 7.2 (1989), ch. 10.

Frost, H., 'Old saws', in *Institute of Nautical Archaeology, Tropis IV Proceedings* (1991), 189–97.

Geus, K., *Prosopographie der Literarisch Bezeugten Karthager* (*Orientalia Lovaniensia Analecta*, 59: Leuven, Peeters: 1994).

Geus, K. and Zimmermann, K., *Punica – Libyca – Ptolemaica. Festschrift für Werner Huß* (Leuven-Paris-Sterling, VA, Peeters: 2001).

Goldsworthy, A., *The Punic Wars* (London, Cassell: 2000) [reprinted as *The Fall of Carthage: the Punic Wars 264–146 BC* (London, Cassell: 2003)].

Gras, M., Rouillard, P. and Teixidor, J., 'The Phoenicians and death', *Berytus* 39 (1991) 127–76 [originally ch. 6 of their book *L'Univers phénicien*: Paris, Hachette Littérature: 1989].

Greene, J., and Kehoe, D., 'Mago the Carthaginian', in in M. H. Fantar and M. Ghaki (eds), *Actes du IIIe Congrès international des études phéniciennes et puniques* (2 vols: Tunis, Institut national des sciences de l'archéologie et du patrimoine: 1995), 2.110–17.

Gsell, S., *Histoire ancienne de l'Afrique du Nord*, 8 vols (Paris, Hachette: 1913–28).

Hackens, T. and Moucharte, G. (eds), *Numismatique et Histoire économique phéniciennes et puniques* (*Studia Phoenicia* 9: Louvain-la-Neuve, Peeters: 1992).

Hannibal ad Portas: Macht und Reichtum Karthagos, ed. S. Peters (Stuttgart, Theiss Verlag: 2005).

Harris, W. V., *War and Imperialism in Republican Rome, 327–70 BC* (Oxford, Oxford University Press: 1979).

Harris, W. V., 'Roman expansion in the west', *Cambridge Ancient History* 8 (1989). ch. 5.

Hopkins, K., *Death and Renewal* (Cambridge, Cambridge University Press: 1983).

Hoyos, B. D., *Unplanned Wars: the Origins of the First and Second Punic Wars* (Berlin and New York, W. de Gruyter: 1998).

Hoyos, D., *Hannibal's Dynasty: Power and Politics in the Western Mediterranean 247–183 BC* (London, Routledge: 2003).

Hoyos, D., *Hannibal: Rome's Greatest Enemy* (Exeter, Bristol Phoenix Press: 2008).

Huss, W., *Geschichte der Karthager* (München, C. H. Beck:1985).

Huss, W., 'Eine republikanische Ära in Karthago?'. in *Studien zur Alten Geschichte S. Lauffer dargebracht*, ed. H. Kalcyk *et al.* (Rome, 1986), 437–42.

Inscriptiones Latinae Selectae, ed. H. Dessau: 3 vols in 5 (Berlin, Weidmann: 1892–1916).

Jacoby, F., *et al.*,eds, *Die Fragmente der Griechischen Historiker* (Berlin, Weidmann: 1923–).

Jenkins, G. K. and Lewis, R. B., *Carthaginian Gold and Electrum Coins* (London, Royal Numismatic Society: 1963).

Kahrstedt, U., *Geschichte der Karthager*, vol. 3 (Berlin, Weidmann: 1913); see also Meltzer.

Kaltner, J. and McKenzie, S. L., *Beyond Babel: A Handbook for Biblical Hebrew and Related Languages* (Leiden: Brill, 2002).

Kleine Pauly, Der: Lexicon der Antike, ed. K. Ziegler and W. Sontheimer, 5 vols (München, Deutscher Taschenbuch Verlag: 1975).

Krahmalkov, C. R., 'A Carthaginian Report of the Battle of Agrigentum, 406 BC', *Rivista di Studi Fenici* 2 (1974), 171–7.

Krahmalkov, C. R., 'Two Neo-Punic Poems in Rhymed Verse', *Rivista di Studi Fenici* 3 (1975), 169–205.

Krahmalkov, C. R., ' "When He Drove Out Yrirachan": A Phoenician (Punic) Poem, ca. A.D. 350', *Bulletin of American Schools of Oriental Research* 294 (1994), 69–82.

Krahmalkov, C. R., *Phoenician–Punic Dictionary* (*Studia Phoenicia* 16: Leuven, Peeters: 2000).

Krings, V. (ed.), *La Civilisation phénicienne et punique: Manuel de recherche* (Leiden, Brill: 1995).

Krings, V., *Carthage et les Grecs, c. 580–480 av. J.-C.: Textes et histoire* (Leiden, Brill: 1998).

Lancel, S., 'Le problème du Ve siècle à Carthage: mise en perspective de documents nouveaux', in Hackens and Moucharte (1992), 269–81.

Lancel, S., *Carthage: a History*, tr. Antonia Nevill (Oxford, Blackwell: 1995) [original French edition: *Carthage*, Paris, Fayard: 1992].

Lancel, S., *Hannibal* (Paris, Fayard: 1995; English tr. by Antonia Nevill, Oxford, Blackwell: 1998).

Lazenby, J. F., *Hannibal's War: a Military History* (Warminster, Aris and Phillips: 1978; reprinted Norman, OK, University of Oklahoma Press: 1998).

Lazenby, J. F., *The First Punic War: a Military History* (London, UCL Press: 1996).

Le Bohec, Y. (ed.), *La première Guerre punique: autour de l'oeuvre de M. H. Fantar: actes de la table ronde de Lyon, mercredi 19 mai 1999* (Lyon, Centre d'études et de recherches sur l'Occident romain: 2001).

Le Bohec, Y., *Histoire militaire des guerres puniques, 264–146 avant J.-C. (L'art de la guerre)* (Paris, Éditions du Rocher: 2001).

Lepelley, C. and Lancel, S. (eds), *Carthage et son territoire dans l'antiquité*: Tome I of *Histoire et archéologie de l'Afrique du Nord: Actes du IVe Colloque International (Strasbourg, 5–9 avril 1988)* (Paris, Comité des Travaux historiques et scientifiques: 1990).

Lewis, D. M., 'Sicily, 413–368 BC', *Cambridge Ancient History* vol. 6 (1994), ch. 5.

Lipiński, E. *et al.* (eds), *Dictionnaire de la civilisation phénicienne et punique* (Turnhout, Belgium, 1992).

Lipiński, E., *Itineraria Phoenicia* (*Studia Phoenicia* 18: Leuven, 2004).

Loreto, L., *La Grande Strategia di Roma nell'Età della Prima Guerra Punica (ca. 273–ca. 229 a.C.): L'inizio di un paradosso* (Napoli, 2007).

Lund, J., 'Phoenician/Punic colonization in Tunisia', in *East and West: Cultural Relations in the Ancient World*, ed. T. Fischer-Hansen (Copenhagen, Collegium Hyperboreum and Museum Tusculanum Press: 1988), 44–57.

Manfredi, L.-I., *La Politica amministrativa di Cartagine in Africa* (Roma, Accademia Nazionale dei Lincei, Classe di Scienze Morali, Storiche e Filologiche: Memorie, serie IX, vol. XVI, fascicolo 3: 2003), 329–532.

Markoe, G., *Phoenicians* (Peoples of the Past series: London, British Museum: 2000).

Masson, O, 'Le "roi" carthaginois Iômilkos dans les inscriptions de Délos', *Semitica* 29 (1979), 53–7.

Meister, K., 'Agathocles', *Cambridge Ancient History* vol. 7.1 (1984), ch. 10.

Meltzer, O., *Geschichte der Karthager*, vols 1–2 (Berlin, Weidmann: 1879, 1896); see also Kahrstedt.

Morel, J.-P., 'Nouvelles données sur le commerce de Carthage punique entre le VIIe siècle et le IIe siècle avant J.-C.', in Lepelley and Lancel (1990), 67–99.

Morstein-Marx, R., 'The myth of Numidian origins in Sallust's African excursus (*Iugurtha* 17.7–18.12)', *American Journal of Philology* 122 (2001), 179–200.

Moscati, S., *The World of the Phoenicians* (English tr.: London, Cardinal: 1968).

Murray, W. M., 'Polyereis and the role of the ram in Hellenistic naval warfare', in *Tropis V: 5th International Symposium on Ship-Construction in Antiquity, Nauplia 1993*, ed. H. Tzalas (Athens, Hellenic Institute for the Preservation of Nautical Antiquity:1999), 299–308.

Oxford Classical Dictionary, 3rd edn. revised, ed. S. Hornblower and A. J. Spawforth (Oxford, Oxford University Press: 2003).

Palmer, R. E. A., *Rome and Carthage at Peace* (*Historia-Einzelschriften* 113: Wiesbaden, F. Steiner Verlag: 1997).

Peters, S.: see *Hannibal ad Portas*.

Picard, G. C., *Hannibal* (Paris, Hachette: 1967).

Picard, G. C., 'Carthage from the battle at Himera to Agathocles' invasion, 480–308 BC', *Cambridge Ancient History* vol. 6 (1994), ch. 9a.

Picard, G. C. and Picard, C., *Daily Life in Carthage in the Time of Hannibal* (Engl. tr.: London, Allen and Unwin: 1961).

Picard, G. C. and Picard, C., *Life and Death of Carthage* (New York, Taplinger Publishing Co., and London, Sidgwick and Jackson: 1968).

Picard, G. C. and Picard, C., *Karthago: Leben und Kultur* (German edn, revised, of *Daily Life*: Stuttgart, 1983).

Picard, G. C. Mahjoubi, A. and Bechaouch, A., '*Pagus Thuscae et Gunzuzi*', *Comptes rendus de l'Académie des inscriptions* 107 (1963), 124–30.

Rhodes, P. J. and Osborne, R., *Greek Historical Inscriptions 404–323 BC* (Oxford and New York, Oxford University Press: 2007).

Rindelaub, A. and Schmidt, K., 'Les fouilles de l'université de Hambourg au-dessous du *decumanus maximus* à Carthage', *CEDAC Carthage* 15 (1996) 44–52.

Quinn, J. C., 'Roman Africa?', in Merryweather, A. D. and Prag, J. R. W., '*Romanization*'?: Digressus: *the Internet Journal for the Classical World*, Supplement 1 (2003).

Sanctis, G. de, *Storia dei Romani*, vol. 3, parts 1–2, 2nd edition (Firenze, 'La Nuova Italia' Editrice: 1968).

Scardigli, B., *I Trattati Romani-Cartaginesi* (Pisa, Scuola Normale Superiore: 1991).

Schmitz, P. C., 'The name "Agrigentum" in a Punic inscription (*CIS* 5510.10), *Journal of Near Eastern Studies* 53 (1994), 1–13.

Schmitz, P. C., 'The Phoenician Text from the Etruscan Sanctuary at Pyrgi', *Journal of American Oriental Studies* 115 (1995), 559–75.

Schwartz, J. H., *What the Bones Tell Us* (New York, H. Holt: 1993; republished, Tucson, AZ, University of Arizona Press: 1997).

Scullard, H. H., 'Carthage and Rome', *Cambridge Ancient History* 7.2 (1989), ch. 11.

Seibert, J., *Hannibal* (Darmstadt, Wissenschaftliche Buchgesellschaft: 1993).

Serrati, J., 'Neptune's altars: the treaties between Rome and Carthage (509–226 B.C.)', *Classical Quarterly* 56 (2006), 113–34.

Shaw, B. D., 'Cult and belief in Punic and Roman Africa', *Princeton/Stanford Working Papers in Classics* (September 2007), 58 pp.

Steinby, C. (2007), *The Roman Republican Navy: From the sixth century to 167 BC* (Commentationes Humanarum Litterarum, 123: [Helsinki], Scoietas Scientiarum Fennica: 2007).

Sznycer, M., 'Carthage et la civilisation punique', in C. Nicolet (ed.), *Rome et la conquête du monde méditerranéen*, vol. 2: *Genèse d'un empire* (Paris, Presses universitaires de France: 1978), 545–93.

Talbert, R. J. A., *Timoleon and the Revival of Greek Sicily, 344–317 BC* (Cambridge, Cambridge University Press: 1974, repr. 2007).

Vegas, M. (ed.), *Cartago Fenicio-Púnica: Las excavaciones alemanas en Cartago 1975–1997* (Barcelona, Cuadernos de Arqueología Mediterránea 4, Universidad Pompeu Fabra de Barcelona: 1998).

Walbank, F. W., *A Historical Commentary on Polybius*, 3 vols (Oxford: Oxford University Press, 1957, 1967, 1979).

Warmington, B. H., *Carthage* (Harmondsworth, Penguin Books: 1964).

Zambon, E., *Tradition and Innovation: Sicily between Hellenism and Rome* (Stuttgart, F. Steiner: 2008).

INDEX

Abdera (Spain) 4, 50, 195
accountants ('treasurers', *mḥšbm, meḥashbim*) 31, 41, 87, 120, 144, 208
Acherbas: *see* Zakarbaal
Acholla 39, 63, 217
Acragas (Agrigentum) 17, 49, 56, 60, 71, 75, 106-7, 112, 133-5, 157, 162-3, 165, 167, 169, 173-7, 180-1, 183, 187
Adherbal (general in 250–249) 34, 187-8
Adherbal (general in 307) 174
adirim, 'drm: see senate of Carthage
Adriatic 168, 197, 199-200, 203
Adys (battle) 185
Aegates Islands (battle) 36, 189
Aelian (writer) 136
Aesculapius (Eshmun) 28, 76, 87, 98; *see also* Asclepius, Eshmun
Agathocles (tyrant and king of Syracuse) 29, 64, 72, 76, 101, 139-42, 145-6, 149, 152-4, 156, 158, 162, 172-7, 181-2, 185-6, 195, 201, 203, 206
agora at Carthage: *see* town square
Alalia (Corsica) 43, 46, 125
Alashiya 4, 9
Alexander the Great 2, 101, 112, 139, 141, 152, 162, 172, 174, 191, 196, 200, 211
Alps 163, 199-200
Ammianus Marcellinus (historian) 105

amphorae 12, 44, 50, 60, 62, 83
Anaxilas (tyrant of Rhegium) 164-5
annals of Tyre 5
Antiochus III 208
Apollo (Reshef?) 15, 77, 94, 98-9, 219
Appian 6, 28, 30, 70-1, 75-6, 75-6, 85-8, 90-2, 113, 135, 142-3, 151, 212-14, 217
Appius: *see* Claudius, Appius
Apthther 212
Apulia 199, 201,205
Arcesilaus 174
Ariana (Sebkhet Ariana) 13, 15, 76, 88
Aristo (Hannibal's agent) 208
Aristotle 6, 17, 22, 24-33, 35-7, 42, 44, 63-5, 124, 135, 137-8, 152, 154, 179, 221, 222
Asclepius (Eshmun) 76, 99, 120; *see also* Aesculapius
assembly, citizen (*'m, ham*) 23, 25, 29-30, 36-8, 50, 208
Assyria 1-2, 4-5, 10-11, 130
Astarte 9-10, 23, 44, 53, 77, 94-5, 99, 110, 121, 147
Ataban (Numidian lord of Thugga) 78, 81, 113, 116
Athens 22, 57, 60, 96, 107, 120, 132, 164, 166-7, 211-12, 220
Augustine, Saint 105, 147, 220
Augustus 2, 220
Autaritus (Gallic mercenary general) 161, 190-2

Avienus, *Ora Maritima* 54
'awakener of the god' (priestly
  office) 99, 148
Azores 209

Baal (except B. Hammon and B.
  Shamim) 23, 77, 94-6, 98, 100,
  194
Baal Hammon 53, 77, 94-5, 98-9,
  100, 102-3, 147, 167, 194, 196,
  220
Baal Shamim 77, 94-5, 98, 194
Baalshillek (ossuary of) 118
Baalsillek (freed slave) 69
Babylonians 1, 55
Baebelo (silver mine, Spain) 195
Baecula (battle) 203
Bagradas (Mejerda, river) 13, 15,
  65, 142-3, 150, 191, 204, 213,
  217
Balearic Islands mercenaries 156-7,
  162
Barca (Elissa's brother) 20
Barca: *see* Hamilcar Barca
Barcid family 33,-4, 37-8, 57, 98,
  121, 144, 158, 163, 193, 195,
  197-8, 202, 204, 207-8
basileus, basileis 25-8, 51
Belus (Elissa's father) 20
Belvédère, Parcu du (Tunis) 192
Bithyas (Bitias?; Numidian officer
  in 148) 210, 218
Bithynia 211
Bitias (in Elissa legend) 10
Boethus the Carthaginian
  (sculptor) 112-13
Bomilcar (general and putschist,
  310–308) 76, 86-7, 140-1, 153,
  155, 173-4
Bomilcar (in Second Punic War) 34
books, Carthaginian 66, 105-6,
  108
Borj-el-Jedid 12, 15, 105, 117
bribery at Carthage 32-3, 168,
  222
Bruttians, Bruttium 201-2, 204,
  206
Bulla (western Libya) 65, 143, 204,
  213
Byblos 1-2

Byrsa (hill and citadel) 7-15, 28,
  36, 73, 75-7, 81, 83-8, 96, 108,
  111, 113, 130, 208, 219
Byzacium 39, 63, 65-6, 142-4,
  147, 161, 192

Caere (Etruria) 43-4
Caesar, Julius 39, 126, 220
Camarina (Sicily) 163, 165, 167,
  185, 188
Campania 60, 157, 176, 179-81,
  190, 201-2, 209, 222
Cannae (battle) 29, 157, 159,
  199-201, 204-5
Cape Bon 13-15, 18,39, 44, 64, 67,
  71, 83, 90, 143, 147, 155, 173,
  185-6, 217
Cape Farina 15, 44-5, 178-9
Capua (Campania) 201-3
Carales (Cagliari) 4, 46, 169
carbon-14 dating 7, 9
Carchedon (Greek name for
  Carthage) 6
Carthalo (general in
  250–249) 187-8
Carthalo (Hannibal's officer) 201,
  211
Carthalo (high priest) 101,
  125-7
Carthalo (politician in
  150s) 213-14
Cassiterides islands 3, 50, 54-5
Cassius Dio: *see* Dio
Cassius Dionysius of Utica 66, 70
Catadas river (Mellane) 13, 65, 77,
  185
Cato the Censor 26, 64, 67,
  215-16, 222
Catulus, Gaius Lutatius 189
cavalry 16, 110-11, 147, 149,
  154-9, 161, 164, 167, 171,
  186, 191, 195, 197-8, 200,
  203-4
Cereres (Demeter and Kore) 220
Chanani (*Kn'nm*) 220
chariots, war 154, 156, 162, 171
child sacrifice, reports and
  allegations 82, 100-5, 174
choma (quay, Falbe's
  quadrilateral) 92

chora (Carthage's home territory) 63-5, 69, 71, 173, 199, 210, 221
Cinyps (river) 40
Cirta (Numidia) 42, 62,105, 147, 212, 214, 217
Cisalpine Gaul (northern Italy) 198
citadel (Carthage): *see* Byrsa
Citium (Cyprus) 4, 9
citizens of Carthage 17, 20-3, 25, 29, 36-9, 63, 65, 69-70, 75, 86, 130, 132-3, 136, 138-41, 143, 150, 154-5, 157, 167, 171, 191, 196, 207, 210, 217-19, 221
Claudius Nero, Gaius (consul) 203
Claudius, Appius (consul) 182-4
Cleitarchus 100
Cleitomachus: *see* Hasdrubal Cleitomachus
Clupea (Aspis, Kelibia) 18, 80, 185-6, 217
coinage, coins 2-3, 11, 25, 57, 62, 68, 92, 98, 112, 120-1, 123, 143, 191, 195, 207, 209
Colaeus of Samos (mariner) 43, 55
Columella (agricultural writer) 65-6
Concessa (at Nicivibus) 103
Constantine (emperor) 127
consuls 28, 33, 130, 181-5, 187-9, 203, 208, 216-18
copper trade 1, 4, 120
Corcyra (Corfù) 176
Cornwall 3, 55
Corsica 43, 46, 60, 112, 157, 165, 184
corvus ('raven', naval weapon) 184-5, 187
Cothon (artificial ports at Carthage) 90, 92-3, 218-19
council, 'more sacred' 30-1
Crimisus (Belice: river and battle) 138, 154, 156, 171
Cronus (Baal Hammon?) 53, 98-101
Croton (Italy) 106, 176
crucifixion (of Carthaginian traitors) 35-6, 127-8, 137-8, 184
curse on Carthage (Scipio Aemilianus') 219-20
Curtius Rufus (historian) 101-2

Cyprus 1-2, 4, 7-9, 11, 196
Cyrene 18, 40, 174, 212
Cyrus the Great 46, 126

Darius 57
deditio in fidem (unconditional surrender) 216
Demeter and Kore 78, 96, 110, 112-13, 115, 123, 147, 168, 220
democracy, 'democrats' (at Carthage) 25, 29, 37, 213-14, 221
Dermech 81
Dido: *see* Elissa
Dio (Cassius Dio) 135, 182
Diodorus 17, 27, 29-30, 34, 41, 47-8, 60, 62, 64, 69, 86-7, 98, 100-2, 104, 106, 131-2, 135-6, 140-1, 145, 151-2, 154-7, 166, 169, 171, 173-4, 176, 178-9, 194-6, 221
Diogenes (Carthaginian general in 147) 218
Dion (Syracusan liberator) 134, 136, 158, 170
Dionysius I (tyrant of Syracuse) 33, 134-6, 151-2, 167-72, 175, 182, 219
Dionysius II (Syracuse) 134, 170-1, 177
Dionysus 98, 113
docks, dockyards at Carthage 67, 73, 90-1, 93, 113, 151, 169-70
Dorieus of Sparta 40, 48-9, 56, 163-4
Douimès 10-12, 15, 108, 110
Drepana (Trápani) 170, 177, 187-9
Duero (river, Spain) 198
Duillius, Gaius 184
dye trade 3, 13, 60

Ebro (river) 197-8
Ebusus island (Ibiza) 4, 41, 50, 54, 56, 59-60, 110, 120
Egypt 1-2, 17, 40, 77, 97, 108, 111,116, 119-20, 130-1, 139, 141, 172, 186-7, 196, 222
elephants, war 42, 88, 162-3, 185-7, 191, 195, 198, 206

El-Haouaria quarries (Cape
Bon) 18, 90
Elissa (Dido) 7-12, 15-17, 20,
23-4, 107,121, 123, 125, 164
Elymi (Sicilian people) 47-8
Emporia (region, gulf of
Sirte) 39-42,45, 5, 65, 79, 163,
212-13
Enna (Sicily) 167, 185
Entella (Sicily) 179, 190
Ephorus (historian) 156
Epicydes (Syracusan-Carthaginian
activist) 161, 201
epikrateia (Carthaginian territories
in Sicily) 49, 164-7, 173, 176-7,
179, 182-3, 186-7
Eryx, Mt (Erice, Sicily) 152, 170,
177, 188-9
Eshmun (and temple) 28, 87, 98-9,
130, 219
Eshmuniaton ('Suniatus', 4th
Century) 134-7, 170
Etruria, Etruscans 3, 43-6, 54,
57, 63, 75, 132, 156, 165,
179-80
Euboea 43, 49
Eudoxus (historian) 6
Euripides 6

Fabian family (Rome) 98
Fabius Maximus, Quintus ('the
Delayer') 201-3, 211
Fabius Pictor, Quintus
(historian) 193, 196
Fair Cape (Cape Bon or Cape
Farina) 44-5, 178
Falbe's quadrilateral
(Carthage) 92, 218
fleet and navy, Carthaginian 10,
34, 36, 41, 52, 56, 72, 90-3,
129, 134, 149-53, 155, 173,
175, 177, 181-3, 185-90, 195,
199-200, 202, 205-6, 209, 214,
218
fleets and navies, foreign 56
(Etruscan); 92, 150, 155, 184-8,
189, 202, 218 (Roman); 168,
170, 176 (Syracusan)
foundries at Carthage 13, 15, 67-8,
73

Gades 3-6, 32, 50-1, 53, 60, 98,
194-5, 199, 222
Gammarth (Cape) 12, 75-6, 85, 88
garum (fish-sauce) 60-1, 221
Gaul, Gauls 43, 60, 126, 157,
161-2, 197-200
Gela (Sicily) 163, 167, 173, 175-6
Gelon of Syracuse 49, 57, 73, 132,
163-5
generals, Carthaginian 17, 27, 29,
32-4, 36, 38, 46, 49, 52, 76, 83,
87, 101, 125, 128, 131, 134,
139-40, 144, 152, 155-6, 161,
168-9, 171, 176, 181, 187-91,
196, 198-200, 202, 206, 210,
217-19
gerousia (Carthaginian senate) 25,
28, 30; *see also* senate of
Carthage
Gibraltar, straits of 3, 41, 43, 45,
52-4
Gisco (Magonid, 4th
Century) 137-8, 140-1, 154,
156, 166, 171-3
Gisco (Magonid, 5th
Century) 131-3, 165, 170
gold trade 11, 51, 60, 132
'Gorillas' 52-3
Great Plains (western Libya) 143,
204, 213
Gry the fuller 69
Guadalquivir (river, Spain) 50, 194
gugga (joke term for merchant?)
62
Gulussa (son of Masinissa) 209,
214
Gunzuzi (Libyan region) 143-4

Hadrumetum (Sousse) 65, 116-17,
142, 144, 146, 173, 204, 216,
221
Halycus, river (Platani) 169, 171,
175-7, 201
Hamilcar (general in 250s) 185-7
Hamilcar (general in 341) 171
Hamilcar (general in
320s–310s) 139-40, 172-3
Hamilcar (general, son of
Gisco) 140, 156, 173, 175, 192,
203

Hamilcar (magistrate of *pagus Gurzensis*, 12 BC) 221
Hamilcar (Magonid, died 480) 17, 24-7, 33, 42-3, 47-9. 52, 56, 63, 101-2, 112, 127-8, 130-2, 157, 164-6,
Hamilcar (secret agent at Alexander's court) 139, 172
Hamilcar 'the Samnite' (politician in 150s) 213-14
Hamilcar (writer on agriculture) 65-6, 105
Hamilcar Barca 16, 22, 24, 142, 157, 159, 161, 163, 188-97, 214, 222
Hammamet, gulf of 18, 21, 79, 143, 196
Hannibal (general in First Punic War) 181, 183-4
Hannibal (son of Gisco, Magonid) 27, 106, 132-3, 135, 156-7, 166-7, 169
Hannibal (son of Hamilcar Barca) 16-17, 20-1, 23-4, 29-30, 32-4, 36-8, 63, 66, 83, 92, 94-6, 98-9, 101, 106-7, 121, 125, 130, 132, 144, 151, 154-5, 157-9, 161, 163, 193-208, 210-11, 215-16, 221-2
Hannibal (trierarch in 250) 34
Hannibal 'the Rhodian' (in First Punic War) 153
Hannibal 'the Starling' (politician, 2nd Century) 213
Hannibal quarter (*quartier Hannibal*), Carthage 83-5, 111,113, 208
Hanno (admiral in 241) 35-6, 189
Hanno (general in 310) 140-1, 173
Hanno (general in 307) 141, 174
Hanno (general in 264–262) 181, 183
Hanno (general in 213–211) 161
Hanno (Hannibal's nephew and lieutenant) 161, 202
Hanno (in *Poenulus*) 61-2, 209
Hanno (Magonid, 5th Century) 106, 135,
Hanno (officer at Messana in 264) 159, 189

Hanno (sufete and chief priest) 32
Hanno (sufete and voyager) 50-5, 59-60, 98, 105, 107, 125, 132; *see also* periplus
Hanno 'the Great' (4th Century) 22, 70-1, 134-8, 140-2, 169-71
Hanno 'the Great' (3rd Century) 30, 34, 135, 142, 144, 188-93, 207
Hanno 'the Great' (2nd Century) 135, 213-14
Hannobaal (freed slave?) 21, 68-9
harbours at Carthage 15, 67, 75, 88, 91-2, 94, 202
Hasdrubal (Carthaginian general 151–146) 17, 29, 214, 217-19
Hasdrubal (Carthaginian general in 250s) 187
Hasdrubal (Carthaginian general in 310) 185
Hasdrubal (Carthaginian general in 341) 171
Hasdrubal (Carthaginian general, grandson of Masinissa) 17, 148, 210, 217
Hasdrubal (Hannibal's brother) 24, 34, 196-7, 199-200, 203-5
Hasdrubal (Hannibal's brother-in-law) 33-4, 38, 193, 195-7
Hasdrubal (Magonid) 24, 47-8, 56, 128, 130-1
Hasdrubal (son of Gisco, general in Second Punic War) 203-4
Hasdrubal 'the Kid' (politician) 207
Hasdrubal Cleitomachus (philosopher) 211-12, 220
Hera 94, 98-9, 211
Heraclea Minoa (Sicily) 158, 170, 185, 187
Heracles, Hercules 5, 7, 48, 94, 98-9, 120-1, 123, 125
Hermocrates of Syracuse 59, 166
Herodotus 2, 24, 27-8, 46, 48, 51, 54-7, 59-60, 101, 128, 144, 164, 222
Hicetas (4th Century) 171
Hicetas (3rd Century) 176

Hiempsal II (king of Numidia, 1st Century) 105
Hiero (king of Syracuse, 3rd Century) 177, 181-3, 187, 189, 192, 201
Hieron (tyrant of Syracuse, 5th Century) 132
Himera (Sicily) 17, 43, 46-7, 52, 57, 73, 101-2, 126, 128, 130-3, 144, 156, 164, 167, 169-70
Himilco (general in 307) 141, 174
Himilco (Iomilkos, in 279) 28
Himilco (Magonid, active 410–396) 27, 33-4, 101, 106, 132-5, 145, 150, 154, 150, 167-9
Himilco (voyager) 54-5, 59, 105
Himilco Phameas (officer, 2nd Century) 210
Hippacra (Bizerte) 4, 9, 13, 40, 65, 141-2, 144, 150, 161, 174, 191-2, 21-18
Hippocrates 161, 201
Hiram (king of Tyre) 3-4
Hittites 1-2
Horoscopa (in Libya: Thubursicu?) 214
hostages 164, 217, 220
Hundred and Four, Court of 35-6, 38, 133-4, 136, 140, 207

Iberian mercenaries 157
Ilipa (battle) 157, 162, 203
Illyria 197, 201-2, 205
Îlot de l'Amirauté (Carthage) 73, 87, 90-1
iron trade 3, 11, 60
Isis 97, 107, 111, 119, 121, 147
Isocrates 25, 33
ivory 3, 42-3, 50, 108-9, 113, 120

Jersualem 3, 81, 100-1
Josephus 4, 8
judges 27, 32, 36
judges, order of (faction, 2nd Century) 32, 207-8
Jugurtha (king of Numidia) 17, 147
Julius Nasif (military poet, 4th Century AD) 106

Juno 44, 53, 95, 98, 220
Junon (hill) 12, 81
Jupiter 8-9, 24, 98-9, 222
Justin 5, 7-12, 16-18, 24-5, 28, 35, 39, 42, 46-51, 56, 62-3, 71, 101-2, 106, 125-37, 139-41, 164

Kerkouane 14, 18, 39, 67. 74. 80, 82-3, 85, 87, 95-6, 99, 111, 113, 146, 159, 162
kings and monarchy at Carthage 24-5, 27-8, 33
Kn'nm (Chanani) 1, 220
kyrious Karchedonious 21

La Marsa 75
Lacinium, Cape (Capo Colonna, Italy) 98, 211
lagoons area at Carthage 14-15, 73, 75, 81, 86-7, 89-90, 93, 196
lake of Tunis 13-15, 67, 75-6, 89-90, 93, 151
Latium (Italy) 44-5, 178-80
lead trade 3, 55
Lepcis Magna 4-5, 11, 39-41, 45, 105-6, 150, 163, 199, 213
Leptis (Minor; Lamta) 217
libri Punici ('Punic books') 105
Libyon (coin-legend) 123, 191
Libyphoenicians 17, 63, 69, 146, 150, 155, 157, 210, 215, 218
Liguria, Ligurians 157, 204
Lilybaeum (Marsala) 61, 150, 161, 168, 170, 177, 180, 187, 189, 196
Lipara (Islands) 181, 187
Livy 10, 17, 23-4, 26, 28, 30-2, 87, 98-9, 135, 157, 180, 200-1, 205, 207-8, 212-14, 221
Lixus 3-5, 50-2
Lucania, Lucanians 201-2

Macedon (kingdom) 21, 94, 112, 199, 201-2
Mactar (Libya) 106-7, 142-3, 189, 191
Mago (admiral in 279) 177
Mago (explorer) 42
Mago (general 344/343) 35, 154, 156, 158, 171,

Mago (general 390s–380s) 27, 33-4, 134, 168-9,

Mago (Hannibal's brother) 24, 197, 199, 204, 206

Mago (ruler of Carthage) 22, 24, 47-8, 55-7, 125, 128-31,

Mago (writer on agriculture) 65-6, 70-1, 124,

Mago 'the Samnite' 159

Magonid family 23-5, 35, 47, 52, 98, 128-33, 135, 157, 163-8, 193

Maharbal (officer of Hannibal) 159, 197, 200

Malaca (Málaga, Spain) 4, 50, 195

'Malchus' 19, 26, 36, 46, 124-5, 127; see also Mazeus

Mamertines of Messana 176-7, 181-3

Manilius (consul in 149) 216

Marcellus, Marcus Claudius 202-3

Marcius Censorinus (consul in 149) 216

Marsala (Lilybaeum) 61, 150-1

Marseilles Tariff 22

Masaesyli (Numidian people) 147, 204

Masinissa (king of Numidia) 17, 99, 105, 143, 146-8, 161, 203-5, 207-10, 212-15, 217-18, 220

Massyli (Numidian people) 147-8, 191, 195, 204, 210, 213

Mastia Tarseion (Spain) 178, 195-6

Mathos (Libyan rebel leader) 131, 190-2, 200

Mauretania, Mauri 3, 16, 42, 51-2, 105, 131-2, 137, 143, 157

mausolea (in Libya) 78-80, 100, 113, 116

Maxula (near Carthage) 15-16

Mazeus ('Malchus') 46-8, 55-7, 101-2, 124-30, 133, 135, 189

Megara (M'rt, suburb of Carthage) 13, 16, 75-6, 81, 85-6, 88, 141, 163, 210, 217-18

Mejerda (river): see Bagradas

Méjerda, Monts de la 142-3, 150

Mellane: see Catadas

Melqart 5, 7, 9, 12, 23, 56, 77, 94-5, 98-9, 102, 111, 120-1, 123, 125-7, 139, 148, 222

Menander of Ephesus (writer) 4, 6-8

Meninx (Jerba, island) 65

mercenaries 33, 56, 72, 120, 141, 149, 153-8, 161-3, 171, 176, 186, 188, 190-1, 194, 198, 209, 222

Messana 17, 35, 159, 164, 168, 173, 176, 180-3, 189, 190, 198

Metaurus (battle) 203

Metellus, Lucius Caecilius 187

Micatani (Numidian people) 195

Micipsa (king of Numidia) 147, 212

Milkpilles 107

Milkyaton (various) 21, 24, 69, 78, 97, 115, 147

mines 1, 55, 195, 207

mlk, mlk 'dm, mlk 'mr, mlk b'l 102-3

Mogod (mountains) 142, 150

molchomor 103

molk: see mlk

Monte Sirai (Sardinia) 45-6

Mottones (later Marcus Valerius Mottones; cavalry officer) 161, 203

Motya (Sicily) 4, 48, 57, 77 100, 102, 112, 167-8, 170, 219

Muluccha river 143

Muthul river 65

Muxsi (region) 143-4

Mylae (Sicily) 184

mzrḥ (mizreh) 22, 106

Naples 3, 12, 17, 132, 165

Naravas (Nrwt: Numidian prince) 161, 191, 193, 195, 203

navy: see fleet and navy

Neapolis (Nabeul, Tunisia) 18, 39, 173, 196

necropolis, necropoleis 14, 75, 80-1, 102, 108, 110, 117-18

Nepheris 217-18

Nepos, Cornelius (writer) 26, 98, 195, 204

New Carthage (Cartagena) 21, 98, 178, 195, 203
New City (district of Carthage) 76, 88, 196, 210
'New City' (name) 4,11, 17-18, 76, 88,167, 176, 195-6, 210
New Gate (at Carthage) 38, 67-8, 75
Nicivibus (Ain N'gaous, Algeria) 103
Nobas son of 'Axioubas' 62
Nora (Sardinia) 4-5, 23, 37, 46, 95, 100, 147

oaths, Hannibal's 94-5, 98-9, 222
Oea 39
Oestrymnides islands 54
Olbia (Sardinia) 4, 27, 45, 169
Old Testament 2-3, 100
olives 60-1, 64, 66, 75, 85-6, 207
One Hundred and Four: see Hundred and Four
Orosius (historian) 46, 48, 125-7, 214
ossuaries 117-18

Paday (Pidia, *Pdy*) 10; *see also* Bitias
pagus, pagi 143-4, 147, 213, 221
Panormus (Palermo) 4, 47-8, 120, 164, 169, 177, 185-8
pavimentum Punicum (tessellated mosaics) 221
pentarchies 27, 31, 35-6, 68, 87, 131-2
Pentathlus of Cnidus 47, 163
penteconter 52, 56, 60, 129, 151-2
periplus 41 (of Pseudo-Scylax); 50-4, 98, 105, 107, 125, 132 (Hanno's)
Persia 43, 46, 55-7, 139, 162, 164, 174, 222
Peter the Great (tsar) 127
pharaohs 1, 120, 131, 139
Pharusii (Mauretanian tribe) 42
Philaenus, Philaeni brothers 40, 45, 105, 139
Philinus of Acragas 107, 180-1, 211
Philip V (king of Macedon) 21, 94, 201-2, 207, 211

Philistus 6
Phintias (Licata, Sicily) 176, 188
Phintias (tyrant of Acragas) 176
Phocaeans 43, 46-7, 54-6, 60, 112, 151, 153, 163
Phoenicia, Phoenicians 1-5, 10-11, 12, 16-17, 48-9, 95, 105, 147, 153, 196
Pithecusae (Ischia) 3, 12, 49
Plato 26, 100, 107, 211, 222
Plautus (playwright) 61-2, 209, 222
Pliny the Elder 5-6, 53-5, 65-6, 105, 136, 195
plostellum Punicum (threshing-cart) 221
Plutarch 100, 102, 106, 221
Poeni 1
Poenulus (comedy) 61-2, 209
Polyaenus 131, 134-5, 169
Polybius 18, 21, 27, 29, 32, 34, 37, 40, 44-5, 59, 63-4, 71-2, 75, 91, 94, 106, 144-5, 149, 154-5, 157-8, 178-80, 184-5, 188m 190, 192, 194, 198-9, 205, 209, 212, 215, 218-19, 221-2
Ponim 1
population 11, 17, 42, 55, 63, 67, 70, 72, 75, 85, 143, 145-6, 170, 199, 210
ports, artificial (Carthage) 73, 77, 86-7, 89-93, 150-1, 202, 209, 218
pottery 4, 7, 9,12, 14, 41, 43, 45, 49, 60, 62, 68, 73-4, 79, 81, 83, 91-2, 95, 112, 209
praetor 28, 33, 189
priests, priesthoods 9, 22, 24, 32, 78, 85, 96, 99, 119, 126, 131-2
Ptolemies of Egypt 119, 139, 141, 172, 187
puinel ('Carthaginian') 43
Pumay 5, 8-9, 23-4, 95, 211
Pumayyaton 8-9
Pygmalion 6-8, 10, 13, 23
Pyrenees 197, 200
Pyrgi (Etruria) 44, 168
Pyrrhus (king of Epirus) 153, 162, 176-7, 179-81, 200

Qart-hadasht (city-name) 4, 6, 9,
  18, 21, 120, 123, 196
quadrireme 152
quaestor (at Carthage and
  Gades) 32, 207; *see also* rb,
  rab
quinquereme 56, 91, 150-3, 167,
  184, 189, 195, 205, 216

rb, rab (offices and title) 27, 31-6,
  99, 106, 134-5, 207
rebellions and revolts, Libyan 33,
  38. 42, 47, 65, 71-2, 76, 88, 96,
  106, 131, 134, 145-6, 154,
  158,161, 168, 173, 179, 185,
  190, 212
Regulus, Marcus Atilius 29, 71,
  161, 163, 185-7, 206
Reshef 5, 77, 95, 98-9, 219
Rhegium (Reggio) 17, 164-5, 172,
  180-1, 183
Rhodes 60, 211
Río Tinto (Spain) 50, 195
Rususmon (Cape Farina) 15

Sabratha 39, 42, 78
Sacred Battalion (*hieros lochos*)
  154, 156, 158, 173
Safot (various) 21, 24, 68-9, 78
Saguntum (Spain) 197-8
Sainte Monique (Carthage) 12, 43,
  87, 117-18
Sallust 5, 39-40, 105
Salombaal (Salammbô) 24
salt on Carthage (legend) 220
Samnites (central Italy) 159, 180,
  201-2
Sardinia, Sardinians 4-5. 13,
  17-18, 26-7, 29, 33, 44-8, 50,
  54, 56, 59, 70, 77-8, 82, 95, 104,
  120, 125-6, 129-30, 153, 157,
  169, 178-9, 183-4, 191, 193-4,
  196-7, 221
Saturn (Baal Hammon) 98, 103,
  220
Savage, Thomas 53
Saw, the (*Prion*) 192, 214
Scipio Aemilianus, Publius
  Cornelius 95, 148, 211, 214-15,
  218-20

Scipio Africanus, Publius
  Cornelius 21, 30, 71-2, 150,
  155, 157, 162-3, 192, 203-8,
  211
Scipio Nasica 215-16
Segesta (Sicily) 48-9, 112, 165-6,
  183-4
Selinus (Sicily) 47-8, 132, 158,
  164-7, 171
Semiramis (legendary queen of
  Assyria) 10
senate of Carthage (*'drm,
  adirim*) 22, 24-30, 35, 37, 72,
  87, 124, 136-7, 139-41, 219
senate-house (*bouleuterion*) 86-7,
  141, 219
shellfish 2, 13, 60
shops, workshops at
  Carthage 13-14, 67, 82-3, 85,
  217
Sicca 142, 144, 189-90, 204
Sicharbas: *see* Zakarbaal
Sidi bou Said 12, 75, 111
Sidon 1-2, 4, 59
Siga (Numidia) 41, 147
Silanus, Marcus Iunius (translator
  of Mago) 211
Silenus (historian of
  Hannibal) 107, 211
Siliana (river) 65
Silius Italicus 20, 101-2
silver trade 3, 50, 55, 60, 194-5
Sirte, gulf of 39-40
slaves 21, 61, 63-4, 66-72, 104,
  137, 158, 168, 170, 174, 184-6,
  192, 195, 210, 217, 219-20
Sophoniba (Saponibaal,
  'Sophonisba') 17, 23, 204
Sosylus (historian of
  Hannibal) 107, 211
Sparta 22, 25, 33, 35, 40, 48, 107,
  158, 158, 161, 164, 166, 186,
  211
Spendius (mercenary rebel
  leader) 190-2, 200
stele, stelae 5, 17, 23-4, 26-7, 32,
  38, 67, 77-8, 81-2, 95-7, 99-100,
  102, 104, 106-7, 111, 113,
  115-17, 162
Strabo 2, 40, 42, 54-5, 65, 85, 210

strategos (Greek term for
general) 33, 141, 196
streets 14, 61, 67-8, 76, 83, 85-6,
130, 173, 192, 219
sufetes 25-30, 32-3, 35, 37-8, 49,
55, 68, 78, 83, 97, 99, 115,
128-31, 136-7, 141, 146-8, 171,
181, 207-8
Sulcis 4, 45-6, 77-8, 169
Suniatus: *see* Eshmuniaton
Synalos (Eshmunhalos, 4th
Century) 158, 170
Syphax (Numidian king) 17, 161,
204
Syracuse, Syracusans 12, 17, 33,
43, 49, 56-7, 62, 96, 121, 132-6,
138-41, 145, 151-2, 156, 161,
163-6, 168-77, 181-3, 90, 192,
199, 201-3, 211

Tagomago wreck (Ibiza) 60, 139
Tagus (river) 196, 198
Tanit *pene* Baal 98-9
Tanit 23, 53, 69, 77, 81-2, 95-6,
98-9, 100, 104, 121, 123, 147,
220
Tarentum 17, 92, 177, 181, 201
Tartessus 43, 50, 55
Tauromenium (Taormina) 156,
170
taxes, Carthaginian 31, 42, 63, 67,
144-6, 188-90, 207-8, 213, 216,
220-1
Téboursouk, Monts de 143
Terillus of Himera 164
Tertullian 101, 104
Thapsus 63, 173, 217
Tharros 4, 45, 100, 102, 169
Thebes (Greece) 62
Thefarie Velianas (king of
Caere) 44
Theiosso (Timaeus' name for
Elissa) 10
Thermae Himeraeae
(Sicily) 169-70, 172, 185, 196
Theron of Acragas 49, 73, 163-5
Theveste 142, 188, 213
Thuburbo Maius 77, 111
Thubursicu 65, 214
Thucydides 17, 59, 166

Thugga (Dougga) 37, 65, 78-9,
100, 113, 116, 142, 144, 146-7,
174, 214
Thusca (*Tšk't*: region) 143-4,
212-13
Timaeus 6-7, 10, 156, 170
Timoleon 150, 154, 156-8, 170-2
tin 1, 3, 40, 54-5
Tingi (Tangier) 51-2, 61
Tocae (Thugga) 142
tombs 50, 52, 69, 80, 82, 97, 99,
108, 118, 120, 133, 220
tophet (children's ritual
cemetery) 14, 17, 75, 77, 81-2,
96, 100-4, 113, 115-16, 219
Toscanos (Spain) 13, 83
town square (*agora*, at
Carthage) 14, 28, 36, 76-7,
86-7, 130, 141, 172, 219
Trasimene, Lake (battle) 199-200,
205
treasurers: *see* accountants
treaties 18, 21, 44-7, 50, 59, 94,
98-9, 129, 138, 166, 178-80,
197, 201, 204-6, 212, 215
Trebia, river (battle) 163, 199
trierarch (naval official) 34
trireme 92, 19, 150-2, 154, 171,
195
triumphal parades (at
Carthage) 49, 130-1, 192
Trogus, Pompeius 6-7, 9-11,
126-7, 130, 134-5, 137
Truceless War 123, 190
Tunes (Tunis) 15, 63, 71, 155,
173-4, 185, 190-2, 200, 202,
217
Tunis, gulf of 6, 12, 15
Tyndaris (Sicily) 170, 184, 187
Tyre (*Sor*), Tyrians 1-11, 13, 20-1,
23-4, 55-6, 69, 85, 94, 101,
107, 125-7, 139, 164, 172, 178,
208

Uchi 65, 78, 144
Ugarit 2, 230
Uthina 185
Utica 3-6, 8-9, 13, 15, 39, 65-6,
110-11, 141-3, 146, 150, 174,
178, 191-2, 204, 215-17, 220

Varro 66, 70
Vicus Africus (Rome) 61, 67

workshops: *see* shops, workshops

Xanthippus of Sparta 158, 161, 163, 186
Xenophon 42
Xerxes 57, 164

Yadomilk 10-11, 23-4, 108
Yehawallon (engineer) 68

Zaghouan (mountains) 143
Zakarbaal (Elissa's uncle) 7-8, 23, 94
Zakarbaal (king of Byblos) 1
Zama (town and battle) 30, 36,142, 154-5, 157, 162-3, 189, 204
Zeugei (region) 143-4
Zeus 9, 94, 98-9, 117
Zilalsan (*Zllsn:* Numidian prince) 146-8, 191
Ziqua (Zaghouan) 144
Zorus 6